Suzy Gershman

BORN TO SHOP

HONG KONG

The Ultimate Guide for
Travelers Who Love to Shop

7th Edition

MACMILLAN • USA

To Diane Freis, with love and thanks.

MACMILLAN TRAVEL
A Simon & Schuster Macmillan Company
1633 Broadway
New York, NY 10019

Macmillan Publishing books may be purchased for business or sales promotional use. For information please write: Special Markets Department, Macmillan Publishing USA, 1633 Broadway, New York, NY 10019.

Find us online at **www.frommers.com** or on America Online at Keyword: **Frommers**

Copyright © 1998 by Suzy Gershman.

All rights reserved. No part of this book may be used or reproduced or transmitted in any form or by any means, electronic or mechanical, including photocopying, recording, or by any information storage and retrieval system, without permission in writing from the Publisher.

MACMILLAN is a registered trademark of Macmillan, Inc.

ISBN 0-02-861770-3
ISSN 1067-3830

Editor: Vanessa Rosen
Map Editor: Douglas Stallings
Production Editor: Chris Van Camp
Design by George J. McKeon
Digital Cartography by Raffaele Degennaro

SPECIAL SALES
Bulk purchases (10+ copies) of Frommer's and selected Macmillan travel guides are available to corporations, organizations, mail-order catalogs, institutions, and charities at special discounts, and can be customized to suit individual needs. For more information write to Special Sales, Macmillan General Reference, 1633 Broadway, New York, NY 10019.

Manufactured in the United States of America

CONTENTS

MAP LIST

WHAT THE SYMBOL MEANS

· ·

 SUZY'S FAVORITES

Stores, restaurants, and accommodations you
should not miss.

TO START WITH

The book you have in your hand is not only new, but the country it represents is under a new flag. At long last, the day we have all been waiting for has come and gone; you'll find scant mention of it in these pages except when it relates to a shopping tidbit such as new laws about exporting antiques.

I consider it business as usual until further notice.

That understood, I welcome you to the last revision in this format because now, more than ever, I am convinced that a trip to Hong Kong also means a trip into China (mainland China that is) or other cities such as Bangkok or Singapore. Perhaps you are on a cruise and also visiting these cities. So by the next book, we'll have much more than just Hong Kong to see and shop. That makes this a collector's edition.

So collect your credit cards, your empty suitcases, and come on down; hop a plane and get on the Pacific Rim team. Prices in Hong Kong have been high lately, but there's still plenty to buy and a grand time to be had by all.

Certainly, I have a grand time every time I visit. Thanks for that must go to Glenn and Lucille Vessa, my dear friends from Honeychurch who are part of my Hong Kong family, as well as to Peter Chan, my Chinese family, and my assortment of girlfriends from Diane Freis to Lynn Grebsted to Sian Griffiths and on and on.

Hoteliers like Thomas Axmacher, Carole Klein at The Regent, and Lucy Lau at the Conrad also help welcome me, feed me, and fill my head with news and tips. A big thank you to all.

CURRENCY EXCHANGE

The currency used in Hong Kong is the Hong Kong dollar, which like the American dollar, is signified with a dollar sign. All prices quoted in this book are in U.S. dollars unless otherwise noted. Prices in Hong Kong are written as $HK.

Although every effort has been made to ensure the accuracy of prices appearing in this book, it should be kept in mind that with inflation and a fluctuating rate of exchange for both the U.S. and the British pound, prices will vary. Dollar estimates in this edition are made at the following rate of exchange: $1 U.S. = $HK 7.

Chapter One

. . . .

THE BEST OF HONG KONG IN A HURRY

According to the Hong Kong Tourist Authority, most visitors to Hong Kong stay only 3 or 4 days. This means you are going to be crazy busy, every moment packed with sights to see, treats to eat and things to buy. While wonders may never cease, your visit will. If you are on a desperate struggle against the clock, I've created this chapter for you.

I will also admit that on my last trip to Hong Kong, I stayed just 4 days plus a few hours. I shopped almost every minute that I wasn't eating or sleeping (and I don't sleep very much), and I still didn't get to every place, see everything, or buy nearly enough.

All resources mentioned here are covered in more detail later in the book and obviously, not every resource in the book has made it to this section.

In a city like Hong Kong that has so many rich and varied shopping, dining, and sightseeing opportunities, it's pretty hard to come up with a single best of anything. Best is a very subjective thing. Each choice is based on a weighted combination of location, value, and energy. I know I'm sounding Zenlike on this one, but it's important to me that you get the right *feel* in your few free moments.

And feelings are in short demand in Hong Kong these days, where there seems to be more emphasis than ever on making a deal, making money, or making China.

1

Airport Warning: Many businesspeople are in such a great hurry getting from meeting to meeting that they save up their shopping errands for the airport duty free as they are leaving town. While I understand this inclination (I've fallen prey to it myself), Kai Tak does not have brilliant shopping, and its duty-free prices are high. I suggest shopping the gift shop at your hotel. That said, I must confess to:

The Best Airport Gift of My Life

In the children's gift section of the DFS store in Kai Tak (who knows what or where or when in the new airport), I found this adorable plastic tote bag filled with small teddy bears, about 4 inches tall. There were five bears, each identical except each was dressed in a different national costume representing the Pacific Rim. Cost: $28. I bought it for my Julia, now four, but I've kept it for myself. Shhhh, don't tell.

Along with my list comes the usual disclaimer—these choices are based on my years on the streets (and in the alleys) of Hong Kong. As soon as we go to press, a bigger or better resource might pop up. Cope.

YOU HAVE 1 HOUR TO SHOP: KOWLOON

The stores here sell everything you need for a successful shopping spree: souvenirs and gifts for everyone you know at low prices, silks and fabrics, herbal medicines and teas, liquors and local wines, jewelry, white cutwork and linens, and arts and crafts. A few of my favorites are: **Yue Hwa Chinese Products Emporium,** 301–309 Nathan Rd. (MTR: Jordan Road); **Chinese Arts & Crafts Ltd.,** 3 Salisbury Rd., (MTR: Tsim Sha Tsui (TST). There is a branch of **Yue Hwa** a block from **the Peninsula Hotel (The Pen)**, but I don't like it and have purposefully sent you to this address, even though it is farther away.

YOU HAVE ONLY 1 HOUR TO SHOP: CENTRAL

. . . .

SHANGHAI TANG
12 Pedder St., Central (MTR: Central).

Holey Moley! You've seen the nightclub now shop the shop! Okay, even if you haven't been invited to owner David Tang's private China Club, his store—Shanghai Tang—is the must-see, must-do of Hong Kong. Souvenirs and fashions, original artwork by contemporary artists—all imported from China; get a load of the gift wrap! Wander, drool, buy, and shop 'til you're late for your next appointment. Clothes are a tad expensive, but there are plenty of giftable quality in the $15–$50 range.

GREAT GIFTS FOR LOVED ONES

. . . .

Jewelry

KAI YIN LO
Mandarin Oriental Hotel, 5 Connaught Rd. (MTR: Central) and Peninsula Hotel, Salisbury Rd., Kowloon (MTR: Tsim Sha Tsui, TST).

PAN AM PEARLS
9 Lock Rd., Kowloon (MTR: TST).

Silk Pajamas or Boxer Shorts

If price is a consideration, check out **Stanley Market,** but make sure you get real silk! The better Chinese department stores also carry these items, but sizes run small and may not fit a western-sized body. Your best bet is **Ascot Chang** for your choice of off-the-peg or made-to-measure and serious quality.

ASCOT CHANG
Regent Hotel Mall, 18 Salisbury Rd., Kowloon
(MTR: TST).

Cigars

DUNHILL
Regent Hotel Mall, 18 Salisbury Rd., Kowloon
(MTR: TST); Prince's Building (MTR: Central).

GREAT GIFTS FOR KIDS

. . . .

Chinese department stores have excellent souvenir
departments where you can find gifts to delight children of all ages. All electronics stores sell video
games, which may or may not be compatible with
your child's game system at home. Know what you're
looking for before you buy; also note that Asian
versions of certain games have different names than
the U.S. or U.K. version. Below are my faves for
American-style gifts and more unique, only-in-Hong-
Kong offerings.

THE LANES
The Lanes, Li Yuen St. West and Li Yuen St. East
(MTR: Central).

TOYS R US
Ocean Terminal (Star Ferry or MTR to Tsim Sha
Tsui, Kowloon).

- **Passport Dolls or Rice Paddy Dolls.** These dolls
  have the potential to become as popular as Power
  Rangers or Cabbage Patch dolls—remember the
  craze from a few years back? Each Chinese baby
  doll comes with her own passport attached to her
  wrist. Beware of fakes, however. The price you
  pay varies with your haggling skills and the nature of the doll's clothing. I always buy mine in
  Stanley and bargain fiercely. Approximately $HK
  200–230.

- **Chinese Hats.** I'm in love with these particular hats or caps. They come in different styles and fabrics with a single long black wool braid attached. The hard sided bowl-shaped cap is called a "watermelon" hat; soft-sided tams are also available. About $3 each. Available in every Chinese department store.
- **Chinese Pajamas.** Yes, they even come in infant's sizes. You can buy these traditional "satin" pjs in Stanley, in almost any Chinese department store, and often in gift shops and tourist traps.

GREAT INEXPENSIVE GIFTS FOR OTHERS

- **Tea Mugs.** Chinese tea mugs (complete with lid) cost about $3 each in any Chinese department store. You'll have to wrap them yourself (pack with care), but they are marvelous gifts.
- **Chinese Tea.** From high-end brands and makers (such as Fook Ming Tong) to any old brand in a great looking package sold from the street or at a Chinese department store, tea doesn't break and makes a very traditional gift. Prices vary with brand and venue.
- **"Jade."** I buy "jade" donuts by the dozen at the **Jade Market** and then string each one individually as a gift. They cost about $1 each and are not real jade. If you're willing to move up to $10–$15 per gift, you can purchase figurines of various animals.
- **Chop.** This is one of those great gifts that you buy because you know no one has one. A chop—a Chinese signature stamp—costs about $25 and can usually be carved while you wait.

THE BEST SHOPPING EXPERIENCES

1. Trolling for bargains on Granville Road or Fa Yuen Street
2. Having a garment made to measure

The 10 Best Stores in Hong Kong

For those in a hurry or those who want to know what I think shouldn't be missed, here's a list to get you started.

Also note that some of the best shopping adventures are actually markets or experiences. These are in alphabetical order, not personal ranking.

1. **Alan Fung, Hyatt Hotel** (basement arcade), Nathan Road, Kowloon (MTR: TST).

   Actually Mr. Fung represents an entire category of stores in Hong Kong, so after you visit this store, you may also want to pop into The Pen where there are several similar stores. The specialty here is now the rage of Hong Kong: large, beautiful, chic, Kelly-style tote bags in a rainbow of colors.

2. **Chinese Arts & Crafts,** Canton Road, Kowloon (MTR: TST).

   Department store of Chinese goodies including silks by the yard or already made into garments, Chinese herbal cures, gifts galore, and everything you can imagine.

3. **Honeychurch,** 29 Hollywood Rd., Central (MTR: Central).

   Sure it's a great store, but part of what's great about it is that the owners are American expats who are warm and funny and wonderful. The main store sells small items but next door is a warehouse for furniture.

4. **Joyce,** 23–25 Nathan Road, Kowloon (MTR: TST).

   No trip to Hong Kong is complete without paying homage to Joyce who imports European clothes and features cutting edge chic. Even if you don't buy, you must have a look! Also try Joyce Cafe, One Exchange Square.

5. **La Place,** Pedder Building, 12 Pedder St., Central (MTR: Central).

This is an outlet of sorts; I don't know how old the clothes are but I do know that I've never seen so many marked down, big-name designer tags in my life. Yes, Chanel!

6. **Mountain Folkcraft**, 12–15 Wo On Lane, Central (MTR: Central).

   Tucked behind the core of Central shopping but worth finding if you love arts, crafts, cut-paper designs and sophisticated folk art.

7. **Seibu**, Pacific Place, 88 Queens Way, Central (MTR: Admiralty).

   Branch of the famous Japanese department store and a wonderland of goodies, many not available in the U.S. I always stock up on Red Earth aromatherapy; many items in the store are expensive but wandering around gives you ideas and inspirations. Also check out the David Chan designed paper goods, T-shirts, etc.

8. **Shanghai Tang**, 12 Pedder St., Central (MTR: Central).

   Possibly the best store in town; certainly the most expensive. Nonetheless, the shopping bags and postcards alone are worth the price of a purchase. The fabrics and tailor made goods are pricey, but downstairs the gift items are more affordable.

9. **Wah Tung**, Aberdeen (no MTR).

   Although Wah Tung has branch stores around town, I vote for their multifloor factory. They have so much china that you will never want to leave, and yes, they will ship for you.

10. **Watsons,** branches all over town.

    I'm not that picky about which branch of Watson's I visit, although the fancy one on Nathan Road is not my favorite. Still, I've never met a Watson's I didn't love. Watson's is a drugstore that sells everything—Chinese herbal cures, makeup, office supplies, dime store goodies, and more. Yes, this is where I buy the soap that promises to make me thin.

3. The Jade Market
4. Temple Street Market
5. Shopping the entire Pedder Building, having tea
   at Mandarin Oriental Hotel, then walking to
   the Star Ferry for the ride home to Kowloon.

THE BEST SOURCES FOR ANTIQUES

Antiques are very tricky in Hong Kong, especially
since the hand–over of the new laws about what
can be exported. I don't advise buying them here
unless you know what you are doing or can afford
to pay what a reputable dealer's experience and
knowledge will cost you.

With that caveat, I rely on **Honeychurch Antiques**
at 29 Hollywood Rd. in Central because I know
and trust the American expatriate owners, Glenn
and Lucille. Hollywood Road (and nearby Cat
Street) is packed with antique dealers.

Hollywood Road is an excellent stroll for antique
shopping but don't buy anything serious from a
dealer who is not known in the trade.

If you can't get uptown to Hollywood Road,
check out **The Silk Road,** a small group of dealers
in Harbour City Shopping Mall (next to Ocean Terminal) and **Charlotte Horstmann & Gerald Godfrey**
in Ocean Terminal. The deal at Horstmann is
simple—the good stuff is put away. You must ask to
see it in the warehouse.

Macau is an excellent source for antiques. That
is, if they haven't made them right there!

THE BEST PLACE TO BUY A CAMERA

New York. However, if you insist, protect yourself
by using only those dealers who have been authorized by the Hong Kong Tourist Authority (HKTA).
HKTA publishes a *Shopping* booklet that lists all

HKTA member stores and can be picked up at the Hong Kong Tourist Authority's office in the arrivals lobby of Kai Tak Airport, open daily from 8am to 10:30pm. If you're in the market to buy a used camera, I can personally vouch for the dealer listed below:

DAVID CHAN
Champagne Court, 16 Kimberley Rd., Kowloon (MTR: Tsim Sha Tsui, TST).

THE BEST PLACE FOR COSMETICS

Prices on cosmetics and perfumes in Hong Kong may be no less than at home, so shop carefully. The most famous discounter is **SaSa**.

SASA
180 Nathan Rd. and 25 Granville Rd., 1 block off Nathan Rd., Kowloon (MTR for both: TST).

THE BEST PLACES TO BUY ELECTRONICS

Please avoid the electronics shops on Nathan Road. By and large, these places are tourist traps. Either use HKTA-authorized dealers (who are, for the most part, dealers who represent a particular brand name and have their own showrooms) or go to the local mall where insiders shop:

GOLDEN ARCADE SHOPPING CENTER
44 B Fuk Wah St. (MTR: Sham Shui Po).

This is a wild and crazy mall of dealers mostly frequented by locals and teenage boys. They've got it here in every international current, fashion, and flavor. Not for the easily intimidated; may be a bootleg version. Know your stuff!

THE BEST SOURCE FOR HANDBAGS

. . . .

MAYER HANDBAG
Mandarin Oriental Hotel, 5 Connaught Rd.,
Central (MTR: Central).

ALAN FUNG
Hyatt Regency Hotel, 29 Nathan Rd., Shop B–15
(basement), Kowloon (MTR: TST).

Unlike in Singapore or Bangkok, there are no decent fake and/or cheap designer handbags on the
streets of Hong Kong. If you wish to have your own
Chanel knockoff, you have to go to a reputable firm
that will make it to measure. This is not cheap. It
means paying between $350–$450 for a handbag
that may look to others like the $1,250 original.

The current rage in Hong Kong however is not
Chanel but Hermès Kelly-style bags, the larger the
better. They are available in a rainbow of colors;
the big ones sell for $1,200HK and $1,800HK—
they are, quite simply, worth coveting in every
color. I didn't get one because I couldn't be happy
with only one and couldn't decide even on two. I
had to walk away, daily, with a headache and a
heartache.

THE BEST TAILORS

. . . .

There is no one best tailor in Hong Kong; there are
three. They stand head and shoulders above all the
others for one simple reason: They are the only
tailors with their own workrooms who do not send
their piecework across to China.

A-MAN HING CHEONG
Mandarin Oriental Hotel, 5 Connaught Rd.
(MTR: Central).

H. BAROMAN
Swire House, Connaught Road (MTR: Central).

W. W. Chan & Sons Ltd.
92 Nathan Rd., 2nd Floor, Kowloon (MTR: TST).

THE BEST TAILORS FOR MEN'S SHIRTS
. . . .

While all good tailors also make shirts, there are two incredibly famous names in shirt making who specialize in men's shirts, shorts, and pajamas only.

Ascot Chang
Ascot Chang, Regent Hotel, 18 Salisbury Rd.,
Kowloon (MTR: TST); Prince's Building,
Chater Rd., Hong Kong (MTR: Central).

David
Mandarin Oriental Hotel, 5 Connaught Rd.
(MTR: Central); 33 Kimberley Rd., Kowloon
(MTR: TST).

THE BEST MARKETS
. . . .

Although Hong Kong is famous for its malls, I'd rather you took the pulse of the city by visiting a market . . . or two. If you can make a day of it, please turn to chapter 13 for tours that include various markets.

If your time is more limited, please consider the following choices for getting to market, to market.

- *The Best Tourist Market for First Timers:* **Stanley Market.** Main Street, Stanley (MTR: None). Hop the bus (no. 6 or no. 6A from Exchange Square in Central or Admiralty MTR) or take a taxi. This market has become soooo touristy that I am reluctant to send Old China Hands here.
- *The Best Fruit and Vegetable Market:* The **Wet Market** adjacent to the **Jade Market** and **Jardine's** in Causeway Bay. Wet market near Jade Market, Shanghai & Reclamation streets, Kowloon (MTR: Jordan Road).

- *The Best at Night:* **Temple Street.** Temple Street, Kowloon (MTR: Jordan Road).

THE BEST SHOPPING MALL

For those who prefer western-style style, I like **Pacific Place** for its mix of stores and totally clean, well-lit, and modern atmosphere. One visit here and you'll leave with a strong sense of Hong Kong's heroes of retail.

PACIFIC PLACE
Pacific Place, 88 Queensway (MTR: Admiralty).

THE BEST DRUGSTORE FOR BASICS

Whether you need toothpaste, deodorant, female supplies, condoms, a birthday card, a pair of panty hose, bottled water, snacks, a toy or bribe for your child . . . or just about anything else, get to the nearest **Watson's.**

WATSON'S
Prince's Building, Central (MTR: Central); Nathan Rd., Kowloon (MTR: TST); Main St., Stanley.

For filling a prescription from home, try the Peninsula Pharmacy, downstairs in the Peninsula Hotel.

PENINSULA PHARMACY
Peninsula Pharmacy, Peninsula Hotel, Salisbury Rd., Kowloon (MTR: TST).

THE BEST SOURCE FOR POSTCARDS

Postcards by David Chan

They're expensive, but to die for. Each card is a reproduction of an old photo from China in the 1930s, sold in assorted venues including at **David Chan** shops at the Star Ferry terminals and inside the **Seibu** department store at Pacific Place.

Also Note: You get a fabulous free postcard with each purchase at **Shanghai Tang;** I asked for extras and got 'em: Shanghai Tang, Pedder Building, 12 Pedder St., Central.

THE BEST FACTORY OUTLETS
. . . .

DIANE FREIS FACTORY OUTLET STORE
Kaiser Estates Phase 1 (10th Floor), 41 Man Yue St., Hung Hom, Kowloon (MTR: None).

While Diane Freis's retail shops in Hong Kong sell her dresses for approximately half their U.S. prices, insiders know about the outlet store where even greater savings are possible. Some of the stock is old, but most are classic styles so it doesn't matter. No public transportation; take a taxi.

PEDDER BUILDING
Pedder Building, 12 Pedder St. (MTR: Central).

Beware that not every store is an outlet but there are plenty of them here and the location couldn't be better. The perfect look-see for someone who wants a taste of outlet shopping.

THE BEST CHINA SHOP
. . . .

WAH TUNG
Wah Tung, Grand Marine Industrial Building, 3 Yue Fung St., Tin Wan, Aberdeen. (MTR: none, take a taxi) ☎ *852-2873-2272; fax: 852-2873-2615.*

Although they have showrooms on Hollywood Road (two of them), head for Aberdeen—you ain't seen nuthin' like this.

THE BEST PLACES FOR A QUICK LUNCH
. . . .

While I recommend several places in the following pages for a quick bite or a more leisurely meal, if you're in Central, the **Mandarin Oriental Hotel** is the best spot for lunch when you don't want to waste a moment and never wish to be disappointed. In Tsim Sha Tsui, you can't go wrong with the Harbourside dining room at **The Regent.**

MANDARIN ORIENTAL HOTEL
5 Connaught Rd. (MTR: Central).

THE REGENT
18 Salisbury Rd., Kowloon (MTR: TST).

Chapter Two

. . . .

DETAILS

WELCOME TO HONG KONG

. . . .

I have been a Hong Kong person for over a decade; I've seen good times and bad times and, hmmm, is this where I sing or dance or just belt it out? Well, I gotta tell you, I ain't never (no, no, no, never) seen times like this—Hong Kong is hot, hot, hot because so much is moving in and out and getting ready for the future . . . the future of China and the entire Pacific Rim.

Hong Kong has the hotels and the bath tubs and the shopping, but it also has the phone lines, the infrastructure, and everything that global business needs to expand not only into China but to Vietnam and points here, there, and on the way to Sydney. (I'm on my way to Shanghai.)

Hong Kong isn't about what flag is flying; it is about the future and it serves as merely the stepping off point. Enter the Dragon.

Hong Kong is known as the "Gateway to the Orient" because more people use it as their Asian base than any other city. Whether they visit on business or on vacation, travelers come to Hong Kong and then fan out: south to Bangkok or Singapore, west to China and Vietnam, or north toward Korea and Japan. Many will change planes in Japan on

Hong Kong Orientation

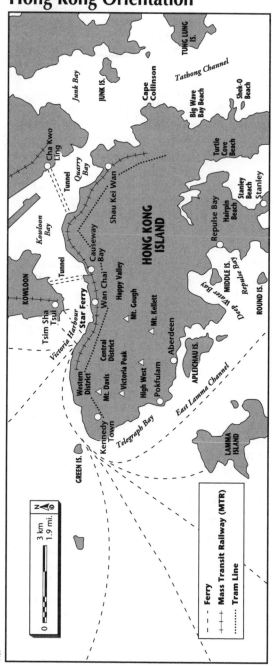

TUNG LUNG IS.

Tathong Channel

Junk Bay

JUNK IS.

Cape Collinson

Big Wave Bay Beach

Shek-O Beach

Cha Kwo Ling

Tunnel

Quarry Bay

Shau Kei Wan

Turtle Cove Beach

Kowloon Bay

Causeway

HONG KONG ISLAND

Repulse Bay

Stanley Beach

Stanley

Harpin Beach

Tunnel

Wan Chai Bay

Happy Valley

KOWLOON

Mt. Gough

Mt. Kellett

MIDDLE IS.

Repulse Bay

Tsim Sha Tsui

Star Ferry

Aberdeen

Deep Water Bay

ROUND IS.

Victoria Harbour

Central District

Victoria Peak

APLEICHAU IS.

Western District

Mt. Davis

High West

Pokfulam

Kennedy Town

Telegraph Bay

East Lamma Channel

GREEN IS.

LAMMA ISLAND

N

3 km
1.9 mi.

0

- - - Ferry
+++ Mass Transit Railway (MTR)
...... Tram Line

1459

arrival in Asia, but they won't actually explore Japan until they are on their way home . . . if ever.

Hong Kong, however, is always home away from home. Despite the existence of direct connections to China from the West Coast of the U.S., when I make plans to fly to China, I usually look at schedules in and out of Hong Kong. When I organize land tours for cruise lines, I make sure everyone stops or starts in Hong Kong. Even though I understand the importance of Shanghai in the future of China, a trip to the Pacific Rim always begins and ends in Hong Kong. And at **Shanghai Tang,** my favorite store. But I digress.

If you can't hack one of those if-it's-Tuesday-it-must-be-Taipei tours, don't worry. Fill your weeks with Hong Kong, Macau, and the Pearl River Delta, so you can at least step into China. Shopping aside, there's simply so much going on in Hong Kong and Macau these days you may just want to enter here and stay put. For quite some time.

HONG KONG IS HOT
· ·

Politics aside, let's look at the politics of fashion and retailing. Because of this thrust into the Far East, designer shops are opening up like mad—Calvin Klein has announced he is not only opening up Calvin Klein Collection stores but also CK stores all over Asia; he just opened in Hong Kong and is about to open in Seoul and Jakarta. In fact, Klein is also doing Paris, London, and Milan—which gives you the whole picture. Isaac Mizrahi has just made a huge deal in the Far East; he, too, will be exploding around the Pacific Basin from Singapore to Seoul. Designers are going global, and the Far East is part of their plan.

But it's a marketing plan for the local population. As an American visiting the area, you are not the target audience. Prices may be high, sizes may be cut differently, styles may not be the same as what you've seen at home. Let the shopper beware.

Meanwhile, there's a huge movement of Chinese and Asian influences as the fashion fad of the moment. This may be over by the time you read this, but suddenly everything in my closet looks dull because the biggest Italian and French designers are telling me that Chinoise is chic, that Mao is of the moment, Suzie Wong is the latest. The Last Emperor has become my guru.

If you think you're going to bop into some of the TT's (Tourist Traps) in Hong Kong, or waltz over to **Stanley Market** or even **The Lanes,** and load up on fads and flash, you can think twice. Even the touristy stuff has gotten expensive, and the good touristy stuff is outrageously expensive—like $200 for a *cheongsam* (Suzie Wong dress) or even a big Mao shirt in silk.

If you are investing, make sure you pick a classic rather than a fad. You want cheap Chinese chic? Try London! Take a walk on the wild side of the next big city you visit—David Tang, creator of **Shanghai Tang,** is taking over, welcoming the Chinese to a high street and a shopping street near you. The Chinese takeover of the island of Hong Kong is nothing; the Chinese have taken over our closets!

A SHORT HISTORY OF HONG KONG TRADE

Hong Kong and the South China Sea have always been a hotbed of commerce because China silk came out of either Canton (now Guangzhou) or Shanghai. You remember the Portuguese and their "black ship"? The black ship brought goods from Europe in exchange for silk from China. This was a lucrative business, and the Portuguese wanted it all to themselves. So did the British, the Spaniards, the French, and, later, the Americans.

The only problem was, the big British ships couldn't get into the shallow waters of Macau (the

Portuguese port), which is somewhat closer to Canton. Happily, they soon discovered that the perfect port was on the island of Hong Kong. So for no other reason than deep water, Hong Kong became the "in" place.

Queen Victoria howled with laughter when in 1842 Hong Kong was given to the British as a prize of war. And it really was a laughing matter. You see, not only were silks and woolens being traded, there also was a thriving business in opium. The first Opium War ended with the British winning and getting Hong Kong, in perpetuity. The second and third times the British won, they got the rights to Kowloon and then certain mainland territories for 99 years.

Strangely enough time flies when you're shopping and shipping, the 99 years ended with the hand over on June 30, 1997. By that time, trade and commerce and money and real estate and infrastructure were all the soul of Hong Kong. Global firms wanted to be in Hong Kong to use her byways into China, and the Chinese wanted to take over, if only for the cash.

The Chinese have made it clear that the future is Shanghai, but Hong Kong will remain a business and cultural (and shopping) destination for years to come.

GET THERE NOW
. . . .

I don't expect anything radical to happen in the next few years. The hand–over is past us. The future is ours. I think Shanghai will take 10 years to get it together.

Nonetheless, knowing what will happen has indeed put the pressure on many tourists to get to Hong Kong before it changes too dramatically. The way I look at it, the real reason to get to Hong Kong before mid-1998 is to use Kai Tak International Airport and not the new Chek Lap Kok International Airport which is far less convenient.

Chek Lap Kok's location (on the island of Lantau) will make the journey from airport to hotel a lot longer than the 15 or 20 minutes it currently takes to get from Kai Tak to most hotels in Kowloon or Central. There is also much discussion these days that the Mass Transit Railway (MTR) system will not be ready when the new airport opens, so there may be a few hectic months until everything is running smoothly.

YOU WERE WORRIED?

If you were worried about the Chinese take over, I suggest you relax and breathe easy. The worst happened long before the official hand–over. You want to know terror? You want to know desperate change on the streets? How about the thought that Bugs Bunny has already taken over Hong Kong!

Does it give you goose bumps or what? Chills or just thrills? No need to fear Chairman Mao when Roadrunner is here. "What's up, doc?," you ask.

Well, **Lane Crawford,** the venerable British department store of colonial Hong Kong, closed its tony doors in Kowloon to make way for a branch of the **Warner Brothers Studio Store,** right there on Nathan Road in the heart of the Golden Mile. I thought I would cry when I saw that Warner Brothers Store.

Planet Hollywood has opened 2 blocks from there in Ocean Terminal. **HMV** is a block from that in the Sands Building, replacing a wonderful Chinese department store that I really miss. **Hard Rock Cafe** is a block away, farther up on Canton Road.

In fact, I spent a lot of my last visit to Hong Kong in tears—so many architectural changes, so much "progress," so many more people, things, and acquisitions. Everything old is being torn down to make way for more of the global bit boys.

CHANGE/NO CHANGE

· ·

Briefly, in case you were wondering, here's what hasn't changed since the take over:

- money, although the queen has come off of the coins;
- visa requirements for Hong Kong (none).

Here's what's changing:

- everyday lives of locals;
- export laws on antiques;
- prices—always going up!

ORIENTATION

· ·

With the new airport on the island of Lantau, shopping destinations spread across major land masses, and folks darting off to Macau, Malaysia, and Mainland China at a moment's notice, you may find yourself asking, "just what and where is Hong Kong?"

Hong Kong encompasses Hong Kong Island, of course, but also the city of Kowloon, the New Territories, and a few hundred islands. Technically speaking what we commonly refer to as Hong Kong is now part of the People's Republic of China (PRC). Still, you need not worry about the mainland, only finding your way across the harbor and in and out of stores and lanes.

When people discuss addresses in the Hong Kong area, they may cite a particular number on a particular street but, more often than not, you will hear your fellow travelers oversimplifying these directions by just naming a building and the neighborhood in which it is located. And they play fast and loose with what constitutes a neighborhood. Some people call all of Victoria Island "Central" and all of the

Kowloon Peninsula "Kowloon." While these terms are technically incorrect, everyone seems to understand this system, so don't knock yourself out trying to be absolutely precise.

Shopping in Hong Kong is concentrated heavily in two areas: Central, the main business "downtown" area on the Hong Kong Island side, and Tsim Sha Tsui in Kowloon. Central is very upscale, civilized, businesslike, and modern. Tsim Sha Tsui (often written TST) is more gritty and more active in a frenetic way.

Please see chapter 8, "Shopping Neighborhoods," for a more detailed discussion of Hong Kong's shopping and commercial districts. When you become an Old China Hand, you'll decide which side of the harbor is more "you" or more convenient to your business or shopping style.

BOOKING HONG KONG

· ·

The **Hong Kong Tourist Association** (HKTA) provides a great deal of very useful information for travelers at no cost. They publish pamphlets on almost every subject imaginable, many of which you can pick up as you exit passport control at Hong Kong International Airport.

The Official Hong Kong Guide is published monthly and contains general information about the city including a short description of Chinese foods, organized sightseeing tours, and a listing of festivals, events, and exhibits being held that month. The HKTA also publishes a weekly newspaper, *Hong Kong This Week*. It contains news of events and shows, along with the usual ads for shops and is distributed free at major hotels and in HKTA offices.

Inside the free packet you can pick up at the airport is the *A-O-A Map Directory*. Maps show both building and street locations. Since so many addresses include the building name, street, and area, it makes finding an address simple.

GETTING THERE

. . . .

When it comes to booking your plane tickets, have I got news for you: There are a confusing number of possibilities and deals and routes and reasons to go with any number of different plans (and planes).

If you are going to Hong Kong via the Pacific Ocean, which is the cheapest and most common route, then what you are looking for is the right combination of ticket price and short layover time. Enter Northwest Airlines. I have now timed this with a variety of airline charts and connection tables and have it down to a science—a Northwest Airlines science.

No one has a shorter connection time through Narita (Tokyo) than Northwest; with the mere legal connection of 1½ hours you hardly have time to wander Narita or feel foggy—you simply stretch your legs, pop back into your seat, and you're off. Arrivals are timed to create minimum effects of jet lag once you are home and on the ground in Hong Kong. It's also a rather social kind of thing in the hub at Narita—people meeting up with colleagues, people connecting on to all sorts of destinations in Asia, not just Hong Kong. And yes, Northwest flies to Mainland China, to Shanghai and to Beijing—even from the U.S.

Also note that technology, peacekeeping efforts, and diplomacy efforts will continue to revise the situation and offer different gateways. American carriers now have rights to fly over Siberia that had never been granted before; United Airlines has recently begun nonstop 747–400 service to Hong Kong from Chicago! This is the longest route segment in history, some 7,788 miles.

Other American airlines have deals with Canada that allow them to offer nice routes from the U.S. with quickie refueling stops on Canadian soil. Canadian carriers are also looking at code shares to increase this marketing effort.

TICKET DEALS

. . . .

Flights on all airplanes to Hong Kong, especially from the West Coast, are packed. One of the reasons for this is that there are lots of businesspeople flying these routes. With China opening up, there are even more of them. Add to that the fact that there are wholesalers who buy blocks of tickets, knowing they will be able to resell them to travel agents and tour groups, and you can see why it may be hard to get the flights you want. Because they buy in bulk, wholesalers often get a better price. And these wholesalers or ticket brokers pass their savings on to their customers. Enter Lillian Fong, my personal secret weapon.

Call or fax Lillian Fong, at **Pacific Place Travel,** 1255 Corporate Center Dr., Suite 203, Monterey Park, CA 91754. ☎ 800-328-8778 or 213-980-8138; fax 213-980-8133. (E-mail: **pacplace@worldnet. att.net**)

Other thoughts:

- If you're flying to Hong Kong from the West Coast, look into what is called a Circle Pacific fare. Most American carriers, and many international ones, offer you this chance to make your own itinerary, traveling to several cities in Asia at package-tour prices. You do not join a group; you set your own pace, but you get a break on the price because you fly all legs with the same carrier.

- Airline miles are a great way to get to an exotic destination that you thought was out of reach. Note that all airline mileage programs have sales and promotions at various times of the year or on certain routes. I was dumbfounded to read recently that American Airlines's frequent-flier program was offering round-trip economy-class tickets to Hong Kong on promotion for a mere 40,000 miles!

Other thoughts:

- Don't be afraid of business class. The trip is a lengthy one; you will be much more comfortable in business class. Furthermore, there are more business-class seats than any other class of seat (you aren't the only person who really doesn't want to do this trip in a coach seat), so there is the possibility of more deals than in coach or first class.
- Don't be afraid of first class. Lillian offered me first-class upgrade tickets if I paid the full fare for business class; this is a pretty good deal. There are all sorts of promotions out there—ask.
- Don't accidentally compare apples to oranges. If you are pricing airfares on several carriers, it is imperative that you understand the quality of the service and what you are getting. Don't assume anything. Virgin has made quite a splash with their extra perks and great entertainment system, but they only offer real value to those travelers willing to fly economy at promotional prices or to those willing to pay extra for their upper class service. The chitchat of the entire Rim is whether American carriers compete with Asian carriers on a service level.
- Consider unusual routing, especially if there are promotional fares. Even if you don't get a price deal, you may end up saving time. For example, the flying time from the West Coast of the U.S. to Hong Kong is approximately 17 hours. The flying time from Toronto to Hong Kong is also 17 hours. You may save time or aggravation if you fly from an East Coast city to Toronto and then catch the Cathay Pacific flight from Toronto to Hong Kong.
- Consider unusual time flights; Cathay now offers a flight that leaves New York rather late at night but gets to Hong Kong first thing in the morning, the *day after* (you do pass the date line, remember?). This is great for jet lag.

• Package tours often offer you the best deals financially, especially if they include airport transfers and some extras. Check them out, especially when you can stay at luxury hotels. Likewise, add-on tours offered by cruise ship lines sometimes have fabulous prices that include promotional events and benefits. More and more cruise ships offer in or out add-ons in Hong Kong.

Promotional Deals

All airlines have promotional deals; Americans have become accustomed to the regular airfare wars, which offer great domestic and European airfares during certain times of the year. Promotional deals to Asia are sometimes harder to find. I was quite amused to read that many of the national carriers of Pacific Rim area airlines offer deals that aren't advertised in America, but you can find them by calling the airlines toll-free number in the U.S. For example, **Air India**, ☎ 800-442-4455, offers "shopping rates" with a 33% discount for women flying between the major shopping cities of the Far East.

Around-the-World Deals

The deal of the century happens to be an around-the-world ticket on British Airways. An around-the-world coach ticket on British Airways is good for 1 year and needs to be bought 14 days prior to departure. The cost is about $3,000 but can be as low as $1,600 if bought during a promotion!

A business-class ticket on British Airways, which routes you from New York to London and London to Hong Kong, is about $4,000 with a 14-day advanced purchase. To put that into perspective, please note that a round-trip business-class ticket from London to Hong Kong is approximately $4,000. Do you smell a bargain or what?

It gets better. A first-class, around-the-world ticket is about $6,000, and a Concorde ticket—you fly Concorde from New York to London only—

comes with an add-on price: $863 for first-class passengers; $1,719 for business-class passengers. Since the ticket can be used over the space of a continuing year, this means that you can book yourself one hell of a deal.

One of the catches is that different priced tickets have different perks: The basic cheapest ticket allows you six stops with use on any of six partner airlines affiliated with BA. You must always travel in one direction, but you can make side trips, which few other round-the-world tickets allow you to do. The number of miles you can travel on the basic ticket is 28,500. Not bad, huh?

Other airlines do offer round-the-world fares and deals, but in most cases, you will code share with two or more combinations. I trust BA and usually use them to get around. I personally find the transpacific trip from New York to Hong Kong to be punishing; I'd much rather go around the world or fly in and out of London or Paris.

Do consider using Cathay Pacific, which can get you to Hong Kong from the U.S. transpacifically and then put you from Hong Kong into any major city in Europe (try London or Paris). All you have to do after that is connect on another carrier for the European-U.S. leg of travel. Or, even better, use a Northwest/KLM code share to go completely around the world and get the benefit of the many Northwest gateway cities that serve various European destinations. You simply connect out of Hong Kong to a chosen European destination on KLM.

Transatlantic Pacific Travel

For me, the secret is often that *transatlantic* is the way to go . . . even come and go! This is true not only if you live on the East Coast of the U.S., but also if you live in Chicago, the Midwest, or Texas. Detroit, Minneapolis, and Cincinnati are now hub cities that offer choices in either direction. Don't be blind to the possibilities.

The day I found out that Hong Kong was a mere 10-hour flight from London was the day I converted. (Note: it takes 11 hours from Hong Kong to London!) A few months after my discovery, I noted that several airlines, led by Singapore Airlines, began advertising their transatlantic routes. Even Delta now has a code-sharing plan with Singapore so that they, too, can offer passengers transatlantic service.

British Airways doesn't have to advertise; they've had the London-to-Hong Kong and the New York-to-London business sewn up for years. Virgin also flies from London to Hong Kong, so there is some competition going on here.

ELECTRONICALLY YOURS

HKTA (Hong Kong Tourist Authority) site: **http://www.hkta.org**

Cyber Deals

Cathay Pacific was one of the first airlines to go on-line and actively recruit travelers. They have many innovative programs, including mileage awards and auctions. They suggest you look at their site: **www.cathay-usa.com** and then use a travel agent for ticketing or finalizing plans.

ARRIVING IN HONG KONG

Hong Kong's Kai Tak International Airport is almost in downtown Kowloon; you're just a few minutes away from The Regent and the Peninsula. The new airport on Lantau Island won't open until sometime in 1998—so we'll worry about that later. Right now, Kai Tak is a breeze.

Car Service

Traveling from the airport to your hotel in the swank car your hotel sends for you is a delightfully elegant way to arrive—if expensive. While public transport is simple and inexpensive, part of the fun of being in Hong Kong is settling into that Rolls or Daimler or Mercedes Benz that your hotel has provided. Expect to pay about $40 (it varies from hotel to hotel) each way for the luxury, but do try to find it in your budget.

While one certainly doesn't pick a hotel based on the cost of its luxury car service, do note that hotels in Central charge more for this service because of the Cross-Harbour Tunnel. The Peninsula, merely a block farther from the airport than the Regent, charges about $15 more for its car—each way! And no, riding in a Rolls isn't any more fun than riding in a Daimler.

Bus

The Airbus is the bus service operating between Kai Tak airport and major hotels. Fares run $HK 12 to Tsim Sha Tsui hotels and $HK 19 to Central. There are four different routes, marked A-1, A-2, A-3, and A-5. Don't ask me what happened to A-4. Also don't ask what the drill will be for the new airport.

A-1 = Airport to Tsim Sha Tsui destinations
A-2 = Airport to Macau Ferry Pier in Central
A-3 = Airport to Causeway Bay
A-5 = Airport to Tai Koo Shing

Buses run every 15 to 20 minutes from 7am until 11:30pm. Check to make certain that your hotel is on the list; up to 20 or 25 hotels may be served on one route. There is an enormous chart at the airport, which even the most jet-lagged can handle. There is also a transportation desk that will help you.

Taxi

Taxi stands are near the arrival lounge. A large sign will give you approximate fares to different areas of

Hong Kong and Kowloon. If you are confused, look for the transportation desk. Taxis usually charge a flat rate: approximately $HK 40 to hotels in Kowloon; $HK 80 to Central.

Officially, the meter on a taxi begins at $HK 14 and turns over at $HK 1.20 per every 200 meters of travel. Drivers charge extra for rides in either direction through the tunnels, additional pieces of luggage, waiting time, and radio calls. The charges for all of these extras are slight, amounting to less than $1 per item. You do tip, but just by rounding up the fare, not by a straight percentage.

GETTING AROUND
· ·

Hong Kong is an easy city to navigate because its transportation options are excellent. It's a good city for walking, true, but you'll also want to enjoy its ferries, kaidos (bigger ferries), trams, double-decker buses, and superb MTR (Mass Transit Railway).

Most rides on the MTR take under 20 minutes; you can cross the harbor in approximately 5 minutes. Crossing the harbor by car or taxi during rush hour is hardest, but it's a breeze doing it on the MTR or the Star Ferry which takes almost the same amount of time. Don't ask me about the hour I spent in a taxi trapped inside the tunnel (!!!) when I was too lazy to take public transportation.

If you intend to sightsee, pick up the HKTA brochure "Places of Interest by Public Transportation" to get exact directions and bus routes throughout Hong Kong Island and Kowloon or consult our Major Transportation Map.

MTR

Before I explain the workings of the MTR, the phenomenally convenient mass transportation system in Hong Kong, I want you to remember one basic rule: When looking up a listing in this book, the

MTR stop at Central will get you to most locations
in Hong Kong and the stop at Tsim Sha Tsui (TST)
will get you to most locations in Kowloon. Unless
otherwise noted in the addresses given, these are the
MTR stops you want. Simple enough.

The MTR is half the fun of getting to great
shopping. Three lines connect the New Territories
to industrial Kwun Tong, to business Central, to
shopping Tsim Sha Tsui, and to the residential eastern part of the island. Each station is color-coded in
case you can't read (English or Chinese).

The longest trip takes less than an hour, and the
ticket's cost is based on the distance you travel. Buy
your ticket at the station vending machines by looking for your destination and punching in the price
code. You will need exact change, which you can
get from a machine nearby. There are also ticket
windows where you can buy multiple journey
tickets.

If you are visiting Hong Kong from overseas, the
best value is a $HK 20 tourist MTR ticket, which
can be obtained from any HKTA office, MTR
station, select Hang Seng banks, or MTR Travel
Services Centres. You must buy your ticket within
2 weeks of your arrival and show your passport at
the time you purchase it. This is for tourists; otherwise stored-value cards come in high denomina-
tions—$HK 70, 100, 200).

Since the MTR is always crowded, you'll be hap-
piest if you buy a stored-value ticket and consider it
a souvenir if you don't use it. I also order $HK 5
coins to use the self-help ticket machines. One-stop
journeys usually cost $HK 3 (less than 50¢ U.S.),
and $HK 6 can get you just about anywhere on
either side of the harbor. Your ticket comes out of
the machine into your hand; insert it into the turnstile and then retrieve it as you go through.

Remember to keep your ticket after you enter
the turnstile because you will have to reinsert it to
exit. If you get off at the wrong stop and owe more
money, an alarm will sound, and you'll have to go

Major Transportation Map

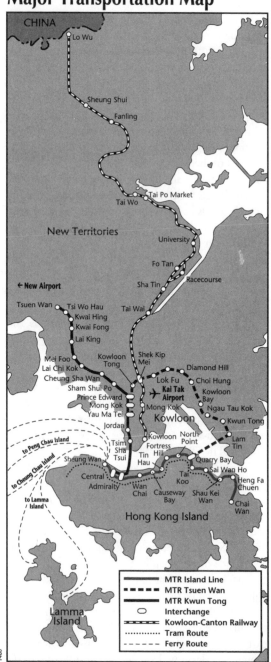

CHINA

Lo Wu

Sheung Shui

Fanling

New Territories

Tai Wo — Tai Po Market

University

Fo Tan

Sha Tin — Racecourse

← New Airport

Tai Wai

Tsuen Wan — Tsi Wo Hau

Kwai Hing

Kwai Fong

Lai King

Mei Foo

Lai Chi Kok

Cheung Sha Wan

Sham Shui Po

Prince Edward

Mong Kok

Yau Ma Tei

Jordan

Kowloon Tong

Shek Kip Mei

Lok Fu

Diamond Hill

Choi Hung

Kai Tak Airport

Kowloon Bay

Ngau Tau Kok

Mong Kok

Kowloon

Kwun Tong

Tsim Sha Tsui

Kowloon

Fortress Hill

Tin Hau

North Point

Lam Tin

Sheung Wan

Central

Admiralty

Wan Chai

Causeway Bay

Tai Koo

Shau Kei Wan

Quarry Bay

Sai Wan Ho

Heng Fa Chuen

Chai Wan

to Peng Chau Island

to Cheung Chau Island

to Lamma Island

Hong Kong Island

Lamma Island

	MTR Island Line
	MTR Tsuen Wan
	MTR Kwun Tong
◯	Interchange
	Kowloon-Canton Railway
	Tram Route
	Ferry Route

1460

over to a window to pay up. Unless you have a stored-value ticket, the turnstile will eat your ticket upon exit, and you will be denied that pretty souvenir you were counting on.

The MTR runs between 6am and 1am. If you need to get somewhere earlier or later, take a taxi.

Taxis

Taxis in Hong Kong are cheap, so go ahead and splurge. The meter starts at $HK 14, and sometimes you simply pay the minimum fare. After that the charge is $HK 1.20 per 200 meters. Taking the Cross-Harbour Tunnel will cost an extra $HK 10 each way, making the total additional fees you pay $HK 20. (As a result, I tend to avoid taking a taxi through the Cross-Harbour Tunnel unless I'm loaded down with packages and have had a long hard day of shopping.) There are surcharges for luggage, waiting time, and radio calls.

If a taxi is in Central and has a sign saying "Kowloon," it means that the driver would like a fare going back to Kowloon and will not charge the extra $HK 10 tunnel fee if he gets such a fare. Shift changes occur at 4pm, and it is sometimes hard to find a cab then. If a taxi doesn't stop for you on a busy road, it is probably because the driver is not allowed to stop.

Look for a nearby taxi stand where you can pick up a cab. Hotels are always good places to find a taxi. Even if you are not staying at that particular hotel, the doorman will help you. Tip him $HK 5 for his services, however.

While English is still the official language, it's always nice insurance to have your destination written in Chinese. Hotels will do this for you on cards they have printed up; the flip side of the card tells the driver how to get you back to the hotel. I was quite shocked on several different taxi trips when the drivers simply put a map-book in my hand and asked me to find the address for them on a map page. If I didn't know my way around town, I would have been sunk. Save yourself the aggravation—get a card ahead of time.

Trains

The Kowloon–Canton Railway (KCR) services the areas between Hung Hom and the Chinese border. Since you can't get into China without a visa, chances are you won't be traveling as far as the border. But do hop on board because you should take this chance to get out into the New Territories and see some of the real world.

If you're expecting an experience out of one of Paul Theroux's books, you'll be disappointed. The KCR is modern, clean, and just like any big-city commuter train. The stations are modern poured concrete, and while some of the passengers may be worthy subjects for a photographer, the train itself is not a romantic experience. But it's cheap, it's fun, and it feels exotic just because there aren't that many tourists on board.

Ferries

The most famous of all the Hong Kong ferries is the **Star Ferry,** with service from Kowloon to Central and back. The 8-minute ride is one of the most scenic in the world. You can see the splendor of Hong Kong Island's architecture and the sprawl of Kowloon's shore. The green-and-white ferries have been connecting the island to the peninsula since 1898.

Billed as the least-expensive tourist attraction in the world, the Star Ferry is a small piece of magic for less than 30¢ a ride. First-class costs $HK 2; tourist-class is $HK 1.50. The difference is minimal except at rush hour, when the upper deck is less crowded. The difference is maximized if you want to take pictures, since you get a much better view from the upper deck, where the first-class passengers loll. The Central/Tsim Sha Tsui (TST) service runs from 6:30am to 11:30pm.

Please Note: The different classes have different entries; on the Kowloon side, you get different shopping opportunities depending on which class of service you use!

Trams

Watch out crossing the streets of Central, or you are likely to be run over by a double-decker tram. Island trams have been operating for more than 85 years, from the far western Kennedy Town to Shau Kei Wan in the east. They travel in a straight line, except for a detour around Happy Valley. Fares are $HK 1 for adults, half fare for children. You pay as you enter. Many trams do not go the full distance east to west, so note destination signs before getting on. Antique trams are available for tours and charters, as are the regular ones.

The Peak Tram has been in operation for more than 100 years. It is a must for any visitor to Hong Kong—unless you are afraid of heights. You can catch the tram behind the Hilton Hotel, on Garden Road. A free shuttle bus will take you from the Star Ferry or Central MTR station (Chater Garden exit) to the Peak Tram terminal. The tram runs to the Peak every 10 minutes starting at 7am and ending at midnight. The trip takes 8 minutes. At the top you hike around to various viewing points or peek in on some of the expensive mansions and high-rises. The best time to make this trip is just before dusk; you can see the island scenery on the trip up, walk around, and watch the spectacular sunset, then ride down as all the city lights are twinkling.

Rickshas

The few remaining rickshas are lined up just outside of the Star Ferry terminal on Hong Kong Island. No new ricksha licenses have been granted since 1972, and the gentlemen who still hold their licenses have been pulling rickshas for some years. Rarely, if ever, do people actually go for a ride around Central. Most people just want to have their pictures taken. The cost for a ride or picture is negotiable. The going rate is $HK 70, however, sometimes you can put $HK 50 in the driver's hand for a few snaps.

Car Rental

Avis, Budget, and Hertz have offices in Hong Kong if you want to drive. I do not advise renting a car in Hong Kong, unless you have a great deal of experience driving in foreign countries. It is far better to hire a car and driver directly from your hotel. Prices vary with the hotel but are approximately $65 an hour. If your hotel gives you a choice between a Mercedes and a Rolls Royce, the Mercedes will generally be less expensive. Remember that you may also make a deal with a taxi driver for several hours or even a day.

PHONING HOME

. . . .

To avoid hotel surcharges on international phone calls, you have a number of options that let you use your credit card or call home collect. I almost always end up using AT&T's USADirect, but there are other games in town. On my last visit, I paid only $2 a minute from Hong Kong to home, which isn't bad considering it was AT&T.

Hongkong Telecom, the local service, allows you to connect to an operator and make a credit card or collect call. You can also buy a stored-value phone card and use a public phone—this is a good value. They are sold at HKTA offices, 7-11 stores, many foreign exchange booths, and all over town.

Otherwise, call these numbers for direct access:

- To call the U.K., dial ☎ 800-0044 for an operator.
- To call the U.S., dial ☎ 800-1111 if your long-distance carrier is AT&T; ☎ 800-1121, if MCI is your carrier; ☎ 800-1877, if Sprint provides your long-distance service; and ☎ 900-1115 if your long-distance carrier is TRT/FTC.

If you wish to make a call to another international country other than home and charge it to your credit card, various cards have world plans that allow you to do this. The savings are not sublime, but they are usually better than direct dialing from a hotel.

Phoning Hong Kong

To get in touch with Hong Kong from the United States, dial ☎ 011-852 followed by the 8 digit number.

STORE HOURS

. . . .

Generally, shops open late in the morning and stay open until late in the evening. The majority of specialty stores open at 10am and close at 6:30pm. However, these are just general guidelines. Some stores open whenever they feel like it. Central tends to open later than Kowloon.

For the most part, stores close at 6:30pm in Central, 7:30pm in Tsim Sha Tsui, and 9pm on Nathan Road in Yau Ma Tei and in Mong Kok. In all honesty, I've been in the stores on Granville Road until 11pm at night. I think that as long as there is traffic, the stores are willing to stay open.

Mall stores are open during regular business hours on Sunday. Most shops in the main shopping areas of Tsim Sha Tsui and Causeway Bay are open 7 days a week. Those in Central close on Sunday.

Major public holidays are honored in many shops. Everything closes on Chinese New Year; some stores are closed for 2 days, others for 2 weeks. Do not plan to be in Hong Kong and do any shopping at this time. The stores that remain open charge a premium. The stores where you want to shop will all be closed.

Store hours are affected by the following public holidays:

- January 1 (New Year's Day)
- January/February (Chinese New Year)
- March/April (Good Friday, Easter Sunday and Monday)
- June (Dragon Boat Festival)
- August 25 (Liberation Day)
- December 25 (Christmas) and December 26 (Boxing Day)

On public holidays, banks and offices close, and there is a higher risk of shops closing as well. Factory outlets will definitely not be open. Many holiday dates change from year to year. For specific dates, contact the HKTA before you plan your trip.

If you are planning a tour of the factory outlets, remember that lunch hour can fall anywhere between noon and 2pm, although 1 to 2pm is most common. Outlet shops will close for 1 hour, along with the factory. Because of this practice, you might as well plan to have lunch then, too.

Department store hours differ from store to store. The larger ones, like **Lane Crawford** and **Chinese Arts & Crafts,** maintain regular business hours, 10am to 5pm. The Japanese department stores in Causeway Bay open between 10 and 10:30am and close between 9 and 9:30pm. They're all closed on different days 1 day of the week, however, which can be confusing. Don't assume because one department store is closed, that they all are.

Market hours are pretty standard. Only food markets open very early in the morning. Food markets are sometimes called "wet markets." There's no point in arriving in **Stanley** before 9am. Even 9:30am is slow; many vendors are still opening up.

The **Jade Market** opens at 10am every day and closes around 3pm; this includes Sunday. The weekend street market on Reclamation is a local market so it opens earlier; there's plenty going on at 9am.

HONG KONG PRIVILEGE

Born to Shop readers who would like some special perks on their next visit to Hong Kong can write to the HKTA for a Hong Kong Privilege card, a discount card which comes with its own little booklet and map, inviting you to discounts in participating stores and restaurants. Discounts are up to 20%, considerable savings. Get the package from the HKTA in the U.S., ☎ 800-282-4582, before you leave for Hong Kong.

If you are a senior citizen (age 60 or over) you qualify for Hong Kong Silver Plus, which also provides discounts.

For both plans, contact your nearest HKTA:
East Coast: HKTA, 590 Fifth Ave., 5th floor, New York, NY 10036; ☎ 212-869-5008; fax 212-730-2605; e-mail: **hktanyc@aol.com.**
West Coast: HKTA, 10940 Wilshire Blvd., Suite 1220, Los Angeles, CA 90024; ☎ 310-208-4582; fax 310-208-1869; e-mail: **hktalax@aol.com.**
Midwest: HKTA, 610 Enterprise Dr., Suite 200, Oak Brook, IL 60521 ☎ 708-575-2828; fax 708-575-2829; e-mail: **hktachi@aol.com.**

CHRISTMAS IN HONG KONG

Christmas decorations go up in Kowloon (it's hard to spot the neon from all the neon) in mid-November as the stores begin their Christmas promotions. Among the best deals in town at this time of year is that many department stores offer free shipping to either the U.K. or anyplace in the world . . . depending on the store.

Marks & Spencer sends Christmas hampers to any address in the U.K. for free, as long as the hamper costs £50 or more. **Chinese Arts & Crafts** stores will ship items as long as they cost $350 or more (U.S., not $HK!).

Christmas permeates the air; even street markets sell decorations—plastic wreaths, silk flowers, ornaments, and more. If you're familiar with the fabulous Christmas ornaments that Pottery Barn sells in the U.S., you'll be thrilled to find some of these Victorian–style embroidered goodies in stores in Hong Kong.

Better yet, Hong Kong is the perfect place to load up on inexpensive presents—what can you find at home that's fabulous for less than $1? Not much! Go to the **Jade Market** and you'll find plenty.

Even when I'm in Hong Kong in July, I start thinking about Christmas.

NEW YEAR IN HONG KONG

I don't mean Western New Year and *auld lang syne*; I mean Chinese New Year and when it comes, you may go crazy if you want to shop. Stores close for days or weeks, depending. Expect most stores to be closed a minimum of 2 to 3 days. The date of the New Year varies because it is based on a lunar calendar; the danger zone falls somewhere between the end of January and mid-February.

HONG KONG ON SALE

Hong Kong has two traditional sale periods: the end of August and shortly before Chinese New Year (January or February).

Everything else goes on sale during this same period. You'll find a lot of no-name merchandise that didn't interest you when it cost $50, but is looking a lot better now that it's marked down to $30.

The best thing about the sales in Hong Kong is that this is your best time to get regular retail merchandise at its lowest price. The real bargains in Hong Kong are not in retail stores; the real bargains in Hong Kong may not be in perfect condition. So if you insist on brand-new, clean, undamaged goods, you should feel safe buying them on sale. If you have teens or are on a limited clothing budget, shop Hong Kong during the sale periods. Check the advertisements in *The South China Morning Post* for special sale announcements.

Remember, the best buys in Hong Kong are not in retail shops. If you crave designer merchandise, about the only time to buy it in Hong Kong is during one of these big sale periods. **The Joyce** sale (see page 254) is an internationally famous event.

TYPHOON RETAILING

. . . .

During the summer (from May to September), Hong Kong falls prey to typhoons. To protect the population best, the Royal Observatory now ranks the typhoons on a scale from 1 to 10. While each number has some significance in terms of the velocity of the wind, we will translate this to you only in terms of shopping habits.

- No. 3 typhoon: The Star Ferry might stop running.
- No. 8 typhoon: All stores are supposed to be closed; everyone is supposed to go home or seek shelter. Offices will not be open during a No. 8. However, hotel stores will stay open and may even jack up their prices.

Tourists are told to stay inside the hotel during a No. 8. The hotels circulate a brochure telling you what to do: Close the drapes, stay away from the windows, etc. You can stay in your room all day reading a book, or you can drink Singapore Slings at the bar. Or you could do what any normal person would do: Go shopping. If you stay indoors, you'll find every shop in the hotel is doing a booming business. We were even offered "special typhoon prices."

FAKES FOR SALE

New York's streets are teeming with vendors selling faux Chanel earrings, T-shirts, and scarves. These goods are easily differentiated from the real thing. While Hong Kong doesn't have a lot of fake Chanel on the streets (it's hidden), there are many items for sale—especially at markets—that appear to be real. But they aren't!

I bought a canvas-and-leather book bag from a street market for the high (for Hong Kong) price of $20 U.S. It had a big and perfect Gap label on the front. It fell apart 36 hours later. Both buckles and one leather strap broke so quickly (in three different incidents) that I am convinced that real Gap labels were sewn on rather ordinary canvas bags. Let the buyer beware.

THE BUILDING SYSTEM

Most of us are used to finding stores on street level, with fancy glass storefronts and large numbers identifying their addresses. There are many such stores in Hong Kong, but many more are operated high up, out of office buildings. You may arrive at an address and see only a cement building. Before you think that the address is wrong, go into the lobby and look at the directory. The store or business will probably be listed with a floor and room number next to it.

Because of this practice of "office shopping," the addresses in Hong Kong usually refer to a particular building. When getting the address of a particular shop, you are likely to be told that it is in the Sands Building, instead of being told that it is at 17 Hankow Rd. Luckily many maps are marked with the actual buildings and their addresses.

Cab drivers are so used to the system that you can usually give them the name of the building, and they will take you right there.

If you are not using one of my tours to plan your shopping expedition, work carefully with a map so that you determine all the shops in one building at one time. Remember that it is not unusual for a business to have a shop on each side of the harbor, so decide if you are going to be in Hong Kong or Kowloon before you make plans. Use the *A-O-A Map Directory* to locate a building before you head off.

SHIPPING

. . . .

Shipping from Hong Kong is easy and it's safe. Container shipping is not inexpensive, but freight is moderate. Whether the item is as cumbersome as a giant Foo dog, as small as a few ginger jars, or as fragile as dinner plates, you can arrange to ship it home. All it takes is a little time and a little more money.

If you anticipate buying an item that needs shipping, do your homework before you leave the U.S. You may need a family member to claim the item at customs if you will still be out of the country, or you may even need a customs agent (see "Bringing it all Back Home," below). You will also want to know enough about shipping costs to be able to make a smart decision about the expense added to your purchase.

To make shipping pay, the item, including the additional cost of shipping, duty, and insurance (and customs agent, etc., if need be) should still cost *less* than it would at home, or should be so totally unavailable at home that any price makes it a worthwhile purchase. If it's truly unavailable (and isn't an antique or a one-of-a-kind art item) at home, ask yourself why. There may be a good reason— such as it's illegal to bring such an item into the country!

If you are indeed looking for a certain type of thing, be very familiar with American prices. If it's an item of furniture, even an antique, can a decorator get it for you with a 20% rather than 40% markup? Have you checked out all the savings angles first? Are you certain the item is genuine and is worth the price of the shipping? There are many furniture fakes in Hong Kong.

There are basically two types of shipping: surface and air. Air can be broken into two categories: unaccompanied baggage and regular air freight.

Surface mail (by ship in a transpacific transaction) is the cheapest. Surface mail may mean through the regular mail channels—that is, a small package of perfume would be sent through parcel post— or it may require your filling an entire shipping container, or at least paying the price of an entire container. Surface mail may take 3 months; I find 2 is the norm. If you are doing heavy-duty shipping, look in the back of the *South China Morning Post* for shippers wanting to fill containers.

If you're shipping by container but can't fill a container, you might want to save even more money by using groupage services. Your goods will be held until a shipping container is filled. The container will then go to the U.S., to one of only four ports of entry (Los Angeles, New York, San Francisco, or New Orleans), where you can meet the container at the dock, be there when your items are unpacked, and then pay the duties due. A full container is approximately 1,500 cubic feet of space (or 8'6" × 8'6" × 20') and will not be delivered to your door (no matter how much you smile). It will cost about $3,000 U.S. to ship a container by sea.

For small items, there are international overnight air package services, like Federal Express, UPS, DHL, etc., that deliver within a day or two. This part of the shipping business is growing just as fast as overnight U.S. services expanded over the past 3 years, so check out the latest possibilities. Crossing the dateline can make "overnight" deliveries seem longer or shorter. Local Hong Kong office numbers for overnight shippers are: **Federal Express:** ☎ 852-2730-3333; **UPS:** ☎ 852-2735-3535; and **DHL:** ☎ 852-2765-8111.

The U.S. Postal Service has international express mail, which is a 3-day service from U.S. post offices. Hong Kong post offices offer a similar program. Ask at the counter.

Do remember that whatever you are sending to yourself is subject to duty when it arrives home. If you've bought a special Hong Kong bargain, leave the price tag on it to prove the price to customs officers who may otherwise value an item at a higher price and charge more duty.

If you want to price a few local freight offices, try: **Unaccompanied Baggage Ltd.,** Counter 330, Departure Hall, Hong Kong International Airport, Kowloon. ☎ 852-769-8275 or **Michelle International Transport Co. Ltd.,** 20 Connaught Rd. West, Room 1002, Western District, Hong Kong. ☎ 852-548-7617.

You can have items shipped directly from shops for you. Many Hong Kong stores, especially tailors, will ship your purchases to the U.S. Most people I know who have done this are surprised when their goods arrive by UPS. Ask about the shop's shipping policies before you decide to ship—some stores will charge you for their trouble (a flat fee), then add the actual shipping rate and an insurance fee.

Try to pay for the purchase with a credit card; that way if it never arrives, you'll have an easier time getting a credit or a refund. Be sure to ask when the store will be able to ship the goods out. I planned to send home some perfume so as not to have to lug it around during a month's worth of touring. The shopkeeper told me she was so backed up on her

U.S. Customs & Duties Tips

To make your reentry into the U.S. as smooth as possible, remember:

- You are currently allowed to bring in $400 worth of merchandise per person, duty free. Each member of the family is entitled to the deduction; this includes infants (but not pets).
- You pay a flat 10% duty on the next $1,000 worth of merchandise. Duties thereafter are on a product-type basis. (For instance, there are hefty levies on hand embroidery!)
- The head of the family can make a joint declaration for all family members. The "head of the family" need not be male. Whoever is the head of the family should take the responsibility for answering any questions the customs officers may ask. Answer questions honestly, firmly and politely.
- You count into your $400 per person everything you obtain while abroad—this includes toothpaste (if you bring the unfinished tube back with you), gifts given to you, items bought in duty-free shops, gifts for others, the items that other people asked you to bring home for them, and—get this—even alterations.
- Have the customs registration slips for things you already own in your wallet or easily available. If you wear a Cartier watch, for example, whether it was bought in the U.S. or in Europe 10 years ago, should you be questioned about it, produce the registration slip. If you cannot prove that you took a foreign-made item out of the country with you, you may be forced to pay duty on it!
- Take two Polaroid pictures of everything you buy—one for your records and one for the shipper. It's very hard to prove damages on an antique piece without a picture.
- Do not attempt to bring in any illegal food items—dairy products, meats, fruits or

vegetables. Liquor-filled chocolates are a no-no for some reason, but coffee is okay. Generally speaking, if it's alive, it's *verboten.*

- Antiques must be at least 100 years old to be duty free. Provenance papers will help. Any bona fide work of art is duty free, whether it was painted 50 years ago or just yesterday; the artist need not be famous.

- Dress for success. People who look like hippies get stopped at customs more than average folks. Women who look like a million dollars, who are dragging their fur coats, who have first-class baggage tags on their luggage, and who carry Gucci handbags, but declare they have bought nothing, are equally suspicious.

- The amount of cigarettes and liquor you can bring back duty free is under state government regulation and varies with your port of entry. Usually, if you arrive by common carrier, you may bring back duty free one liter of alcoholic beverages. You may bring back an additional 5 liters on which you must pay duty—at $10.50 per gallon on distilled spirits—so obviously you don't want to go over your allowance unless you are carrying some invaluable wine or champagne.

  You may also bring back 100 cigars and one carton of cigarettes without import duty, but there will be state and local taxes on the smokes.

- Environmental and endangered species no-nos are a big problem in Hong Kong, so U.S. customs agents will be watching carefully.

- Ivory cannot legally be imported into the U.S. unless it is antique and comes with papers.

- Tortoise shell is also forbidden, no matter where it comes from (unless, that is, it comes from a plastic tortoise).

- If you are planning on taking your personal computer with you (to keep track of your budget, perhaps), make sure you register it before taking it out of the country. If you buy a computer abroad, you must declare it when you come in.

shipping that it would take her at least 6 weeks to mail our order. Then, it would take several weeks or months for the package to arrive by surface mail. I took it with me.

The U.S. Postal Service automatically sends all incoming foreign-mail shipments to customs for examination. If no duty is being charged, the package goes back to the post office and will be delivered to you. If duty is required, the customs officer attaches a yellow slip to your package, and your mail carrier will collect the money due when the package is delivered to you. If you feel the duty charge is inappropriate, you may file a protest, or you don't have to accept the package. If you don't accept it, you have 30 days to file your objection so the shipment can be detained until the matter is settled.

Be sure to keep all paperwork. If you use a freight office, keep the bill of lading. If the shop sends your package, keep all receipts.

Ask about the policy on breakage from any shop that ships for you.

Know the zip code to where you are shipping in the U.S. and insure for replacement value, not Hong Kong value.

LEAVING TOWN BY PLANE
· ·

Exit tax is usually paid at the airline desk—in cash in Hong Kong dollars, so don't spend all your money thinking you don't need it. I noticed that the **Conrad Hotel** gave guests the opportunity to pay for the departure tax at checkout by adding it to the guest's bill—a brilliant notion. I don't know if other hotels provide this service or not.

Also note that the Chinese laws on exporting of antiques are now in place; these laws are not as lax as the former ones. Don't try to smuggle anything, please.

LEAVING TOWN BY CRUISE

More and more cruise ships are using Hong Kong as a turn around hub for their Far Eastern adventures; the exit tax has been paid in your port taxes, and you need not ante-up in order to ship out.

INSURANCE

Insurance usually is sold per package by your shipper. Do not assume that it is included in the price of delivery because it isn't. There are several different types of insurance and deductibles, or all-risk (with no deductible); you'll have to make a personal choice based on the value of what you are shipping. Remember to include the price of the shipping when figuring the value of the item for insurance purposes.

BRINGING IT ALL BACK HOME

Because I travel to Hong Kong regularly and because most of my good clothes have been made and/or bought in Hong Kong, a few years ago I began to worry that U.S. customs would think my clothes were new and that I was trying to run them.

To prevent a problem from even happening, I began to take Polaroid pictures of any foreign-made or foreign-bought merchandise with which I routinely travel. I simply took a snapshot as I packed each item. Then I took the snapshots to the bank and had them notarized.

Now I have a card file of photos of most of my clothes and jewelry items. I've never had to show them to officers, but I consider it cheap insurance.

Chapter Three

· · · · · · · · ·

MONEY MATTERS

MONEY ANNOUNCEMENT

· ·

Don't Fret! The Chinese did not change currency in Hong Kong. We are still dealing in Hong Kong dollars, not yuan, and the paperwork is relatively simple compared to the whole rigamarole involved in getting yuan.

PAYING UP

· ·

Plastic is easy to use, provides you with a record of your purchases (for customs as well as for your books), and makes returns a lot easier. Credit-card companies, because they are often associated with banks, may give the best exchange rates. The price you pay, as posted in dollars or sterling, or whatever your hometown currency is, is translated on the day of your purchase.

Let's say the Hong Kong dollar is trading at $HK 7.80 to $1 U.S. Your hotel may only offer an exchange rate of $HK 7.40 when you convert your money. American Express will probably give you a higher rate of exchange.

The bad news about credit cards is that you can overspend easily, and you may come home to a stack of bills. But one extra benefit of a credit card is that you often get delayed billing, so that you may have a month or two to raise some petty cash.

If possible, travel with more than one credit card. Some stores will only take MasterCard or Visa. Others will accept only American Express. Traveler's checks are a must for safety's sake.

CASH & CARRY

While cash has many benefits, and often greases the wheels of bargaining, it puts you in the most vulnerable position in cases of exchanges, rip-offs, or returns. Once you have paid cash for an item—especially a camera or an electronic goodie which is going to be pricey—you can kiss that money good-bye.

Remember, credit-card companies may help you out if you dispute a charge; once you pay cash you will never see it again. Especially in Hong Kong.

PERSONAL CHECKS

Always travel with your checkbook. End of story. Yes, even to a foreign country. Period.

You see, in many places in the world (and Hong Kong is one of them), retailers are very happy to take your check. In fact, they may prefer it to a credit card.

I did get a letter from a reader, Richard Sungaila, who noted that he and his wife had a very successful visit at one of my favorite jewelry shops in Hong Kong and were shocked and dismayed that the firm did not take their personal check.

Should you have a certain firm or two targeted for big business transactions, you may want to write ahead or fax them to ask if they will accept your personal check.

FLUCTUATING DOLLARS

. . . .

There is no question that the dollar dances, so don't let anyone tell you that the Hong Kong dollar remains constant at $HK 7.80 to the U.S. dollar. True, it generally hovers around $HK 7.80, but this is not a hard-and-fast rule.

If you happen to be in Hong Kong during a time when the U.S. dollar is weak and the Hong Kong stock market is going strong (as it has been recently), you may find that the official rate is $HK 7.60 or $HK 7.70 and that your hotel will give you no more than $HK 7.30. In truth, it is smarter to divide by 7 and be happily surprised rather than upset. If you divide by 8, you are actually getting too good of a price and one that will not be reflected in your cash flow or on your statements.

CURRENCY EXCHANGE

. . . .

As I've already mentioned, currency exchange rates vary tremendously. The rate listed in the paper (the *South China Morning Post*) every day is the official bank exchange rate and does not apply to tourists. Even by trading your money at a bank, you will not get the rate of exchange that's announced in the papers.

- You will get a better rate of exchange for a traveler's check than for cash because there is less paperwork involved for banks, hotels, etc.
- Hotels generally give the least favorable rate of exchange.
- Don't change money (or a lot of it, anyway) at airport vendors; they have the worst rates in town—even higher than your hotel.
- Never change more money than you think you will need since you will pay a higher rate to change Hong Kong dollars back to U.S. dollars when you leave.

- Have some foreign currency on hand for arrival, especially if you are taking a taxi to your hotel. After a lengthy flight you will not want to have to stand in line at some airport booth to get your cab fare.

BARGAINING AS A WAY OF LIFE

When you walk into a store in New York, Paris, or London, you ask the price of an item, whip out your credit card or cash, and say "Thank you very much." No bargaining, no haggling.

Not so in Hong Kong, where life is based on bargaining. Hong Kong society revolves around the art of the bargain. You want to buy a mango at the corner stand? Buy two and offer a little less than double; you will probably be successful.

Bargaining does not take place on buses, in the MTR, or in taxis (unless you are going for a long drive or are hiring the car for a day). Hotel rooms are a flat rate. Your tailor has a flat fee. After that, you're on your own.

In the recent past, I have found tourists plenty and deals scarce. I've fought with vendors in **Stanley** over $HK 5 and not won out. I once left a fancy store in **The Pen** because they would not take $10 U.S. off a high-priced item.

The problem with bargaining is that you can get so wrapped up in the drama that you lose sight of what you wanted to buy or the amounts you are fighting over.

Nowhere is bargaining more important, however, than in the various markets (see page 217). Here, it is open season on tourists, and you are expected to bargain fiercely to get the best deal. Unless you come from a similar background, you will very likely become exhausted and give up. Once you give up, it's guaranteed that you have just gotten the bad end of the bargain. In fierce bargaining you will know that you are getting near the fair price when the shop owner becomes less gracious and more grudgingly quiet.

HOW TO BARGAIN IN HONG KONG

If you are hoping to bargain successfully, I have a few tips for you to follow:

- Do not try to bargain while wearing expensive jewelry or clothing. Go to the market in jeans and a T-shirt or old slacks and a nondescript sweater. Likewise, don't be plain and simple yet have a Nikon around your neck or a Rolex watch on your wrist.
- If you can shop with a Chinese friend, let him or her do the talking. Prices will drop magically.
- If you are bargaining for an expensive item like a carpet, camera, or piece of jewelry, have some background knowledge. If you can find a fault with the product and emphasize that you are doing the merchant a favor by relieving him of inferior goods, you will be in a stronger bargaining position.
- Never chat with the shopkeeper, argue, or show that you are passionately interested in the item. The more businesslike and disinterested you appear to be, the less quickly the merchant will think that the cash is in his pocket.
- Always try to bargain alone (unless you have turned negotiations over to a Chinese friend). If you are with your spouse or friend, take the white hat/black hat positions. If you are the one looking at the item, have your friend talk about how he/she saw the same thing in New York and it was less money, better looking, and easier to buy.
- Ask to see the inside of the item (watch, camera, or electronic device). Most shopkeepers won't want to bother. If they do, look like you know what you are examining and make clucking noises as if something is wrong. If the shopkeeper says

"What?" just shrug knowingly. The trick is to be on the offensive, not the defensive.

• You must have a lot of time available to bargain well. Wearing down the opponent is the key to success. If you're not ready to sit there and squabble, pay the asking price and get out.

• Decide how much you are willing to pay, or what you think is fair. Put this amount of money (exactly) in your palm before you start the dance. After a while, offer that amount on a take it or leave it basis.

• As a last resort in bargaining, walk away. But don't ever walk away from something you can't live without. If you're just bluffing, the shopkeeper will know, and you will lose ground in the bargaining. If you are serious about walking away, the shopkeeper will more than likely offer you a final deal, with the understanding that if you do walk away the price will not go that low again. Don't be too surprised if the price the shopkeeper offers you as you start away is much lower than where the bargaining had broken off. If the item is so special that you can't live without it, pay that price. If not, then be prepared to do without.

TIPPING TIPS

. . . .

Tipping rituals in Hong Kong are complicated because you pay a service charge at your hotel. Yet I find every time I check in or out of a hotel, the $HK 100 bills seem to disappear.

Here's the system I go by:

• I do not tip the driver of the Rolls or the Daimler that the hotel has sent.

• I do not tip the front-desk person who shows me to my room as this is a management type person.

• I tip $HK 10 per suitcase when the luggage arrives in the room. (If tipping in U.S. dollars, I cut that back to $1 per suitcase.)

- I tip $HK 50 to the person who performs the welcoming tea ceremony upon arrival in the room. If tipping in U.S. dollars, I give $5.
- I tip $HK 5 for each taxi hailed at a hotel (any hotel).
- I tip taxi drivers by rounding off to the next convenient figure, not by any scientific formula or percentage.
- I tip the floor boys $HK 100 when I check out.
- If the concierge staff has been helpful, I leave an envelope containing anywhere from $HK 100–200 on the dresser with the words: "With Thanks for Your Help—Suzy Gershman, Room 841" written across the front.
- I tip the same $HK 10 per item on my baggage as I check out.
- I do not tip the driver of the hotel car on arrival at the airport.
- I do tip the hotel baggage representative at the curb at the airport if he takes charge of the luggage and really helps out. The guy from The Pen who was there waiting for me on the last trip was fabulous. I gave him £5. ($8, all my Hong Kong dollars had been spent.) I'm not sure if the other hotels have a man at the airport; that was the first time I experienced this extra service.

EXIT TAX & DUTY-FREE DOLLARS

While you're figuring out what to do with your spare Hong Kong dollars, make sure that you have tucked aside $HK 100 in cash. You will need this for your exit tax, per person.

There is no tax for children under 12. The tax must be paid in local currency, not foreign; credit cards are not accepted. Verify the amount with your hotel concierge, since it can change when the flags change and then you won't have change.

Chapter Four

· · · · · · · ·

SHOPPING STRATEGIES

THE YIN & YANG OF SHOPPING

· ·

Two questions I am most frequently asked are: "Are there any bargains left in Hong Kong?" and "Is Hong Kong still worth visiting for shopping, or is China or Bangkok better?"

Bargains, of course, are in the eye of the beholder. I see bargains in junk in bins and in street markets, and bargains in very high-end items, tailor-made clothing, and custom-made jewelry. Beyond that, I think it takes luck and a sharp eye.

I've been on the streets long enough to know two important yin and yang facts:

- The good stuff is often hidden. Either it's put away, or it goes to those who have custom work done and know how to go after real value.
- You have to go back to the same places constantly and hope to get lucky. Or you have to hit it just right. It's just like shopping at an off-pricer like Loehmann's—hit or miss.

It is virtually impossible to go to Hong Kong and not find anything to buy, but the days of deals galore may be over. Savvy shoppers are off to China with empty suitcases. The best values in

Hong Kong can be found at the extremes of the retail spectrum:

- High-end: The tailor who custom makes you a $2,000 suit for the same price as an off-the-rack suit in the U.S. offers a genuine bargain as does the jeweler who creates one-of-a-kind jewelry for you at better-than-at-home prices.
- Low-end: Anything from a famous name shop or maker that sells for $10–$20 and is reasonably well made is a bargain to me. That hand-knit cotton designer sweater with the intricate floral pattern that I bought for $22 was a steal. Ditto for the Gap shirt for $10 and the white linen dress for $20. I even consider certain items without a name or a label I've purchased in Hong Kong bargains. I recently bought a silk chenille sweater (gorgeous dark turquoise color) for $10. It's the most fabulous thing you've ever seen. Who cares if it has no label inside? It's deals like this that remind us that Hong Kong is still the shopping capital of the world.

WHEN A BUY IS A GOOD-BYE

A true-blue shopper has been known to lose his or her head now and again. And no place on earth is more conducive to losing one's head than Hong Kong. You can see so many great "bargains" that you end up buying many items just because the price is cheap, not because you need or want them. Or you can fall into the reverse trap, seeing nothing to buy, getting frustrated, and then buying the wrong things. When you get home, you realize that you've tied up a fair amount of money in rather silly purchases.

Shopping in a foreign country is much more romantic than shopping at home; there's no question about it. And face it, most people expect to shop in Hong Kong. Even nonshoppers want to shop when away from home; they, too, love Hong Kong. But if

A Few Tips for the Value-Conscious

Value is important. Over the years, I've developed a few strategies to ensure I take it into consideration when shopping in Hong Kong. In the hope that these strategies may prove useful to you as well, I've distilled them into the following points:

- Buy items that have been made in Hong Kong that will cost more in the U.S. once U.S. customs and duties have been applied, Stateside.
- Try to catch the sale periods: the end of August and right before the Chinese New Year.
- Travel with price lists and even catalogs that carry major designer brands so you can compare prices on the spot.
- Target goods you wish to buy in Hong Kong at home before you leave, obtain their U.S. retail prices (with tax), and compile these items into a personalized shopping list. You can whip it out, ever so discreetly, when you're on the scene to be sure what appears to be a bargain actually is one.
- Watch prices on European designer items carefully. Most cost *more* in Hong Kong than in the U.S. or the country of origin! For the most part, avoid European designer goods!
- Let go. Saving money isn't always paramount among my concerns. The reason one shops in European designer boutiques in Hong Kong isn't to save money but to find goods that simply are not sold in the U.S. Some haven't made their American debut, others are for various reasons deemed inappropriate for the American market, and still others don't pass FDA regulations. It's selection, not savings.

you make a mistake while shopping in another American city, you can usually return the merchandise and get a credit with just a small amount of hassle. On a foreign trip, returns can be a major problem and usually aren't worth the effort. So, to keep mistakes to a minimum, I've got a few rules of the game:

- Avoid buying cameras and electronics in Hong Kong. Period. If you are bound and determined to ignore this gem of advice, see pages 140 and 150 on how to buy cameras and electronics in Hong Kong and hope you don't get taken.
- Figure the price accurately. Despite rumor to the contrary, the Hong Kong dollar does fluctuate.
- Try not to make decisions based on labels; let the quality of the item speak for itself. Last time I was in Hong Kong I saw a surprising number of British name-maker labels, the kinds of names most Americans would not recognize. Likewise, Brits may not recognize American designer names. Eliminate the name factor in decision making and go by the correlation between quality and price.
- If you ignore this advice and buy a gift by the label, make sure the person who is receiving the gift knows the value of the name or the brand. I've given many a gift to a variety of international friends who went blank when confronted with a label they didn't know.
- Figure in the duty. U.S. citizens are currently allowed $400 duty free. If you are traveling with your family, figure out your family total. Children, even infants, still get the $400 allowance. If you have more than $400 worth of merchandise, you pay a flat 10% on the next $1,000; after that you pay according to various duty rates.
- Calculate what your bargain will cost you in aggravation. Will you have to schlep the item all over the world with you? If it takes up a lot of suitcase room, if it's heavy, if it's cumbersome, if it's breakable and at risk every time you pack and unpack or check your suitcase, if it has to be hand-held—it might not be worth the cheap price tag. Estimate your time, trouble, and level of tolerance per item. Sure, it may be inexpensive, but if it's an ordeal to bring it home, is it really a good buy?

- Likewise, if you have to insure and ship it, is it still a bargain? How will you feel if the item never makes it to your door?
- I am ambivalent about the value of counterfeit merchandise and cannot advise you whether to buy it or to walk away from it. If you suspect an item to be a fake, you must evaluate if this is a good buy or a good-bye. Remember that fakes most certainly do not have the quality of crafts-manship that originals have. You may also be asked to forfeit the item at customs or pay duty on the value of the real object. But you may have a lot of fun with your fakes.
- My rule of thumb on a good buy is that 50% (or more) off the U.S. or British price is a valuable saving. I think that a saving of less than 20% is probably not worth the effort. If the saving is be-tween 20% and 50%, judge according to the de-gree of your personal desire for the item and the ratio of the previous points. If the saving is 50% or better, buy several and whoop with joy. That's a good buy!

BE PREPARED CULTURALLY

. . . .

Unless you are accustomed to traveling in the Far East, you may find Hong Kong extremely different from anyplace you've ever been before. Depending on how sheltered your life has been, you may even go into culture shock. I don't preach about politics or the poor, but I do suggest that you be mentally prepared for what you are about to experience. There are a few particularly important cultural details:

- Chinese street vendors and retailers may be rude to Anglos. I try not to generalize about a thing like this, but you'll soon discover it is a common thread of conversation among tourists and expa-triates alike. There is a two-class system at work.

Face it. Furthermore, it's gotten ruder out there ever since the hand over.

- The world works best with "tea money"—tip everyone and anyone if you want favors, information, or even a smile. Yep, those ricksha drivers want money if you plan to take their picture.
- As a tourist, you will never get the cheapest price possible, so forget it. Even if you are an American Born Chinese (called "ABC" by locals), you will not get the local price. Speak Cantonese perfectly? Great, you're on your way to a better price.
- You are a rich American (or Brit) and will never miss what you overpay, according to many vendors. Take heart, prices are highest for Germans and then Swiss. Americans ranks about fourth or fifth on the local list of rich catches.

MADE IN HONG KONG

There is a caveat about those famous words, "Made in Hong Kong." Just because an item is made there does not mean you will find it in local stores or outlets. Many garments are shipped directly to the overseas stores, with only dust left behind in the warehouse.

Toys, which are made in Hong Kong, are sent out to be packaged and therefore are imported back into Hong Kong at prices pretty close to those at home. Don't expect any great deals.

Whenever I look in my closet and see all the "Made in Hong Kong" labels, I wish I had bought those items in Hong Kong (on Granville Road in a bin, of course), yet the chances of making a match are pretty slim.

EUROPEAN-MADE BARGAINS

There are few European-made bargains in Hong Kong. The only exceptions can be found during a sale period. But for the most part, it is wrong to assume that Hong Kong prices are cheaper than U.S. or U.K. prices.

My rule is that you don't buy European designer merchandise in Hong Kong unless you are equipped with a price list from home. Expect prices to be high; be ready to pounce when a bargain shows itself.

Hermès scarves and enamel bracelets cost less than in the U.S. and the U.K.; Chanel makeup also costs less, although all Chanel items are not necessarily less. I priced a pair of Ferragamo shoes last trip: they cost $170 in the U.S. (then add sales tax); they cost £100 in Britain (slightly less than in the U.S. considering you will get a VAT refund) and $280 in Hong Kong. And folks, that's $280 U.S. not Hong Kong!

SECONDS FOR SALE

· ·

I've heard that the first words a manufacturer learns in Chinese are "no problem," which is all that can be said when faced with samples that aren't quite right. What happens to these samples or all the items that just don't quite cut the muster? They hit the shelves and streets of Hong Kong.

In the industry, this merchandise is called seconds, irregulars, or imperfects. In Hong Kong, this merchandise is sold on the streets or in factory-outlet stores and may not be marked with tape or tags to tell you it is less than perfect.

Depending on the brand, the "inferior" merchandise may not have anything wrong with it. With name-brand goods in particular, the quality controls are so incredibly strict that when a unit does not pass inspection, it still may *appear* to be perfect. Possibly only the maker could find the defect.

"Damages" almost always have something wrong with them, but often it's fixable or something that doesn't upset you considering how good the bargain is.

Here are some of the flaws that may send a unit to the seconds or damages bin; watch for them in your inspection of lower-priced name goods:

- A dye lot that does not match other dye lots
- Stripes that are not printed straight or do not match at seams
- Prints that are off-register
- Bubbles in glass or plastic
- Uneven finish
- Unmatched patterns at seams
- Broken or poorly set zipper
- Puckered stitching
- Belt loops that don't match

Remember, seconds are not sale merchandise that hasn't sold; they are stepchildren. Most stores will not admit that they sell seconds. If you are shopping in a seconds resource or a factory outlet, remember to check for damages or slight imperfections. Some imperfections are more than slight.

THE BEIJING RULE OF SHOPPING

The Beijing Rule of Shopping is the Asian version of my Moscow Rule of Shopping:

Now: The average shopper, in pursuit of the ideal bargain, does not buy an item he wants on first seeing it, not being convinced that he won't find it elsewhere for less money. This is human nature. A shopper wants to see everything available, then return for the purchase of choice. This is a normal thought process, especially in Hong Kong, where every merchant seems to have exactly the same merchandise. If you live in Beijing, however, you know that you must buy something the minute you see it, because if you hesitate it will be gone. Hence the name of our international law. If you live in Hong Kong, you know the guys from Beijing can come over the hills anytime soon and take it all away. So you buy it when you can.

When you are on a trip, you probably will not have time to compare prices and then return to a certain shop. You will never be able to backtrack cities—and if you could, the item might be gone by the time you got back. What to do? The same thing they do in Beijing: Buy it when you see it, with the understanding that you may never see it again. But since you are not shopping in Beijing and you may see it again, weigh these questions carefully before you go ahead:

- Is this a touristy type of item that I am bound to find all over town? Are there scads of shops selling this kind of stuff, or is this something few other vendors seem to have?
- Is this an item I can't live without, even if I am overpaying?
- Is this a reputable shop, and can I trust what they tell me about the quality of this merchandise and the availability of such items?
- Is the quality of this particular item so spectacular that it is unlikely it could be matched anywhere else or at this price?

The Beijing Rule of Shopping breaks down totally if you are an antiques or bric-a-brac shopper, since you never know if you can find another of an old or used item, if it would be in the same condition, or if the price would be higher or lower. It's very hard to price collectibles, so consider doing a lot of shopping for an item before you buy anything. This is easy in Hong Kong, where there are a zillion markets that sell much the same type of merchandise in the collectibles area. (This includes the entire Hollywood Road area.) At a certain point, you just have to buy what you love and not worry about the price. Understand that you always will get taken; it's just a matter of for how much.

THE TIANANMEN SQUARE RULE OF SHOPPING

· ·

This is a very simple and very important rule for all shoppers in Hong Kong: When things get violent—run. You think I'm kidding? I wish!

I had a very difficult experience in one of those electronics stores on Nathan Road, during which much drama was enacted—there was yelling and screaming, laying on of hands and attempts to physically threaten and bully me. When I told *Born to Shop* British correspondent Ian Cook of the encounter, he looked at me as if I was utterly stupid and said simply "Why didn't you just run?" Indeed.

If you are shopping for cameras, watches, or high-ticket electronics, you must go through a very elaborate bargaining process before you ever get to the price you might pay if you were going to buy. This makes comparison shopping very difficult and, when you are nearing a decent price, puts you in a vulnerable position. Beware.

Vendors know how to make it even more difficult by putting the screws to you. For example, you want a camera. You have done your homework and know that the camera you want costs $275 from 47th Street Photo in New York. You decide to go to a few shops in Hong Kong to find out how prices compare and what's available before you make the big purchase.

You walk into Shop A, which you have chosen at random, since there are several million such shops within shouting distance. The marked price on the camera is $300. You begin to bargain because you know that $275 is the U.S. price. You finally get the price down to $250. You think this is a pretty good price, but you want to try some other shops. You thank the vendor and say you want to think about it. He says, "If you buy it right now, I'll make it $225. No one else would take this loss, but I've spent all this time with you already, and my time is valuable. If you come back later, the price will be $250."

How to Spot a Scam

Hong Kong is the original Scam City. If you think you are street smart, you can still learn a trick or two in Hong Kong. If you know you are naive, get smart now.

The wise man asks, "How can you tell if you are being cheated in Hong Kong?"

The philosopher answers, "How can you tell how much you are being cheated in Hong Kong?"

I list only shops we have done business with or that readers have recommended. But I don't guarantee anything, and it doesn't hurt to be on the ball.

Markets and street vendors are more likely to con you than established retail outlets that are members of HKTA or have a reputation to lose. Whatever the source, here are a few basic tips you can take to protect yourself when making a purchase:

- Feel the goods and carefully inspect any item wrapped in plastic—even go so far as to open the plastic. There is a good chance that the item you have been given is exactly like the sample on display in every way—except that the silk is of an inferior quality. Not everyone will cheat you. But many will try.
- Pick the skins for shoes or leather goods that are being custom made, and make it clear that you expect the skins you pick to be the skins in your garment. Have them marked with your initials. If you go for a fitting, before the linings are added, check your skins to make certain they are the same.
- Jade is very difficult to buy. A true test requires scientific measurement of hardness, specific density, and light refraction. If it's not incredibly expensive and guaranteed, walk away.
- Never trust anyone, no matter how much you think you can. Murphy's Law of Hong Kong: If you can be taken, you will be.

Now you are in hot water. Is this a con job to get you to commit, or must you take advantage of a great bargain when it comes your way and get on with living life? Well, I can't decide this one for you because there are many values at stake here—which include the fun of the chase, your time, and the camera. I can tell you that I was cheated on the purchase of a fax machine in a very elaborate con and that there are times when the bargaining and the shopping aren't fun, and you have to listen to that tiny voice within you, especially if it whispers, "Run."

If you are verbally or physically threatened in the bargaining process, leave at once.

If you are frightened, if things don't seem kosher, run.

Please note that it is unlikely that these tactics will be practiced in any store that features a red junk on it and the HKTA label of membership.

WHO YA GONNA TRUST?

Trust being such a desirable commodity (since it's also so elusive), I've developed a few simple guidelines for those who are concerned and don't know whom to trust in Hong Kong.

- The Chinese System of Trust: The Chinese know that you can't trust anyone except family. As a result, nepotism reigns supreme. Rich people in Hong Kong (whether Anglo or Chinese) do their business within a small cadre of those they trust, most of whom are interrelated. On high-ticket items, they never take risks on outsiders or unknown vendors.

- The HKTA System of Trust: The HKTA is the Hong Kong Tourist Association. They are a heavy-duty presence in Hong Kong and are uniformly referred to as the HKTA. Because rip-offs are so common in Hong Kong, the HKTA put together a merchants' association. They make merchants swear to be honest when they join. In exchange, the merchants get a little red Chinese-junk sticker (it's about 8 inches high) to put in their window, signifying that they are approved by the HKTA and therefore honest.

This is nice in theory, but let's face it, honesty can't be policed. However, if you have problems in one of the HKTA-approved shops, you have recourse. If you have a problem, call the HKTA. They have set up a special shopper's hotline for consumers with questions or complaints. Call the main number (☎ 852-2524-4191) and ask for the Membership Department. If the shop is not a member of the association, there's little that can be done.

Chapter Five

· · · · · · · ·

SLEEPING IN HONG KONG

SUITE DREAMS

· ·

I can't think of any other city in the world, and that includes Paris, where your choice of hotel is a more integral part of your stay than in Hong Kong.

Although I am incredibly picky about hotels, I have found several in Hong Kong that offer the most important factor in a shopping hotel—location—and still have all the luxury you can lust after. Asian hotels are famous for their deluxe standards and fabulous service; enjoying these perks is part of the whole pleasure of staying in Hong Kong.

I recently read that grand hotels are where memories are made, and I think I believe that. Surely I've had memories made in stores, in restaurants, on street corners, and in alleys, but the right hotel is very much a part of the whole. Choose yours with the same care you would use in buying any precious memory or souvenir.

HOTEL TIPS

· ·

Many tour companies and large hotel chains offer shopping packages for Hong Kong, but few of these include the kind of five-star hotels I depend on. If you're a sucker for luxury, don't fight it—but shop around so you can get the most for your money. Hong Kong has a good base of luxury hotel rooms, and when things aren't too busy, there are big-time deals to be made.

I find official rack rates that hotels publish very irritating and refuse to quote them in these pages— few people pay the official rates; there are almost always deals to be made. Hong Kong is deal city.

Promotional rates can be as low as $149 a night at the Omni (Kowloon); I once saw an ad for Mandarin Oriental touting their Oriental Interlude Leisure breaks at which prices per room (not per person) were $HK 1,100 ($142). Rates are on the rise in Hong Kong and rooms can be dear, especially when trade fairs are in town. It pays to shop around for rates and for the right time of year to visit, as rates do change with the seasons.

NOW YOU SEE IT, NOW YOU DON'T

. . . .

If it's been a year or more since your last trip to Hong Kong, you might want to check to see if your favorite hotel is still standing. I wish I was joking. There's been a big bid to tear down hotels and replace them with office towers because real estate is so dear. **The Hongkong Hilton** is long gone— although there are rumors that a new Hilton will be born at the new airport. Every day I hear that **The Sheraton** in Kowloon is living on borrowed time.

Don't assume a hotel is there just because you stayed there before or because friends have mentioned it. Before you get too far into planning your trip, use a toll-free phone number to verify the dates you are thinking about. Also note that several new hotel projects are coming onboard, in town and near the new airport—don't assume that a hotel that carries a brand name is located where it was years ago. New affiliations may have new addresses.

Tricks of the Trade

Some secrets that might make booking your hotel easier:

- Ask about inclusive packages that may include breakfast, airport transfers, and other items that are usually charged as extras. Almost every luxury hotel in the world offers a Honeymoon Package. As long as you don't show up with the kids, you're on your honeymoon.
- Mileage awards can be used to pay for hotel rooms, to obtain discounts on rooms, or to accrue more mileage for your favorite frequent-flier account.
- Always ask the hotels if they are offering weekend or 5-day rates. Almost all hotels discount rooms during the off-season or when there is not a lot of business in town. Hong Kong has so many conventions that you may get a low-price convention rate.
- Peak season in Hong Kong is October and November; you'll pay top dollar for rooms during these months. Summer rates are usually the least expensive although there are often discounts beginning the first week in December.
- Watch out for Japanese holidays which are usually not on U.S. and U.K. calendars; they fill up Hong Kong hotels.
- The Hong Kong Tourist Association ☎ 800-282-4582 publishes a brochure called *Hong Kong Hotel Guide*. This publication provides a comprehensive list of all the possibilities, including addresses, phone numbers, room rates, fax numbers, and services offered.
- Check the big chains for promotional rates. Often you can prepay in U.S. dollars and save . . . or they'll have a deal in the computer that your travel agent doesn't know about. A telephone operator from Hilton told me about an exceptional value at **The Conrad.** Ask!

THE BEST SHOPPING HOTELS OF HONG KONG

. . . .

There are several hotel enclaves on Hong Kong Island; one in Causeway Bay and two in Central. In the heart of Central, pick from those hotels right at the base of the Star Ferry in downtown Central or from those grouped slightly off to the side at Admiralty. How does one decide among them? It all depends on price, style, and location. Don't worry—you can't go wrong with any of the choices below.

Central

I've actually found three hotels that serve as one since all three are in the same location: **Pacific Place,** right above a mall of the same name. They all have entrances within the mall as well as front doors on the street.

THE ISLAND SHANGRI-LA
Pacific Place, Supreme Court Road
(MTR: Admiralty).

When I visited The Island Shangri-La for Richard Branson, I fell in love with this location and with **Pacific Place,** the mall, and the exotic architecture and style of The Island Shangri-La. There actually wasn't a location problem; I found ease in getting around simply by hopping in a taxi or even walking.

Note that **The Marriott** and **The Conrad** also have hotels in this cluster and are also connected to the mall. You may want to price all three hotels, if price becomes an issue.

For U.S. reservations for **The Island Shangri-La,** call ☎ 800-942-5050. Local phone: ☎ 852-2877-3838; fax 852-2521-8742.

THE CONRAD
88 Queensway (MTR: Admiralty).

I tried to book The Island Shangri-La on my last visit, but they were full. So I called Hilton's reservation number in the U.S. and immediately realized that The Conrad not only had space, but had a better deal. Not only are prices less, but the operator on the phone very quickly explained several price options in package deals, telling me where the best buys and values were. There was even a rate that included the limousine transfer to and from the airport—it was simply the best rate in Hong Kong.

Yet I found the best part when I got to my room— each room is provided with a complimentary teddy bear in the bed and a yellow rubber ducky in the bathtub. You can buy more ($3 each), but the first set is on the house.

The hotel also has a businessy atmosphere to it that I really like; it's a luxury hotel, but they are organized to help you get things done—they provide a booklet with the bus transport information right in your key card; the business center is open 24 hours a day; you can pay the airport departure tax when you check out. The hotel is structured to compete with fancier hotels by offering more business perks and conveniences; I'm hooked.

Call ☎ 800-HILTONS for toll-free reservations. Local phone: ☎ 852-2521-3838; fax 852-2521-3888.

THE MANDARIN ORIENTAL
5 Connaught Rd., (MTR: Central).

If your motto is "Location, location, location" and you also care for Old-World service, fabulous hotel restaurants, power breakfasts, and sensational afternoon teas, rooms with a view, and an indoor swimming pool, then it must be Mandarin. You'll pay for the privilege, but this is the single best shopping location in Central.

While Mandarin Oriental has a forbiddenly formal reputation which may lead you to believe you cannot afford their services, I beg you to think again and reconsider. If you book during one of their promotional periods, they are practically giving away rooms. When you can stay in a Mandarin Oriental for less than $150 per night, they are giving away rooms.

For U.S. reservations, call ☎ 800-526-6566 or Leading Hotels of the World ☎ 800-223-6800. Local phone: ☎ 852-2522-0111; fax 852-2810-6190.

Even if you aren't staying here, please come use parts of the hotel and check it out: go upstairs for cocktails and a view; use the coffee shop for lunch; have formal tea (it's a meal unto itself), and shop the hotel's mall.

Kowloon

THE REGENT HOTEL
18 Salisbury Rd., Kowloon (MTR: TST).

Still considered to be one of the most scenic locations in Hong Kong, The Regent occupies the tip of Kowloon Peninsula; the views from the lobby bar at night are nothing short of spectacular.

In addition to its spectacular views, I consider The Regent home because they have Hong Kong's best hotel shopping mall, which has now replaced the one at the Peninsula Hotel as the chicest address. Every big-name European designer has a shop here, but so do other big names—from Chanel to Donna Karan! Not to mention my regular hairdresser, Hair Image (see page 139). And I dote on the concierge. There's also a less fancy mall (New World Shopping Centre) attached to The Regent's three-level mall and a new underground road of dreams—The Palace Mall, right alongside The Regent and somewhat hidden by the fact that it's underground and will eventually connect The Regent and The Pen.

The Regent also has one of my favorite quick-bite places to eat in Hong Kong—the coffee shop (called Harbourside; it's downstairs). Try the smoked chicken salad. They have serious restaurants here, too (see page 78), but this one is a great shopper's special because it is quick and well priced.

Part of what's so interesting about this hotel is that it is both formal and casual at the same time. The pool is great, but the hot tub is what you'll come away raving about. Indeed, I can't consider a trip to Hong Kong to be a success until I've spent some time in The Regent's hot tub. Also note The Shanghai Club, a must-do for a drink if you aren't staying at this hotel.

Regent and Four Seasons have merged management; for U.S. reservations, ☎ 800-545-4000. Local phone: ☎ 852-2721-1211; fax 852-2739-4546.

THE PENINSULA HOTEL
Salisbury Rd., Kowloon (MTR: TST).

The Pen, as it is called, is the most famous hotel in Hong Kong and in Kowloon as well; it continues in its friendly competition with **The Regent,** as the two vie for international titles as the best hotel in town . . . or the world.

The only way to decide is to stay in both of them—preferably during the same stay—so you can see how uniquely different the two properties are. (This is not as nutty as it sounds, especially if you are going to Macau in between for a few days.)

The Pen built a new tower with health club, pool, and view firmly in place . . . as well as a Philippe Starck–designed restaurant (**Felix**) to add to their galaxy of gourmet stars. And yes, there's a helicopter pad on the roof.

The Pen prides itself on its Old-World charm and classy elegance; the crowd is much more dressed up than at The Regent. The lobby, where tea is the most famous beverage, is the best place for spotting rich, beautiful local women, called *tai-tais*. **Gaddi's** is the single most famous French restaurant in town and a living legend in its own merit.

Now then, in case you're tacky and care only about the bottom line, here's the dish you've been waiting for. Yes, The Pen is more expensive than **The Regent** and yes, they pride themselves on this fact. A deluxe harbor-view room will cost close to $500 a night. Even their car service is more expensive than anyone else's. However, if you show your copy of this book upon check-in, the general manager will be delighted to send you a box of Peninsula chocolates to welcome you to Hong Kong.

For U.S. reservations, ☎ 800-262-9467 or Leading Hotels of the World, ☎ 800-223-6800. Local phone: ☎ 852-2366-6251; fax 852-2722-4170.

THE KOWLOON HOTEL
19–21 Nathan Rd., Kowloon (MTR: TST).

If you want the best location in town but don't feel up to springing for a five-star hotel, perhaps you should consider The Kowloon Hotel, whose secret is the simple fact that it is owned by the Peninsula Group. It is a four-star hotel rather than a five-star hotel and is more in keeping with an American-style big hotel than a palace, but it's got advantages.

You're next door to **The Pen** (this means you are in the middle of a shopping neighborhood), and the hotel is built in a slim tower, so view rooms are available. Locationwise, I don't need to get more explicit, do I?

Now let's talk about price. The rooms are half the price of those at The Pen. Best of all, a suite here costs the same as a regular room at The Pen or The Regent. A harbor-view double costs about $150 a night. Also, because the clients are mostly businesspeople, there are fax and computer terminals in the rooms and all sorts of modern, up-to-date electronic gadgets.

For U.S. reservations, ☎ 800-262-9467. Local phone: ☎ 852-2369-8698; fax 852-2369-8698.

Chapter Six

· · · · · · · ·

DINING IN HONG KONG

BORN TO EAT

· ·

If you think Hong Kong is most famous for its shopping, think again. The international word is that the number-one attraction in town is its culinary pleasures—from five-star restaurants in the most elegant hotels to Chinese restaurants somewhat off the beaten path. There are certain places in town that are so fabulous you just have to try them in order to complete your Hong Kong experience.

While I have developed my own list of favorites, I've also had a few whispers in my ear from Fred Ferretti, an editor at *Gourmet* magazine. I'm lucky enough to bump into Fred and his wife a few times a year—she's Eileen Yin Fei Lo, one of this country's well-regarded cookbook writers—they always are generous with their thoughts on best bets and best buys. Because Fred and Eileen spend part of each year in Hong Kong, be sure to check back issues of *Gourmet* for Fred's latest finds.

LEGENDS & LANDMARKS

· ·

When I pick a restaurant for this category, my selection is based on a combination of factors: the length of time the establishment has been in operation, the quality of its food, location, and ambience. Some of these places so typify what is special about Hong Kong, I consider them "don't miss" experiences. These establishments are designated with a shopping-bag icon.

JUMBO FLOATING RESTAURANT
Shum Wan, Aberdeen (MTR: none).

My first thought about Jumbo was that only tourists go here and, therefore, it wasn't worth my time. It took me years to get up the nerve to come here and, now that I've done it, I feel like a fool. Why did I wait so long? I can't wait to come back and bring my son! If ever there was a fantasy place to bring your kids, this is it.

Jumbo, as you may already know, is the most famous of the floating restaurants in Aberdeen Harbour. It is best seen at night when all the lights are aglow, but you can go for lunch and take advantage of the various souvenir vendors who set up shop in junks and on the pier that provides service from Aberdeen Harbour to the floating restaurant. (There's more shopping when you get into the restaurant, but all these prices are marked in yen.)

The place is enormous and has a fun, almost silly atmosphere. This is not intimate dining, but if dressing up in a mandarin's outfit and having your photo taken sounds like fun to you (or your kids), this is the place. Menus feature pictures, so you just point to what you want. Dinner for two with beer is about $40. The food is American-style Chinese. To get here: Take a taxi to Jumbo Pier and hop aboard Jumbo's tender. For reservations, ☎ 852-2553-9111.

GADDI'S
The Peninsula Hotel, Salisbury Rd., Kowloon (MTR: TST).

From Jumbo to Gaddi's is surely going from the ridiculous to the sublime: Gaddi's is known to visitors and locals alike as the best French restaurant in town; serious foodies wouldn't consider a trip to Hong Kong complete without a visit. It's much like a private club of local and visiting firefighters.

Lunch and dinner are both popular; lunch is less expensive. However, we have indeed found a deal: The house offers a set dinner menu of five courses, each with its own wine, for approximately $125 a person, an excellent value.

This may be the most elegant restaurant in Hong Kong; an evening spent here will send you home with delightful memories (be sure to dress the part). The maitre d' is named Rolf; ☎ 852-2366-6251 for reservations.

THE PEAK CAFÉ
121 Peak Rd. Also: Café Deco, Peak Galleria (MTR: none, take the tram).

Although there are now two landmark restaurants atop the Peak (**Café Deco** is the other one), I prefer The Peak Café because it is not part of the tacky mall that houses Café Deco. It has a chic and accessible quality that makes it perfect for anyone and any occasion. The food is a mixed bag of continental with some Pacific Rim thrown in.

And yes, darlings, of course there's shopping up here. It's touristy, but the Peak Café logo souvenirs are tasteful and there's even an outlet store. Could I make this up? ☎ 852-2849-7868. For **Café Deco**, ☎ 852-2849-5111.

LAI CHING HEEN
The Regent Hotel, 18 Salisbury Rd., Kowloon (MTR: TST).

Patricia Wells, food critic for the *International Herald Tribune*, has named Lai Ching Heen one of the top 10 restaurants in the world; this accolade alone should be your reason to book. The fact that every other food critic in the world agrees with her is your second reason.

Located downstairs in The Regent Hotel, this restaurant is so famous that it helps to book ahead. You don't get the same view of Central that comes with dinner at **La Plume** or **Yu,** but you do get a view of Causeway Bay. Last time we were there, we also got to watch a full moon rise over Causeway Bay. Talk about perfect!

But it's the food, not the view, that draws people from all around the world in droves. They are known for their fresh seafood and wide selection of dishes.

During hairy crab season (October to November) there was no hairy crab on the menu; nonetheless, at our request, the kitchen prepared them. Then the waiters gave us lessons in how to dismantle the crabs. For reservations, ☎ 852-2721-1211.

SNACK & SHOP
. . . .

It's quite easy to get a snack while shopping in Hong Kong. It's simply a question of how adventurous you are. *Dai pai dong* is the Chinese name for the street vendors who cook food from carts in street markets or corners. Although I have pictures of my sister, the late great Dr. Debbie, eating from assorted dai pai dong, her advice to me on how to stay healthy has remained in the back of my head:

"Always eat lunch in the best hotel in town."

Hong Kong has lots of great hotels and each has several restaurants, so you'll have no trouble sticking to this simple piece of advice. While I have also ferreted out a few other places in "Other Restaurants" below, those of you who dislike surprises should remember that a five-star hotel offers your best shot at happiness.

From a price point of view, hotels usually have a coffee shop or one restaurant with moderate prices amid their galaxy of four or five eateries. But, for a shopper's lunch, I'm often at:

THE MANDARIN ORIENTAL COFFEE SHOP
*The Mandarin Oriental Hotel, 5 Connaught Rd.,
(MTR: Central).*

HARBOURVIEW COFFEE SHOP
*The Regent Hotel, 18 Salisbury Rd., Kowloon
(MTR: TST).*

THE LOBBY
*The Peninsula Hotel, Salisbury Rd., Kowloon
(MTR: TST).*

FAST-FOOD NOTES

If this kind of conservatism is not your cup of tea
and you'd like to watch your purse (or you have the
kids with you!), there are tons of franchised American fast-food joints in Hong Kong. You'll have no
trouble finding a **McDonald's** or **Kentucky Fried
Chicken** anywhere you turn.

One night in Kowloon, we found a local diner
where there were no other *gwailo* (foreigners) and
then went for a stroll on Nathan Road and had
dessert from **Häagen-Dazs** . . . and I didn't feel as
though I'd sold out on the local experience in the
slightest.

OTHER RESTAURANTS

Below is a selection of restaurants outside the hotel
circuit that are appropriate for lunch or even a quick
dinner, listed by the shopping neighborhood in which
they are located.

Central

JOYCE CAFÉ
*The Atrium, One Exchange Sq.
(MTR: Central).*

Maybe this is the time to tell you that I got lost trying to find this cafe, even though it's not very hard to find (that's Hong Kong for you). Located right in Central, one building over from the Star Ferry terminal, Joyce Café is a sensation and worth walking around and hunting down—even if you keep walking by the House of 1,000 Assholes and feel like one yourself. Joyce Café is in the building next door to the one unkindly known as the House of 1,000 Assholes.

But enough about them. Let's talk about Joyce, my heroine. She will probably take the Joyce Café concept global—yes, I plan to find one in Paris in no time at all. The decor is fabulous; the views are pretty good; the people watching is sublime; and the food is hotshot Pacific Rim.

This is a place to be seen and to consider yourself part of the scene. The food is good and moderately priced. There is also take-out service. For reservations call ☎ 852-2810-0807. Reservations are accepted by fax, 852-2810-0165.

Luk Yu Teahouse

📋 *24 Stanley St. (MTR: Central).*

It's not the teahouse of the August Moon, but Luk Yu could be a movie set. Order dim sum from the menu in Chinese, and try not to take pictures since that's what all the other tourists are doing. Go for an early lunch (locals eat between 1– 4pm, so if you're there by noon, you should be able to get a table without much of a wait) or at teatime when you can get a table easily.

Dim sum is served until 5pm. A perfect location in Central makes this a good stop for shoppers; it's halfway to Hollywood Road and not that far from The Landmark.

Do note that waiters at Luk Yu make it a policy to be rude to Westerners. A recent attempt to order in Cantonese brought on scowls. For reservations, ☎ 852-2523-5464. Cash only.

Western

YAT CHAU HEALTH RESTAURANT
*262 Des Voeux Rd. (MTR: Central or
Shueng Wan).*

The gimmick is that you see a doctor when you enter; the doctor diagnoses you, and then you choose
your menu according to your personal needs. Based
on ancient Chinese medicine, the practice is sound
to those who believe. The examination is free; lunch
or dinner can get pricey if you pick dishes with civet
cat, ginseng, or even more exotic ingredients. Our
rather bland meal was about $40, including a single
glass of three penis wine. Credit cards accepted. The
English-speaking doctor is not in-house on Saturday. Conveniently located between Western and
Central, a few blocks short of Western Market.
Credit cards are accepted.

Okay, so we know you're dying to know: What's
the three penis wine for? Backache, of course. Ian
has had a bad back since a car accident several years
ago. Did it do any good? Well, no. But then he didn't
drink every drop. If you are traveling with preteens,
they will eat this place up. And never stop talking
about it.

Pacific Place

GOLDEN LEAF

🛍 *Conrad International, 88 Queensway
(MTR: Admiralty).*

If you think the entry above sounds like a hoot but
you really don't fancy going into the Western District or trying your luck with people who speak no
English, then you need a visit to Golden Leaf, an
upscale, very fancy Chinese restaurant with a
similar twist. The top-of-the-town chef (best of
the year for 4 years in a row says Hong Kong *Tatler*)
believes in gourmet health foods with a thera-
peutic bend, so each dish is chosen to better your

health. You self-prescribe; there is no doctor in the house. Top it all off with detoxifying dessert—a black jellylike roll smothered in honey and trail mix, served warm, which is actually quite nice.

Hollywood Road/Midlevels

PETTICOAT LANE & THE PAVILLION
2 & 3 Tun Wo Lane, Central (MTR: Central).

This place, with two different menus and two different names, is located in an alley right off Hollywood Road and is truly a find, if only because it's so hidden. But everyone knows how to get here, so ask any of the stores on Hollywood Road if you feel frustrated. The hole in the wall eatery is adorable in a baroque bordello fashion; it's a gay scene at certain times of the day but straight for lunch. Really a treat!

The two places have different types of formality to them—Petticoat is informal whereas Pavilion has a fancy menu with salads, pasta, and main courses; reservations for Petticoat Lane, ☎ 852-2973-0642; The Pavilion, ☎ 852-2869-7768.

LE TIRE BOUCHON
9 Old Bailey St., Central (MTR: Central).

Right off Hollywood Road's antiques row is this very authentic little French bistro that will completely dissuade you that you are in China. Charming, with good food, and intimate—you can even try out your high school French. This is a popular dinner spot but a real find at lunch. Reservations ☎ 852-2523-5459.

Stanley

STANLEY'S ORIENTAL
90B Stanley Main St., Stanley (MTR: None, take bus no. 6 from Exchange Sq. in Central to Stanley).

Part of my ritual when I visit Stanley is to have lunch at Stanley's Oriental. There is also **Stanley's French,** virtually around the corner, and **Stanley's Fukashima,** a Japanese restaurant; but I like the Oriental because of its colonial feel, view of the beach, and quiet corner location. It has quick bites, salads, sandwiches, and more. Sometimes we go for a late lunch to avoid crowds; they'll take the last lunch order at 2:45pm. We don't usually reserve, but you can, ☎ 852-2813-9988. If you want to eat on the balcony, a reservation is a must.

TABLES 88
88 Stanley Village Rd., Stanley (MTR: None, take bus no. 6 from Exchange Sq. in Central).

My friend Pat Altman came home from Hong Kong raving, I mean gushing and waving her arms, and all but demanding that I tell you about this new restaurant, right in the heart of the restaurant neighborhood of Stanley. Erica also came back from Stanley waving her arms and raving about the oldest police station in Hong Kong turned restaurant; a mere 20 paces from where you enter the market. Great buffalo wings; tons o' tasteful logo merchandise. Open 11:30am–10:30pm. Reservations, ☎ 852-2813-6262.

Kowloon

FELIX
The Peninsula Hotel, Salisbury Rd., Kowloon (MTR: TST).

So it's like this. You're only in Hong Kong for a few days, and you're faced with an overwhelming number of shopping and eating experiences. You want to take advantage of all of them, yet you can't quite get your priorities straight. Step this way. Felix should be high atop your priority list if you like the young and hip and can take a little bit of noise and a few out-of-towners staring out the windows.

(Speaking of staring out the windows, be sure to do so from the men's toilet.)

Named after the former general manager of The Pen, Felix was designed by Philippe Starck and created atop the new Pen tower to offer view, view, view and something for everyone—which means a large menu, moderate prices, and casual dining. Felix is not intimidating, and it is a once-in-a-lifetime must-do; use the special elevators to the side.

TST East

SHANG PALACE
Kowloon Shangri-La, 64 Mody Rd. (downstairs), Kowloon (MTR: TST).

Fred Ferretti from *Gourmet* tells me that Shang Palace gets his vote for best Chinese restaurant in Hong Kong. It gets my vote just for decor alone. Eating in this restaurant is like being in an exquisite Chinese dream.

Meanwhile, Fred's wife, Eileen Yin Fei Lo, also votes for Shang. Note that Fred's wife is one of the most famous Chinese cooks alive, and if she gives the nod, the place has to be great.

The walls are made of the most beautiful carved and lacquered wood. The dining room features both small and large tables so, regardless of the size of your party, you can have a Chinese family-style dinner and really get into it. For more intimate dining, ask for a private room. Extensive menu, quite moderate prices. Lunch and dinner. For reservations, ☎ 852-2721-2111, ext. 8401.

Chapter Seven

· · · · · · · · · ·

HONG KONG DICTIONARY OF STYLE

TALK THE TALK

· ·

Nothing tells a merchant you are an insider faster
than your ability to "talk the talk": to mention a
few buzzwords that immediately convey the message that you are not a fool and are, therefore, a
force to be reckoned with. While nothing replaces
true expertise, herewith is a short dictionary of local customs, products, and practices that will give
you some inside knowledge and, I hope, a little extra power at the bargaining table.

Entire books have been written on almost all of
these subjects, so if you really want to learn more,
stop by your local library or bookstore. You'll also
find that major booksellers in Hong Kong have lots
of books on local subjects that you might not find
at home. Books are not cheap in Hong Kong, but
the selection on specialty topics may be worth the
price differential.

AN ALPHABETICAL GUIDE

· ·

Part of this alphabet was originally created for *Born
to Shop* by my former partner, Judith Thomas, a
debt I'd like to acknowledge. While I have added to
it, much of the original text is hers. Good going and
good joss, Jude.

ANTIQUES

. . . .

According to the U.S. government, an antique is any item of art, furniture, or craft work that is over 100 years old. The reason the U.S. government cares is simple: You pay no duty on genuine antiques. However, with the Chinese takeover, the laws about the export of antiquities are changing, so there's a whole new world of definitions of what's an antique and what isn't and an even grayer area in which you can be cheated, especially if illegal activities are taking place. Watch it!

True antiques are a hot commodity, and unscrupulous dealers take advantage of that need by issuing authenticity papers for goods that are not old. To make matters worse, Hong Kong does not require its dealers to put prices on their goods. Depending on the dealer's mood, or assessment of your pocketbook, the ginger jar you love could cost $HK 100 or $150 U.S.; it could be 10 years old or 10,000. If 1,000-year-old eggs, sold in all markets, aren't really 1,000 years old, imagine what they do to antiques.

Only you can determine if you feel like you're getting a good deal. Pick a reputable dealer, and ask a lot of questions about the piece, its period, etc. If the dealer doesn't know and doesn't offer to find out, he probably is not a true antique expert. Get as much in writing as possible. Even if it means nothing, it is proof that you have been defrauded if later you find out your Ming vase was made in Kowloon, circa 1995. Your invoice should state what you are buying, the estimated age of the item (including dynasty, year), where it was made, and any flaws or repairs done to the piece.

I've noticed that there is a characteristic particular to most quality antique shops, which is never even imitated in bad shops. In good shops, the dealers want to tell you everything they know about a piece or a style you have expressed interest in; they are dying to talk about the items; they are dying to educate you. They take pleasure in talking about and explaining the ins and outs of entire categories of goods. If you don't find these free lessons readily offered, don't spend a lot of money in that shop.

The center of international trade in Oriental antiques is actually London; all the big dealers come to Hong Kong to buy. Hong Kong is the crossroad for goods coming out of China (usually illegally) and for those goods already brought out. Grave robbing has been going on like mad.

BLUE-AND-WHITE

Blue-and-white is the common term given to Chinese export-style porcelain, which reached its heyday in the late 17th century when the black ships were running "china" to Europe as if it were gold. After 1750, craftspeople in both England and continental Europe had the secret of creating bone china and were well on their way to creating their own chinoiserie-styles and then manufacturing transfer patterns for mass use.

In those years before westerners were on to the secrets of the Orient (and still believed porcelain was created from baked eggshells), there was such a huge business in export wares that European shapes and styles were sent to Canton for duplication. Thus, a strong knowledge of these forms is required by the shopper who wants to be able to accurately date a piece.

Glenn Vessa of **Honeychurch Antiques** tells me that after you've handled a few thousand pieces of blue-and-white, you will have complete confidence in what you are doing. I can only tell you that I flunked the test he gave me, and I had studied beforehand.

The untrained eye needs to look for the following: pits and holes that indicate firing methods; the nonuniform look of hand drawing versus stencils;

the shades of blues of the best dyes; the right shades of gray-white as opposed to the bright white backgrounds of new wares. Marks on the bottom are usually meaningless. Designs may have European inspiration (look at those flowers and arabesques), which will help you determine what you are looking at.

Be careful that you are not looking at English-made blue-and-white passed off as export wares. I saw some in an antique shop in Macau, and while it was nice, it wasn't what I came to China to buy.

BRONZES

Antique Chinese bronzes are featured at several Hong Kong museums, making them an easy art form with which to commence your education in Chinese art. Visit several local museums to sharpen your eye so you can understand the difference between what will cost you thousands of U.S. dollars and what you can buy for a few hundred. The lesser price indicates a fake. As with all Chinese art, you must be able to recognize subtle changes in style and form that indicate time periods and dynasties in order to properly date your fake.

Glenn Vessa says that Japanese bronzes are still a good investment; bronze incense burners begin around $3,000 and go up. Stop by **Honeychurch** to talk to him about it.

CAMERAS

Can we tell you about cameras? You probably don't want to know everything that we can tell you about cameras.

First off, we have to deal with fantasy. For some reason, every shopper who comes to Hong Kong thinks he's going to get a great deal; that this is THE place to buy a camera. WRONG! Unless you are a pro, you may not even want to bother with the exercise. But if you insist on playing the game, pay attention.

Start by doing research at home as to what equipment you need. DO NOT allow a Hong Kong camera salesperson to tell you what he thinks you should buy, or what is a good deal. Once you feel comfortable that you know what you are looking for, visit several shops (and not all on Nathan Road) comparing prices. Try the stores on Kimberley Road off of Nathan Road. We have discovered that prices can vary by as little as $10 and as much as $200 before negotiations even begin.

Be sure to ascertain that the price for the camera includes a manufacturer's worldwide guarantee. The store's guarantee (even if printed on fancy paper) is worthless; the manufacturer's guarantee may prove worthless, too, but at least get it.

As soon as you start serious negotiations, examine the camera very carefully. It should still be in its original box, complete with the original packing material that holds it tightly. Remember that camera boxes can be repacked to look like new. Check to make sure yours was not. Look at the guarantee to verify that it is a worldwide guarantee and is authentic. There must be a stamp from the importing agent on the registration card. The dealer will add his stamp upon conclusion of the sale. If you are really careful, you will call the importing agent and verify the sale. Check the serial numbers on the camera and lens with those on the registration card to make certain that they match. Take out the guarantee before the camera is repacked and ask to have it packed in front of you. This way the merchandise can't be switched. Ask to have the following information included in the store receipt: name and model of camera, serial numbers of each part, price of each item, date of purchase, itemized cost of purchase with total sum at the bottom, and form of payment you are using.

CARPETS

. . . .

As the Persian carpet market has dried up, the popularity of Chinese carpets, both new and old, has escalated. China still has a labor pool of young girls who will work for very little money and sit for long periods of time tying knots. Carpets come in traditional designs or can be special ordered. Price depends on knots per square inch, fiber content, complexity of design, how many colors are used, and city or region of origin. Any of the **Chinese Arts & Crafts** stores is a good place to look at carpets and get familiarized with different styles and prices ranges. You can visit the **Tai Ping Carpets** showroom in Central or TST East and then make an appointment to visit the factory in Kowloon to watch work in progress.

When considering the material of the rug, consider its use. Silk rugs are magnificent and impractical. If you are going to use the carpet in a low-traffic area or as a wall hanging, great. Silk threads are usually woven as the warp (vertical) threads and either silk or cotton as the weft (horizontal). The pile, nonetheless, will be pure silk. Wool rugs are more durable.

Chinese rugs come in every imaginable combination of colors. No one combination is more valuable than the next. Some older carpets have been colored with pure vegetable dyes; more modern ones use sturdier synthetics in combination with vegetable dyes. Avoid carpets that were made with aniline dyes, since these are unstable. These dyes were used on older rugs that were crafted at the beginning of the century. To test for aniline dye, spit on a white handkerchief and then rub the cloth gently over the colors. If only a little color comes off, you are safe. If the carpet has been dyed with aniline dyes, a lot of color will come off on the handkerchief.

CERAMICS & PORCELAIN

· ·

Ceramic and porcelain wares available in Hong Kong fall into three categories: British imports, new Chinese, and old Chinese. For a short lesson in buying blue-and-white, see page 90.

New Chinese pottery and porcelain is in high demand. Although much of the base material is being imported from Japan and finished in Hong Kong, it is still considered Chinese. Most factories will take orders directly. There are numerous factories in Hong Kong where you can watch porcelain wares being created and place your personal order.

Porcelain is distinguished from pottery in that it uses china clay to form the paste. Modern designs are less elaborate than those used during the height of porcelain design in the Ming Dynasty (A.D. 1368–1644), but the old techniques are slowly being revived. Blue-and-white ware is still the most popular. New wares (made to look old) can be found at the various Chinese government stores, including **Chinese Arts & Crafts,** in zillions of little shops on and off Hollywood Road, in **Stanley Market,** in Macau and just about everywhere else. Fakes abound; buy with care.

CHEONG SAM

· ·

You really already know what a cheong sam is; you just don't know the word so you're temporarily thrown. Close your eyes and picture Suzie Wong. She is wearing a Chinese dress with Mandarin collar and silk knot buttons that buttons from the neck across the shoulder and then down the side, right? Possibly in red satin with a dragon print, but that's an extra. The dress style is called a cheong sam. Really touristy ones come in those silk and/or satin looks, but you can buy a chic one or you can have one custom made. **Irene Fashions** made me a drop-dead elegant one in navy wool crepe. It was inspired by the dress Demi Moore wore in *Indecent Proposal*. Even though I don't quite look like Demi in it, I'm still amazed at the curves the tailor was able to cut in the garment.

CHINESE NEW YEAR

During the Chinese (Lunar) New Year, most stores will close. For a few days preceding the festivities, it is not unusual to find prices artificially raised in many local shops, as shopkeepers take advantage of the fact that the Chinese like to buy new clothing for the new year.

CHINESE SCROLLS

Part art and part communication, Chinese scrolls are decorative pieces of parchment paper, rolled around pieces of wood at each end. They contain calligraphy and art relating to history, a story, a poem, a lesson, or a message. Some scrolls are mostly art, with little calligraphy, but others are just the opposite. Being able to identify the author or artist makes the scroll more valuable, but it is usually not possible. Chinese scrolls make beautiful wall hangings and are popular collector's pieces.

CHINOISERIE

Exports from Asia were so fashionable in Europe that they started their own trend. Western designers and craftspeople began to make items in the style of Asia. Much was created from fantasy and whimsy; there is also a mixture of influence of Indian and other styles with the purely Chinese. Works made in an Asian style are considered chinoiserie. Chinoiserie is not actually made in China.

CHOPS

. . . .

A chop is a form of signature stamp on which the symbol for a person's name is carved. The chop is then dipped in dry dye and then placed on paper, much like a rubber stamp. The main difference between rubber stamps and chops is that rubber stamps became trendy only in the 1980s, whereas chops were in vogue about 2,200 years ago. Since chops go so far back, you can choose from an antique or a newly created version. (For more on chops, see page 149.)

CLOISONNÉ

. . . .

The art of cloisonné involves fitting decorative enamel between thin metal strips on a metal surface. The surface is then fired under just the right temperatures, and the finish is glazed to a sheen. It sounds simple, but the handwork involved in laying the metal strips to form a complicated design, and then laying in the paint so that it does not run, is time-consuming and delicate and is an art requiring training and patience.

Antique works by the very finest artists bring in large sums of money. Most of what you'll see for sale in Hong Kong (outside of the finest galleries) is mass-produced cloisonné and is very inexpensive— a small vase sells for about $20; bangle bracelets are $3. You can also find rings, mirrors, and earrings for good prices at most of the markets. These make good souvenir gifts to take home. Frankly, I prefer the Hermès version.

COMPUTERS

. . . .

All the famous brands, makes, and models of computers can be found in Hong Kong, but you had better be computer literate to know if you are getting a better deal than you could get back home. Be sure to check the power capacity, voltage requirements, guarantees, and serial numbers of every piece you buy. Clones are also available and at very good prices. However, "Buyer Beware" applies doubly in this category.

Various software programs are also available; prices are not much less than in the U.S., but can be substantially less than in the U.K. The biggest problem is that you simply must know what you are doing and what you are buying; the more you rely on the sales help, the more likely you are to be taken.

There are several office buildings that specialize in computer showrooms: try the **Silvercord Building** in Kowloon and **Golden Arcade Shopping Center** in Sham Shui Po.

DIM SUM

Dim sum is a Hong Kong specialty and is easily ordered in any western-style restaurant where someone speaks English or the menu is printed in dual languages. If you go for a more adventurous meal, you may need a few basic tips. You may also buy a book on the subject or carry around pictures with you. Some people show photos of the grandchildren. I have in my wallet a picture of my favorite dim sum. The best bet is to learn what you like at home, under western-style conditions, then learn the names of the items in Chinese or have them written out for you. Of course, that's too easy. It's much more fun to go someplace where they will allow you to stand next to the dim sum cart and point.

EMBROIDERY

The art of stitching decorations onto another fabric by hand or machine is known as embroidery. Stitches can be combined to make abstract or realistic shapes, sometimes of enormous complexity. Embroidered goods sold in Hong Kong include a variety of items: bed linens, chair cushions, tablecloths, napkins, runners, place mats, coasters, blouses, children's clothing and robes—all of these items are new. There is another market in antique embroidered fabrics (and slippers) which is, of course, a whole new category, price-wise. Antique embroidery items can be very expensive.

Traditionally, embroidery has been hand sewn. However, today there are machines that do most of the work. Embroidery threads are made from the finest silk to the heaviest yarn. Judge the value of a piece by whether it is hand stitched or machine stitched and what kind of thread or yarn has been used.

One of the most popular forms of embroidered work sold in Hong Kong is whitework, or white-on-white embroidery. Most whitework is done by machine, but the workmanship is very good. Hand-embroidered goods are hard to find today and very expensive. Try **Chinese Arts & Crafts.** Most of these goods come out of Shanghai and may be competitively priced in your hometown. Don't assume you're getting a bargain.

FENG SHUI

· ·

Feng Shui (translates as wind, water) is an important cultural concept related to keeping the spirits happy. It has to do with the positioning of human-made objects—especially buildings—that must remain in harmony with the earth and not disturb the spirits which inhabit that space. Harsh angles upset the spirits; the building, its doors, its windows, and its core must be in alignment so the spirits can flow. This means that before any project is built or any room designed, a Feng Shui expert must be called in for advice.

FURNITURE

Chinese styles in furniture caused a major sensation in the European market. Teak, ebony, and *padouk* were all imported from the Far East and were highly valued in the West. Yet the major furnishing rage was for lacquered goods, usually in the form of small chests of cabinets that were placed on top of stands, which were built to measure in Europe.

True Chinese antique furniture is defined by purity of form, with decorative and interpretive patterns carved into the sides or backs. Antique furniture is a hot collector's item. Dealers and collectors alike are scouring the shops and auction houses. It is better to find an unfinished piece and oversee its restoration, than to find one that has already been restored. If it has been restored, find out who did the work and what was done. Some unknowing dealers bleach the fine woods and ruin their value. Others put a polyurethanelike gloss on the pieces and make them unnaturally shiny.

If you do decide to buy, decide beforehand how you will get the piece home. If you are shipping it through the shop, verify the quality of their shipper and insurance. If you are shipping it yourself, call a shipper and get details before you begin to negotiate the price of the piece.

HAPPY COATS

One of the hottest-selling tourist items is the "happy coat," a padded jacket with a stand-up mandarin collar, usually made of embroidered silk with decorative flowers, animals, and birds. They make great souvenirs of Hong Kong but all too often are the kind of thing that you can't (or don't) wear in the real world. When picking fabric, try for something classic that works with a western-style wardrobe.

The Lanes is your best bet for these coats.

IVORY

. . . .

One Word of Warning: No. It's that simple. Articles made from ivory will not be allowed into the U.S. It is not smart to try to run them. Only antique pieces with proper paperwork will be allowed in.

Carvers in Hong Kong are currently using dentin from walruses, hippopotamuses, boars, and whales as substitutes for elephant ivory. If you want to make sure you are not buying elephant ivory, look for the network of fine lines that is visible to the naked eye. If the piece you are buying is made of bone, there will not be any visible grain or luster. Bone also weighs less than ivory. Imitation ivory is made of plastic, but can be colored to look quite good. However, it is a softer material than real ivory and less dense.

There are very few antique ivory pieces left in Hong Kong. If someone claims to be selling you one, be very wary. Should you snag one, you'll want provenance papers.

JADE

. . . .

Jade was originally used solely in rituals for the dead. In the late Chou Dynasty it became a source of delight acceptable for the living to appreciate; interest in intricately carved jade ornaments, sword fittings, hairpins, buttons, and garment hooks took off.

The term *jade* is used to signify two different stones, jadeite and nephrite. The written character for jade signifies purity, nobility, and beauty. It is considered by some to be a magical stone, protecting the health of one who wears it. The scholar always carried a piece of jade in his pocket for health and wisdom. Jade is also reported to pull impurities out of the body; if you buy old jade that is red-brown in color, it is believed that the jade absorbed the blood and impurities of its deceased former owner.

Jadeite and nephrite have different chemical properties. Jadeite tends to be more translucent and nephrite more opaque. For this reason, jadeite is often considered to be more valuable. Furthermore, really good jade—imperial jade as it is sometimes called—is actually white, not green.

If you are shopping for jade, you need a quick lesson in Chinese: *chen yu* is real jade; *fu yu* is false jade. Jadeite comes in many colors, including lavender, yellow, black, orange, red, pink, white, and many shades of green. Nephrite comes in varying shades of green only. The value of both is determined by translucence, quality of carving, and color. Assume that a carving that is too inexpensive is not jade. "Jade" factories work in soapstone or other less valuable stones. Poor quality white jade can be dyed into valuable-looking shades of green. Buyer beware.

Jade should be ice-cold to the touch and so hard it cannot be scratched by steel. I always produce my trusty Swiss Army knife and ask the dealer if I can cut into a sample. If he nods yes, then his merchandise is real.

Some shoppers make it common practice to quick touch or lick-touch a piece. This is not a real test of good jade although stone will certainly feel different to the tongue than plastic. You may also want to "ring" a piece, since jade, just like fine crystal, has its own tone when struck.

The **Jade Market** (see page 224) is a fun adventure and a good way to look at lots of "fake" and real jade. Test your eye before you buy. If you are determined to buy a piece of genuine jade, I suggest that you use a trusted jeweler or other reputable source; you'll pay more than you might in a market or a small jewelry shop, but you'll be paying for peace of mind. Please note that jade (real jade) is very, very expensive. Fake jade may be what you really have in mind. Don't be shy.

If you are interested in carved jade figures, bring out your own jeweler's loupe and watch the dealer quake. If the carving is smooth and uniform, it was done with modern tools. Gotcha! A fine piece and an old piece are hand cut and should be slightly jagged on the edges.

What are those green circles you see in the market and often in the street? They are nephrite and should cost no more than $1 per circle. They make fabulous gifts when tied to a long silken cord and turned into a necklace.

I've been buying brown jade over the last few years—I don't know if it's real or not; dealers claim it is "antique." I pay between $10 and $20 per piece and am happy with what I've got. What's it's really worth is anyone's guess. I've been attaching my jade pieces to the zippers or straps of various handbags—very chic. But heavy.

JOSS STICKS

Although there is a method of telling fortunes with joss sticks, these long, thin, skewerlike pieces of wood are meant to be burnt in a Buddhist temple with prayer or thanks. You buy them in the temple. There are various methods—I plant all of mine in one clump of sand in a chosen area; Ian separates his and does them individually.

The concept of joss is related to luck; it is proper to wish a person good joss.

LACQUER

No, I don't mean nail varnish. I'm talking about an ancient art form dating as far back as 85 B.C. when baskets, boxes, cups, bowls, and jars were coated with up to 30 layers of lacquer in order to make them waterproof. Each layer must be dried thoroughly and polished before another layer can be applied. After the lacquer is finished, decoration may be applied. Black and red are the most common color combinations. (Black on the outside, red for the inside.)

You may date an item by the colors used; by the Han Dynasty metallics were used in the decorative painting. Modern (post-1650) versions of lacquer may be European inspired chinoiserie; beware.

MONOCHROMATIC WARES

. . . .

You may adore blue-and-white porcelains, but please remember they were created for export because locals thought they were ugly. The good stuff was usually monochromatic. Go to a museum and study the best and brightest before you start shopping because, again, fakes abound.

Celadon is perhaps the best known of the Chinese porcelain monochromes. It is a pale gray-green in color and grew to popularity because of the (false) assumption that poisoned food would cause a piece of celadon pottery to change color. The amount of green in the piece is based on how much iron is in the glaze.

NINTENDO

. . . .

I am very sorry to report to you that my regular reporter for this section, Aaron Gershman, is now more interested in girls than Nintendo. I think this means that one of us is getting older.

If you are planning on buying any Nintendo games in Hong Kong, have an up-to-date *Nintendo Power* issue with you so you can show it to salespeople, who might be able to match up the games in case of different names.

You must buy a converter ($8–$10) in order to use Japanese–style game cartridges on a U.S. Nintendo because you can't use the Japanese size on your machine. The converter attaches to the cartridge to make it compatible with your machine. This is technology at its best. Take advantage of the opportunity to get a new game and get something your friends don't have. You can have games before anybody else gets them. Buy the converter in Hong Kong, because they aren't sold in Japan.

Super Nintendo games are available in Hong Kong; you will also need a converter.

OPALS
. . . .

Hong Kong is considered the opal-cutting capital of Asia. Dealers buy opals, which are mined mainly in Australia, in their rough state, and bring them to their factories in Hong Kong. There they are judged for quality and then cut either for wholesale export or for local jewelry. Black opals are the rarest and, therefore, the most expensive. White opals are the most available; they are not actually white, but varying shades of sparkling color. The opal has minuscule spheres of cristobalite layered inside; this causes the light to refract and the gem to look iridescent. The more cristobalite, the more "fire." An opal can contain up to 30% water, which makes it very difficult to cut. Dishonest dealers will sell sliced stones, called doublets or triplets, depending upon the number of slices of stone layered together. If the salesperson will not show you the back of the stone, suspect that it is layered. There are several opal "factories" in Hong Kong. These shops offer tourists the chance to watch the craftspeople at work cutting opal and offer opal jewelry for sale at "factory" prices. It's an interesting and informative tour to take, but we couldn't vouch for the quality of any opal you might buy from a factory.

PAPER CUTS
. . . .

An art form still practiced in China, paper cuts are hand-painted and hand-cut drawings of butterflies, animals, birds, flowers, and human figures. Often they are mounted on cards; sometimes they are sold in packs of six, delicately wrapped in tissue. We buy them in quantity and use them as decorations on our own cards and stationery.

PEARLS

. . . .

Pearls have been appreciated and all but worshipped in eastern and western cultures for centuries. Numerous famous women in history have had enviable pearl collections—from Queen Elizabeth I to Queen Elizabeth II, to say nothing of Elizabeth Taylor, Coco Chanel, and Barbara Hutton, whose pearls were once owned by Marie Antoinette.

The first thing to know about shopping for pearls in Hong Kong is that the best ones come from Japan. If you are looking for a serious set of pearls, find a dealer who will show you the Japanese government inspection certification that is necessary for every legally exported pearl. Many pearls cross the border without this, and for a reason.

Pearls are usually sold loosely strung and are weighed by the *momme*. Each momme is equal to 3.75 grams. The size of the pearls is measured in millimeters. Size 3s are small, like caviar, and 10s are large, like mothballs. The average buyer is looking for something between 6 and 7 millimeters. The price usually doubles every half millimeter after 6. Therefore, if a 6mm pearl is $10, a $6^{1}/_{2}$ mm pearl would be $20, a 7mm $40, and so on. When the size of the pearl gets very high, prices often triple and quadruple with each half millimeter.

Most pearls you will encounter are cultured. The pearl grower introduces a small piece of mussel shell into the oyster, and then hopes that Mother Nature will do her stuff. The annoyed oyster coats the "intruder" with nacre, the lustrous substance that creates the pearl. The layers of nacre determine the luster and size. It takes about 5 years for an oyster to create a pearl. The oysters are protected from predators in wire baskets in carefully controlled oyster beds.

There are five basic varieties of pearls: freshwater, South Sea, *akoya*, black, and *mabe*. Freshwater pearls are also known as Biwa pearls and are the little Rice Krispies-shaped pearls that come in shades of pink, lavender, cream, tangerine, blue, and blue-green. Many of the pearls larger than 10mm are known as South Sea pearls. They are produced in the South Seas, where the water is warmer and the oysters larger. The silver-lipped oyster produces large, magnificent silver pearls. The large golden-colored pearls are produced by the golden-lipped oyster. The pearls you are probably most familiar with are known as akoya pearls: These range from 2mm to 10mm in size. The shapes are more round than not, and the colors range from shades of cream to pink. A few of these pearls have a bluish tone. The rarest pearl is the black pearl, which is actually a deep blue or blue-green. This gem is produced by the black-lipped oyster of the waters surrounding Tahiti and Okinawa. Sizes range from 8mm to 15mm. Putting together a perfectly matched set is difficult and costly. Mabe pearls (pronounced *maw-bay*) have flat backs and are considered "blister" pearls because of the way they are attached to the shell. They are distinguished by their silvery-bluish tone and rainbow luster.

Pearls are judged by their luster, nacre, color, shape, and surface quality. The more perfect the pearl in all respects, the more valuable. Test pearls by rolling them—cultured pearls are more likely to be perfectly round and will, therefore, roll more smoothly.

You needn't be interested in serious pearls, whether natural or fake. In fact, prices being what they are, I'm in favor of fakes. Hong Kong sells fake versions of cultured pearls rather readily; specialty items such as baroque style or gray pearls are hard to come by. Chanel-style pearl items may be found in fashion stores, but not at pearl dealers.

SILK

. . . .

Anthropologists will tell you that silk is China's single greatest contribution to world culture. The quality of Chinese silk has always been so superior that no substitute has ever been deemed acceptable; thus trade routes to bring silk around the world were established—the same routes that brought cultural secrets from ancient worlds into Europe's own local melting pots.

The art of weaving silk originated some 4,000 years ago in China. Since that time it has spread throughout Asia and the world. China, however, remains the largest exporter of cloth and garments. Hong Kong receives most of its silk fabric directly from China. Fabric shops in the markets sell rolls of silk for reasonable prices, although silk is not dirt cheap and may be priced competitively in your home market.

Be sure, when buying silk, that it is real. Many wonderful copies are on the market today. Real silk thread burns like human hair and leaves a fine ash. Synthetic silk curls or melts as it burns. If you are not sure, remove a thread and light a match.

SNUFF BOTTLES

. . . .

A favorite collector's item, snuff bottles come in porcelain, glass, stone, metal, bamboo, bronze, and jade. They also come in old and new old-style versions. In short, watch out; this is a category that has been flooded with fakes, due to tourist demand.

A top-of-the-line collectible snuff bottle can go for $100,000, and that is American moolah; so if you think you are buying a fine example of the art form for $10, do reconsider your position. The glass bottles with a carved overlay are rare and magnificent; there are specific schools of design and style in snuff bottles that are especially valuable to collect.

You can find more ordinary examples in any of the markets. If you just want a few ornaments for the house (or tree), the markets or shops on Hollywood Road will have plenty.

SPIRIT MONEY

Colorful fake paper money to be burned for the dead. Sold in any of the old-fashioned paper shops, which are fast fading out. There are a string of such paper shops on Shanghai Street in Kowloon; you can also find them in Causeway Bay near Jardine's Bazaar and in Macau, in the antique stores neighborhood.

SPORTS SHOES

If you haven't shopped with a preteen recently, you might not know just how important it is to be wearing the "right" sports shoes to school. Indeed, there are tons of name-brand sports shoes sold everywhere, from stores to **Stanley Market** to the street. For the most part, they cost 20% more than they do in the U.S. We know they are made in Korea and should be cheap, but so far our findings have been sorry.

TEA

The Museum of Tea Ware in Flagstaff House, Cotton Tree Drive, Hong Kong, is a good place to start an exploration into the mysteries of tea. Tea has been grown in China for over 2,000 years and reflects the climate and soil where it is grown, much as European wines do. There are three categories of tea: unfermented tea, fermented tea, and semifermented tea.

It is customary to drink Chinese tea black, with no milk, sugar, or lemon. Cups do not have a handle, but often do have a fitted lid to keep the contents hot and to strain the leaves as you sip. Since Hong Kong was a British colony, you may also find many hotel lobbies and restaurants that serve an English high tea (a great opportunity to rest your feet and gear up for a few more hours of shopping).

Because tea is relatively inexpensive and often comes in an attractive package or tin, it makes an excellent gift. Your choices are wide—there are many fancy tea shops selling high-priced and well-packaged goods, but there are also many choices in grocery store and local herbal/medicine shops that are equally attractive. All the Chinese department stores have a wide selection of teas and tea containers.

XIYING POTTERY TEAPOTS

Tea utensils are a popular item to purchase in Hong Kong, with Xiying pottery teapots being one of the most popular and expensive. They are made from unglazed purple clay and are potted by hand to achieve different forms of balance. They often resemble leaves, trees, or animals. Proportion is achieved by changing the balance of the base, top, and handle. Xiying teapots are always signed by the artist who made them, and the more famous artists' pots sell for over $1,000.

Chapter Eight

. . . .

SHOPPING NEIGHBORHOODS

A WORD ABOUT NEIGHBORHOODS
. . . .

The island of Hong Kong (Central) and Kowloon (TST), on the Kowloon Peninsula, are the most popular areas and your two basic shopping neighborhoods.

Just because they are the best known and the handiest doesn't mean you should stop learning your neighborhoods. I will send you everywhere from TST East to the New Territories; I'll also tell you how to get into some factory districts and a lot of other neighborhoods outside the merely obvious.

The more I visit Hong Kong, the more comfortable I am with getting away from tourists and the commercial main streets of Central and Kowloon; define a successful visit to Hong Kong as one in which you've spent at least a little bit of time in the real-people neighborhoods. But I also have to admit that during my last trip to Hong Kong with only 4 full days in town—anything in a weird or out of the way neighborhood quickly disappeared from my must-do list.

GETTING AROUND THE NEIGHBORHOODS
. . . .

The MTR will get you almost everywhere, or at least into the main neighborhoods and basic shopping areas. Unless I specifically note otherwise in an address, the MTR stop at Central gets you to most locations in Hong Kong; the MTR stop at Tsim Sha Tsui (TST) services most Kowloon shopping areas.

There's also excellent bus service and ferries to outlying islands where you can just roam around upon arrival. Getting to specific addresses in the New Territories can be difficult without a car; consider hiring a taxi or a car (with driver) from your hotel.

I really think that if your time is limited and you want to see a lot, a car and driver is an economical luxury. The price ranges from $250–$350 per day. If you can't afford the whole day, hire car and driver up until lunch, or half a day. Then, you can finish off on foot. The time you'll save with your own personal chauffeur will permit you to get to a number of out-of-the-way neighborhoods and enhance your enjoyment of the shopping time that you have.

Whatever you do, don't take a taxi through the Cross-Harbour Tunnel if you can help it. I once painfully sat in traffic for an hour trying to get through it!

A WORD ABOUT ADDRESSES

Although I have already warned you that the address you will be given is most often the name of the building and not the street address, I want to stress that when street addresses are written out, they may designate a specific door or portion of a building. So you may see different addresses for the same buildings, like **The Landmark, Swire House,** or **Prince's Building.** Don't freak out or assume it's an error. Simply check your trusty map. If an office building takes up a city block, as many do, shops can claim different street addresses on all four sides!

The same is true when cruising the boutiques in a shopping center like **The Landmark:** Often the shop's address will simply be the name of the building. The easiest way to find what you're

looking for is to check the directory on the main
floor of the mall.

HONG KONG ISLAND NEIGHBORHOODS

· ·

The island of Hong Kong actually makes up only a
portion of what most tourists refer to as "Hong
Kong." While government, business, and "downtown" functions take place on the island, much of
the local population live elsewhere in neighborhoods
that do not seriously feature shopping and, therefore, are not included in these pages.

The island is divided by a ridge of hills topped
by the famous Peak. The rich and famous live in
villas lining the roadway up the Peak; the almost
rich and famous (as well as the upper-middle class)
live in what's called the Mid-Levels, the area of the
hills above Central but below the Peak.

To get to most other portions of the island you
can either go through a tunnel under the hills toward Aberdeen, or take the tram or MTR along the
shoreline to the housing estates, where middle-class
people live in housing blocks and "mansion" or
"estate" developments.

Central

Central is the part of Hong Kong that refers to what
we used to call "downtown" when I was growing
up. It's the main business and shopping part of town:
It's the core of Hong Kong Island.

Shopping in Central is mostly westernized and
even glitzy, but wait, you round a corner and voilà—
it's **The Lanes:** real people galore. You walk up
Pottinger to Hollywood Road and, again—the real
thing. Central seems to house the ridiculous and
the sublime within the same city block; it's your
opportunity to mix westernized shopping with Eastern lifestyles.

The Landmark, (see map) a shopping mall of mythic proportions, houses 5 floors of shopping including stores in the basement, at street level, on a mezzanine above the street shops, and up in two towers that rise above the main floors of shopping. European designers have their shops here or across the street in **Swire House,** the **Prince's Building,** or the **Mandarin Oriental Hotel.**

The Lanes are two little alleys (Li Yuen West and Li Yuen East, see map) half a block away from each other—they are lined with storefronts and then filled in with stalls so you have to look behind the stalls and poke into nooks and crannies to get the full flavor. Each is teeming with people and product. One lane specializes in handbags (most imitations of famous brands and styles, few of good quality); the other, underwear.

The **Pedder Building** (see page 237) is a must: This one building is conveniently located across the street from The Landmark and in every shopper's direct path. There are enough outlets here to empty your wallet and keep you satisfied, even if you have no more time for stores. **Shanghai Tang** is also here, alongside the outlet building—this is the best one stop you will make, especially if you are in a hurry.

Hollywood Road: Although it's in Central, I consider this street more of its own neighborhood (see page 115).

Western

The Western District is adjacent to Central and can be reached on foot or via MTR. Take the MTR to Sheung Wan to get to central Western. Despite the decidedly touristy flavor in the renovation of **Western Market,** the Western District is a lot more Chinese, in both appearance and attitude, than Central. This is really the district to see before it is ruined; as the modernization continues, the Western as I know it will disappear within the next few years.

al & Western Districts

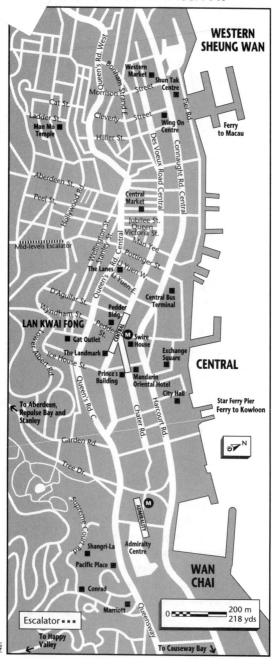

WESTERN
SHEENG WAN

Queen's Rd. West
Bonham Strand E.
Western Market
Shun Tak Centre
Morrison Street
Cat St.
Cleverly Street
Ladder St.
Man Mo Temple
Wing On Centre
Hillier St.
Des Voeux Road Central
Pier Rd.
Connaught Rd. Central
Ferry to Macau

Aberdeen St.
Peel St.
Hollywood Rd.
Central Market
Jubilee St.
Queen Victoria St.
Man Yee
Mid-levels Escalator
Wellington St.
Stanley St.
Pottinger St.
The Lanes
Queen's Rd. Central
Li Yuen W.
Li Yuen E.
D'Aguilar St.
Central Bus Terminal
Pedder Bldg.
Pedder St.
Wyndham St.
LAN KWAI FONG
Gat Outlet
M
Swire House
Ice House St.
The Landmark
Exchange Square
CENTRAL
Tower Albert Rd.
Prince's Building
Mandarin Oriental Hotel
City Hall
Star Ferry Pier
Ferry to Kowloon
Queen's Rd. C.
Chater Rd.
Harcourt Rd.
To Aberdeen, Repulse Bay and Stanley
Garden Rd.
N
Tree Dr.
Supreme Court Rd.
M
ADMIRALTY
Shangri-La
Admiralty Centre
Pacific Place
WAN CHAI
Conrad
Marriott
Queensway
Escalator ∎∎∎
0   200 m
           218 yds
To Happy Valley
To Causeway Bay

1461

Here you'll feel less like a sightseer and more like a visitor to the Far East. Western used to represent the real part of town, but the high-rises and the glitz are encroaching quickly.

It's moving fast, so strike out to find the shops with snakes in cages and little restaurants where you're not sure if the snacks are snacks or snakes. There's an electronics district in Western, as well as old-fashioned Chinese medicine shops, and the terminal for heading off to Macau.

Going west from Central, the area begins shortly after **Central Market,** at Possession Street, and continues to Kennedy Town, where most of the local working people live. Western includes the famous **Man Wa Lane,** where you can purchase your own personalized chop (see page 150), the **Shun Tak Centre** (off to Macau), and **Bonham Strand East,** where you'll find scores of Chinese herbalists. The farther west you wander, the more exotic the area becomes.

My best way of "doing" Western is to combine it with a trip to Hollywood Road; if you walk downhill from Hollywood Road, you'll automatically end up in Western. Then you can take in the **Western Market** before walking back to Central or hopping in the MTR station right there at Shun Tak.

Hollywood Road

Up above Central, and technically within the Central District, Hollywood Road is a shopping neighborhood unto itself. You can reach it from either the Central or Sheung Wan MTR stops. It's within walking distance, if you're wearing sensible shoes and have the feet of a mountain goat; you can also tell your taxi driver *"By Fa Gai"* (meaning "white flower") and be dropped off in the core of the antique area, in what used to be the neighborhood where the white prostitutes plied their trade.

Or you can simply take the Mid-Levels outdoor escalator—just make sure you get it during an "up" hour as the stairs only go "down" during rush hour in the morning. You shop your way right up to the top; although I admit that I did it, and after Hollywood Road, it sort of loses its zip, and then you are rather in the middle of nowhere looking for a taxi. Still, you must ride up at least to Hollywood Road.

Hollywood Road is Hong Kong's antique neighborhood. Because of the escalator (a moving staircase to the heavens that moves pedestrian traffic from the Mid-Levels down into Central), the arrival of the Chinese with new laws on antiquities, and the ever rising rents in Hong Kong, the area has changed tremendously and will continue to do so. There are antique stores elsewhere, but Hollywood Road is still a great place to get to know.

Hollywood Road isn't hard to get to, but it is not necessarily on the way to anywhere else you're going, so it's essential that you specifically plan your day or half a day to include this outing. The idea is to walk the 3 blocks of Hollywood Road from Wyndham to the Man Mo Temple. Then you'll hit Cat Street and the flea market before descending into Western (see page 113).

As charming as this area is, I must warn you up front that much of what is in these shops must be considered imitation, or at least faux. If you are looking to do anything more serious than browse, I suggest you make your first stop **Honeychurch Antiques** (no. 29), where the expat American owners Glenn and Lucille Vessa are bright, honest, and always willing to help. They know who's who and what's what in their world of dealers and will tell you about their stock and everyone else's. Their look is an eclectic blend of antiques from around the Orient (kind of Country chinoiserie); however, they know who has the more formal pieces. In fact, they know who has everything.

If you are spending big bucks, it is imperative that you buy from a reputable shop. Ask Glenn and Lucille for guidance.

The most visually arresting "store" on the street has a quasi–flea market feel and the name **Low Price Shop** written in scrawl across the door. Bird cages, beads, old clothes, new snuff bottles, all spill out onto the sidewalk at no. 47, where prices range from dirt cheap—about $3 (U.S.) for an American bestseller paperback, used but recent—to outrageous. Most of the so-called antiques are not so old, and the prices can be rather high. Old-looking postcards and photos (newly made, my friend) are sold here and make very popular souvenirs. Despite the fact that the place is of questionable authority, it's still a heap of fun. A great photo opportunity.

Many dealers sell what look like reproductions to me (although they swear this is the real stuff), and I get that empty feeling in the pit of my stomach as I work these stores, trying to discern real treasures from imagined finds. I must also tell you that Glenn Vessa gave me a blue-and-white ceramics test (after I read and studied four books on the subject) that I flunked outright. I could not accurately ID a piece that was 300 years old. Glenn says knowing what you're doing with ceramics is easy (that's what brain surgeons say about their job as well), but I beg you to be careful.

There are serious porcelain dealers on Hollywood Road, and then tourist traps that sell porcelains and then some factories. It all starts to look alike to me, and that's why I know you should worry. **Hwa Xia** sells only blue-and-white and looks very important (no. 56); **The Place** (no. 81A) is very western-looking in style and sells lots of porcelains, but also other objects and some furniture, too.

But wait! **Wah Tung**, my favorite porcelain shop in Hong Kong, has opened a showroom on Hollywood Road, and while nothing will replace the experience of being lost in an industrial flat, there's a lot to be said for convenience. Don't miss it: 148 Hollywood Rd. The entrance is small and not very warm; you may be put off. Go upstairs, relax.

Lan Kwai Fong

Take the MTR to the Central station and you'll find Lan Kwai Fong, which is right in the heart of Central, beneath Hollywood Road in an alley right off D'Aguilar Street. This area is more of an eating neighborhood than a shopping neighborhood. Look carefully or you will miss it.

Lan Kwai Fong is where everyone goes to party and to see and be seen; where everyone wants to know which of the clubs or eateries you think is best so they can judge their own chicness (and yours). There are only a few boutiques; I know the area well because there's a **GAT** factory-outlet store in one of the buildings here. There are other outlet shops nearby. Jammed on Friday and Saturday nights.

Wan Chai

Wan Chai these days means Convention Center. It means Hyatt hotel—one of the best hotels in Hong Kong. It means great location between Central and Causeway Bay, and it means expensive real estate. It does not particularly mean shopping, despite a gigantic **Chinese Arts & Crafts** store.

The Star Ferry provides direct access from Kowloon Peninsula as it travels from Tsim Sha Tsui to Wan Chai Pier. Old Wan Chai has been pushed back from the waterfront and will continue to be developed. If you want to see some of the original architecture and shops, prowl Queen's Road East and the lanes connecting it to Johnston Road. Shopping in the convention center is decidedly unexciting, but if you move on to the Hopewell Building, there is a **street market on nearby Fenwick Street** that is fabulous—no other tourists in sight, and a great place for taking pictures.

Causeway Bay

Causeway Bay features one deluxe hotel (the Excelsior) and many tourist package–style hotels. This area is far funkier than Central. The MTR stop is Causeway Bay. Bordered by Victoria Park on the east, and beyond that, Aw Boon Haw (Tiger Balm) Gardens, the whole area was once a bay until land reclamation turned the water into soil several decades ago. Home to the **Royal Hong Kong Yacht Club,** one of the most colorful parts of Causeway Bay is its typhoon shelter, where sampans and yachts moor side by side. You can have dinner on a sampan while cruising the harbor.

Shopping here breaks down into four different categories:

- Funky street shopping which includes plenty of medicine shops, snake soup cafes, a great market, and **Jardine's Bazaar.**
- Hip, young, and with-it Hong Kong boutiques, where new designers (who can't quite afford Central) open shops.
- **Times Square,** a relatively new giant mall that has taken the town by storm because it has 4 floors of local and western brands. Even if you don't want to shop here, you may want to visit to check out the scene and people watch—the young, hip Chinese yuppies who are cruising . . . and shopping.
- There are four big Japanese department stores in Causeway Bay: **Sogo, Daimaru, Mitsukoshi,** and **Matsuzakaya.** I think Sogo is the best. Note that each one is closed 1 day of the week; they work on a rotation system. There are a few Japanese department stores in Kowloon, and the very delicious **Seibu** is in Pacific Place, but this is the concentrated neighborhood for *depato.* That's Japanese for department store.

Continue your shopping spree in Causeway Bay away from the modern stores and onto Lockhart Road—sort of a main drag down the backbone of Causeway Bay—for a good look at some lost Chinese arts. This street is crammed with herbal and medicine shops and yep, snake shops. Pick your fave from the cage.

A great nearby photo opportunity is the fresh food market right before Jardine's. **Jardine's Bazaar** is alive with action from the early morning into the night. This is the Hong Kong I want you to see. It features a produce market, a clothes, fabrics, and notions market, and an indoor meat market; but I only suggest a visit to the latter if you are very strong and not at all squeamish. I did it once and once was enough.

Many of the shops in Causeway Bay stay open until 10pm, due to the street action. Causeway Bay lacks the expensive sheen of Central, but still has a lot of glitter packed in with the grime. The **Excelsior Hotel**—the fanciest hotel in the area—has a huge shopping arcade that most would call a mall.

Happy Valley

Happy Valley is situated directly behind Causeway Bay (no MTR—take a taxi) and is well known for its racetrack, amusement park, and shoe shops. Horse-racing season lasts from September to June, and during this time thousands of fans stream in and out of the area.

I've only tried shopping in Happy Valley once because this is home to a number of infamous shoe shops, and I thought I should give it a whirl. Wrong. Cheap, ugly shoes. And no big sizes for my big American feet.

Aberdeen

Say "Aberdeen" to most tourists, and they think of the floating restaurants this waterside community is famous for. Say "Aberdeen" to me, and I nod and smile and whisper **"Wah Tung,"** my favorite pottery and porcelain factory. Aberdeen is also the home of the **Joyce Warehouse Store**—but it's in yet another part of Aberdeen, so plan your attack carefully. Consider going with a car and driver for several quick hits (then continue on to Stanley and Repulse Bay).

Wah Tung is one serious shopping adventure. Send the husband and kids off in their own taxi to play at **Ocean Park** at the edge of Aberdeen (see next listing) while you hop a taxi for china (not China). You may dash off to **Wah Tung China Company** in a taxi, but plan on needing a truck to get home—this is the place for pottery. There's some 30,000 square feet of breakables here. They claim to have the largest selection in the world, and they ship (see page 149). Hours are 9:30am to 5:30pm from Monday through Saturday, and 11am to 5pm on Sunday. This happens to be a great Sunday adventure, by the way. You can even call **Wah Tung** (☎ 852-2873-2272), and they'll come and fetch you.

This is a fabulous way to shop. The showroom is in a warehouse; follow the signs to the elevator. There are 4 floors of glorious finds. Pay no mind to the price tags; negotiate for a discount.

For more on the **Joyce Warehouse**, see page 254.

Stanley/Repulse Bay/Ocean Park

It seems to be very "in" to bash **Stanley Market** and say it isn't up to the old standards. I have my own love-hate relationship with this tourist trap. Last trip, I loathed it. I actually had tears streaming down my face. It's very touristy . . . and I couldn't find anything to buy.

In my opinion, Stanley Market, in the heart of downtown Stanley (no MTR; take a taxi or bus no. 6), is indeed a tourist trap. However, I spoke to some British first-timers a week later; they couldn't stop raving about Stanley. My Hong Kong shopping friends still claim to find bargains here. Maybe it's a matter of perspective.

Part of the pleasure of a visit to Stanley is the drive across the island, especially the view as you go around some of those coastal curves. If you find Stanley to be overly touristy, simply get back in the taxi, go to Repulse Bay, shop the snazzy stores, eat lunch, and then return to Hong Kong proper.

Stanley is exceedingly crowded on the weekends, but delightfully quiet midweek. Note that Stanley is not one of those markets where the early bird gets the worm. The early bird gets to sit and sulk until the shops open around 9:30am.

Now then, about Repulse Bay and Ocean Park. They are theme parks of different sorts. Repulse Bay is no longer a hotel but a very tony residential address with a fancy restaurant (**The Verandah**) and a mini-mall of very, very upscale shops. Ocean Park is a water park for the kids. Both are conveniently combined with Stanley, although it's unlikely that the same person will want to do all three in 1 day.

KOWLOON NEIGHBORHOODS

· ·

The peninsula of Kowloon was ceded to the British during the Opium Wars, in one of three treaties that created the Royal Crown Colony of Hong Kong. We think it was the best gift Britain ever received; too bad they had to give it back.

Kowloon is packed with shops, hotels, excitement, and bargains. You can shop its more than 4 square miles for days and still feel that you haven't even made a dent. Like Hong Kong Island, Kowloon is the sum of many distinct neighborhoods.

Tsim Sha Tsui

The tip of Kowloon Peninsula is made up of two neighborhoods: Tsim Sha Tsui and Tsim Sha Tsui East. It is home to most of Hong Kong's fine hotels, and the home of serious tourist shopping in Kowloon. The Tsim Sha Tsui (TST) station on the MTR will get you into the heart of things. There's also the Jordan Road station for when you're traveling a bit farther into Kowloon and working your way out of the tourist neighborhoods.

At the very tip of Tsim Sha Tsui are the **Star Ferry Terminal** and the **Harbour City Complex.** This western harbor front includes **Ocean Terminal, Ocean Galleries, Ocean Centre,** the **Omni Marco Polo Hotel, Omni the Hong Kong Hotel,** and the **Omni Prince Hotel.**

The heart of Tsim Sha Tsui, however, is **Nathan Road,** Kowloon's main shopping drag; Ian says it's the equivalent of London's Oxford Street. Nathan Road stretches from the waterfront for quite some distance and works its way into the "real-people" part of Kowloon in no time at all.

The most concentrated shopping is in the area called the **Golden Mile,** which begins on Nathan Road perpendicular to Salisbury Road. Both sides of this busy street are jam-packed with stores, arcades, covered alleys, and street vendors. There are also some hotels here, each with a shopping mall and enough neon to make Las Vegas blush from embarrassment.

If you are walking north (away from the harbor), you'll pass the Golden Mile. Then you reach a mosque on your left and then the **Park Lane Shopper's Boulevard,** also on your left. To your right, across the street from the Park Lane, is **Burlington Arcade.** The next street on your right is **Granville Road,** which is famous for its jobbers, where brand-name goodies are sold from bins.

While Nathan Road is the core of Kowloon, my favorite part of Tsim Sha Tsui is actually a bit off the beaten path, although directly in sight. In the Golden Mile section of Tsim Sha Tsui, there are two streets that run parallel to Nathan Road and are centered between the Golden Mile and Ocean Terminal: Lock Road and Hankow Road.

If you have adventure in your soul, we ask that you wander this area with your eyes open. It's crammed with shops, neon signs, construction, and busy people and does not get so many tourists because it has the aura of being hidden. At the top of Lock Road, right before you get to Haiphong Road,

Kowloon

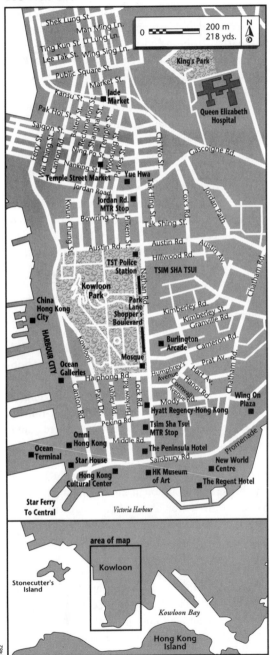

Shek Lung St.
Man Ming Ln.
Ting Kun St. Li Lung Ln.
Lee Tak St. Wing Sing Ln.
Public Square St.
King's Park
Market St.
Kansu St.
Jade Market
Pak Hoi St.
Queen Elizabeth Hospital
Saigon St.
Battery St.
Reclamation St.
Shanghai St.
Temple St.
Woosung St.
Portland St.
Chi Wo St.
Nanking St.
Shing Po St.
Gascoigne Rd.
Temple Street Market
Yue Hwa
Jordan Road
Jordan Rd. MTR Stop
Tak Hing St.
Cox's Rd.
Bowring St.
Kwun Chung St.
Parkes St.
Pilem St.
Tak Shing St.
Jordan Path
Jordan Rd.
Austin Rd.
Austin Rd.
Austin Av.
TST Police Station
Hillwood Rd.
TSIM SHA TSUI
Kowloon Park
Nathan Rd.
Chatham Rd.
China Hong Kong City
Park Lane Shopper's Boulevard
Kimberley Rd.
Kimberley St.
Granville Rd.
HARBOUR CITY
Kowloon Park Dr.
Mosque
Burlington Arcade
Cameron Rd.
Ocean Galleries
Haiphong Rd.
Humphrey's Avenue
Hart Av.
Hanoi Rd.
Cornwall Avenue
Prat Av.
Chatham Rd.
Canton Rd.
Park Dr.
Ashley Rd.
Hankow Rd.
Lock Rd.
Mody Rd.
Wing On Plaza
Peking Rd.
Hyatt Regency-Hong Kong
Omni Hong Kong
Middle Rd.
Tsim Sha Tsui MTR Stop
Promenade
Ocean Terminal
Star House
The Peninsula Hotel
Salisbury Rd.
New World Centre
Hong Kong Cultural Center
HK Museum of Art
The Regent Hotel
Star Ferry To Central
Victoria Harbour

0   200 m
    218 yds.
N

area of map
Kowloon
Stonecutter's Island
Kowloon Bay
Hong Kong Island

1462

look to your left, where you'll find a small alley that leads all the way through to Hankow Road. This is called the **Haiphong Alley,** and it is crammed with vendors. Many of these vendors do not speak English and will drive a very hard bargain, if they bargain at all. Who cares?

Once you become an Old China Hand, you'll note that prices on Nathan Road are for tourists, and you may disdain the whole Golden Mile area.

Near Jordan Road the atmosphere is more real. Be sure to get to the **Temple Street Market** (see page 222). And, of course, you can't miss the **Jade Market.** If you have a true spirit of shopping and adventure, you'll also make sure you get to Fa Yuen Street (see page 128).

Harbour City

Although technically still part of Tsim Sha Tsui, I count the western portion of Kowloon as a separate neighborhood, since it is basically one giant shopping mall—or, actually, several giant interconnected shopping malls. I call the whole entire stretch of Canton Road—from the Star Ferry to China Hong Kong City—Harbour City. This definition includes the buildings across the street on Canton Road, like **Silvercord** and the **Sun Plaza Arcade.** Many *gweilo* big names have opened in this area including **HMV** and **Planet Hollywood.** This whole area has changed dramatically and will continue to do so.

Note: If you are arriving from the Hong Kong side, it's easier to get to the Harbour City part of Tsim Sha Tsui by the Star Ferry. You'll be right there when you land.

The denser shopping is on the Ocean Terminal side, where (walking away from the Star Ferry) the buildings, in order, are: **Star House, Ocean Terminal, Ocean Galleries, Ocean Centre, World Financial Centre, Omni Prince Hotel,** and **China Hong Kong City,** which is a mall-and-towers complex and ferry terminal. This entire stretch of shopping buildings also includes office space and residential towers, as well as some of the well-known tourist hotels in this area: **Omni Marco Polo, Omni Hong Kong Hotel,** and **Omni Prince Hotel.**

Antique aficionados should check out the mall called **The Silk Road** (see page 138). Photographers should note there's **Robert Lam,** the professional lab which Ian uses, is at 116–120 Canton Rd., across from The Omni Prince Hotel.

Tsim Sha Tsui East

If you have Hong Kong Harbour at your back, Ocean Terminal to your left, and The Regent to your right, you are looking at the heart of Kowloon, or Tsim Sha Tsui. As the Kowloon peninsula curves around the harbor and the land juts away from Kowloon and The Regent, the area just east of Tsim Sha Tsui but before Hung Hom and the airport is known as Tsim Sha Tsui East.

Because it is waterfront property, it has become known mostly for its string of luxury hotels.

Although the MTR does not come over in this direction, the walk to Tsim Sha Tsui station is not unreasonable, even in the noonday sun. You may also get here via a specific routing of the Star Ferry.

Tsim Sha Tsui East has come to fascinate me as a miniature version of the greater Hong Kong. You can find almost everything you need right here. Mobbed on weekends by local shoppers, its various buildings include **Auto Plaza, Houston Centre,** and, of course, the enclosed mall itself, which is **Tsim Sha Tsui Centre.** There is street-level shopping all along Mody Road, in the various buildings, inside the mall itself (of course), and then on street levels of the buildings behind the Nikko.

There is also some shopping inside each of the hotels; I often take a lunch break at the **Kowloon Shangri-La** coffee shop and hit the hotel stores before returning to the malls.

Yau Ma Tei

Remember when I was telling you about Jordan Road and the area north of Tsim Sha Tsui? Well, this is it. Take the MTR to Jordan Road. Above Tsim Sha Tsui, north on Nathan Road or Canton Road, is the district of Yau Ma Tei.

The most famous shopping site in the area is the well-known **Jade Market** at Kansu and Battery streets; look for the overpass of the highway, and you'll then spot the market right below it.

Here you can shop from 10am until 2:30pm, going from stall to stall, negotiating for all the jade that you might fancy (see page 224). There are two different tents filled with vendors. The experience is just short of mind-boggling. You'll never be strong enough to do both tents.

Alongside the **Jade Market,** on Shanghai Street, is a "wet market"—real live Chinese green market worthy of exploration with or without camera.

At night you will want to visit the **Temple Street Market.** As you push your way through the shoulder-to-shoulder crowds you'll have the chance to buy from the carts, have your fortune told, or enjoy an open-air meal. I had a reader write in and say she couldn't find the fun parts, so check out the details (see page 222).

I went to the **Jade Market** on a Sunday last time and walked there via Reclamation Street, which was filled with stalls heaped with market goods, from fruits and vegetables to chicken feet and dried lizards and finally cheap T-shirts and socks. I had a ball.

Hung Hom

Home of Hong Kong's original outlets, this part of town will disappear once the new airport is fully functional and this part of town can be rehabbed. Factories have already moved out, and the outlet scene is bad. If you have tons of time on your hands, maybe—but most agree with me, don't waste your time checking this out unless you are doing a dissertation on Hong Kong real estate.

The most famous address in Hung Hom is **Kaiser Estates,** an industrial development of factories and factory-outlet stores with a few fancy outlets—when you look at **JBH/Fashions Of Seventh Avenue,** you'll be seeing a boutique as smart as anything in Central. There's no MTR stop; you'll need to take a taxi.

Prince Edward & Fa Yuen

Even though Fa Yuen is just a street and not a true neighborhood, it is enough of an event unto itself that it should be considered as a separate destination. Fa Yuen is so great, I consider it my favorite new neighborhood in Hong Kong. On a recent visit, I bought so much, I truly could not fit down the stairwell to the Prince Edward MTR in order to return to The Regent.

To put it in a nutshell, Fa Yuen is the newer version of Granville Road. It's farther "uptown," deeper into the real Hong Kong, and a good bit cheaper than Granville Road, while still offering much of the same style of shopping—storefront after storefront of racks and bins filled with no-name and designer clothing for as little as $10 U.S. an item. Silk blouses cost a tad more, but not much.

Fa Yuen has been blossoming for several years now; no doubt it will become too commercial and a new place will sprout. Until then, what are you waiting for? Bring plenty of cash because most of these stores do not take plastic. Consider bringing airline wheels with you or a donkey. It is time to shop 'til you drop, Hong Kong style.

When I study my shopping bags from Granville Road, I note that some of the jobbers who sell U.S. name clothing on Granville also have a store on Fa Yuen Street. But names and addresses are truly meaningless; you go, you see, you shop.

You must be prepared to rummage at Fa Yuen, but because you won't see guests from your hotel, you will feel like a real China Hand for having come here and outsmarted everyone else you know.

If you need a jumping-off place, head for **Come True,** 146 Fa Yuen St. Then there's **Kwong Shui Hong** at 190 Fa Yuen St. These 2 blocks are dense with great stores; just walk from one to the next. They truly all look alike, but by now, you're getting used to this kind of thing. Besides, after you've done Granville Road, this will come naturally to you.

From here, you can wander over to the nearby **Ladies Market** (see below). It's 2 blocks away on Tung Choi Street, which opens around 4pm. Don't confuse these two different shopping venues. This Ladies Market is mostly a street market with stalls on the road, while Fa Yuen Street consists of traditional retail with actual shops. Look at a map.

Also note that the new **Bird Market** is in this neighborhood, Yuen Po Street.

To get there: Take the MTR to Prince Edward.

Mong Kok

Mong Kok is very gritty but easier on the nerves than **Sham Shui Po** (see below). Clustered around upper Nathan Road, where the tourists thin out fast, the **Mong Kok Market** at Tung Choi Street is an afternoon market that is also called the **Ladies' Market** (see map).

If you have evening plans and can't make it to the **Temple Street Market,** then Mong Kok is the afternoon market you should plan to visit. In addition to stands selling alarm clocks that cluck, blaring Canto-pop, and fake designer scarves, you'll find everything you could ever need.

To get there: Depart the MTR at Mong Kok station and find Hong Lok Street, which is more of an alley on the south side of Argyle Street. It's 2 blocks west of Nathan Road (if your back is to the harbor, then west is to your left).

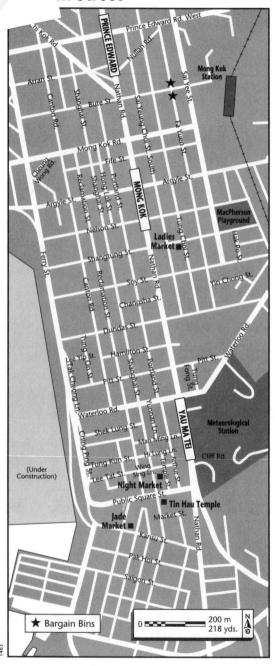

en Street

PRINCE EDWARD

Prince Edward Rd. West

Chi Kok Rd.

Nullah Rd.

Arran St.

Sai Yee St.

Mong Kok
Station

Canton Rd.

Shanghai St.

Bute St.

Nathan Rd.

Sai Yeung Choi St. South

Fa Yuen St.

★
★

Cheung Wong Rd.

Mong Kok Rd.

Fife St.

MONG KOK

Argyle St.

Argyle St.

Reclamation St.

Shanghai St.

Hong Lok St.

Portland St.

MacPherson
Playground

Hak Po St.

Nelson St.

Ferry St.

Shangtung St.

Tung Choi St.

Ladies
Market

Canton Rd.

Reclamation St.

Soy St.

Nathan Rd.

Yin Chong St.

Changsha St.

Dundas St.

Waterloo Rd.

Tung On St.

Tak Cheong Ln.

Lee Yip St.

Hamilton St.

Shanghai St.

Portland St.

Pitt St.

Pitt St.

Tung Fong St.

Waterloo Rd.

Ching Ping St.

Shek Lung St.

Man Ming Ln.

YAU MA TEI

Meteorological
Station

Tung Kun St.

Hi Lung Ln.

Cliff Rd.

Lee Tat St.

Wing Sing Ln.

Temple St.

Arthur St.

Night Market

(Under
Construction)

Public Square St.

■ Tin Hau Temple

Jade
Market ■

Market St.

Nathan Rd.

Kansu St.

Pak Hoi St.

Saigon St.

★ Bargain Bins

0   200 m
    218 yds.

N

1463

Sham Shui Po

For more adventures of a very real kind, head out a little farther to hit the food markets in the streets just down from the Sham Shui Po MTR station, where Kwelin Street crosses Ki Lung Street. You can walk around this city block to see live fish wriggling in red plastic bins, heaps of bok choy, and cages of bound bamboo sheltering fowl of every type. Watch more carefully to see the true details of market life. This is not for young children or the squeamish.

Sham Shui Po is also headquarters to the wholesale computer world, where you can bargain for video games that cost anywhere from 25% to 75% less than U.S. prices. Head for **Golden Arcade Shopping Centre,** at 44B Fuk Wah St.; you'll see it from the MTR station.

In fact, Sham Shui Po is getting more and more socially acceptable—now the fabric dealers and trim sellers are beginning to move in. Many relocated when Cloth Alley was abandoned; some went into Western Market, others not.

This is not a neighborhood I recommend for everyone, especially those with only half a day for shopping; but it is the kind of place the stout-hearted, with 2 or more days to shop, will enjoy exploring. This is also one of the few remaining patches of the "old" Hong Kong.

OUTER ISLAND NEIGHBORHOODS

. . . .

The more I visit Hong Kong, the more I need to get away from the touristy places and the malls and find the true spirit of China. Or at least, Hong Kong. Often this means a day trip to an island. However, I don't mean a day trip to the new airport!

The great thing about the outer islands—all technically part of the New Territories—is that they make fabulous little side trips. Since being on the water is so much a part of the Hong Kong experience, being able to take local ferries and *kaidos* (flat barges used as ferries) will add to the pleasures of your visit. Shopping, eating, and simply wandering these islands can make a perfect day trip; some hightail it to Lantau, especially for the beaches. I prefer to wander the little village streets on other islands and poke into the shops.

Lamma

Lamma doesn't have any shops that I've noticed, but there are a few vendors here and there to add to the colorful scene. They sell things like waxed parasols, plastic back-scratchers, and straw hats, but hey, isn't that what you came here to buy anyway?

There are two main towns on Lamma, but the place you want to be is Sok Kwu Wan, with its view of the harbor (and the cement factory) and its stretch of outdoor cafes (everyone goes to Lamma to eat at one of the harbor-front dives where the food is fresh and the clientele is local). It's the second stop on the kaido from Aberdeen; there is direct service from Central.

Cheung Chau

Don't go to Cheung Chau in May because of the famous Bun Festival (it's way too crowded). Do go when no one else wants to go, so you have the full glory of the place all to yourself. Take the ferry from Central.

This island has banned cars, so all you can do is walk the garden paths. There are temples, shops (lots of porcelain shops), and restaurants. There is also a market along the Praya (beach front) in Cheung Chau Village.

Lantau

This is the airport island.

Chapter Nine

· · · · · · · ·

THE HEART OF HONG KONG: SHOPS & STORES

ATTENTION, PLEASE

· ·

There are so many kinds of shopping experiences in Hong Kong, each so different from another, that, in order to cover this material thoroughly, I have grouped all these experiences into the following categories: shops and stores, markets and malls, and factory outlets . . . stretching through the next few chapters.

This chapter covers the basic resources available in storefronts: small boutiques, medium-sized shops, and department stores. Organized alphabetically by goods, it presents the best of these forms of Hong Kong retail. Some of my absolute favorite shops are marked with a shopping-bag icon. Hong Kong's numerous malls present another distinct experience, based on architecture, ambience, and location of each. And yet another shopping experience, with its own look and feel and energy, is Hong Kong's many open-air markets. Some are gritty and very real world; others are more commercial and touristy. These shopping experiences are covered in chapter 10, "Markets & Malls."

Finally, Hong Kong's newest and most exciting retail trend, factory outlets, are treated in chapter 11, "Factory Outlets."

ART & ANTIQUES

. . . .

While there are many places to buy art and antiques in Hong Kong, I have purposely created a somewhat small section, for several reasons:

- The bulk of the internationally famous dealers in Asian art are in London, New York, Tokyo, Vancouver, Taipei, Brussels, and places other than Hong Kong, especially now that Hong Kong is under Chinese rule and there are new laws governing what can be taken out of the country.

- The amount of fakes and frauds in the art business is infamous. The situation is even more intense in Hong Kong, and in no way can I confirm the authenticity of your purchase.

- The antiques scene in Hong Kong has shifted, due to new laws imposed by Chinese; many dealers have left, many are poised to do so if things get tough. Some dealers have moved from Hollywood Road; Ocean Terminal is holding its own with a space politely called **The Silk Road** (third floor), which holds many dealers as well as the internationally famous **Charlotte Horstmann & Gerald Godfrey gallery.**

Buy what you know; if you don't know much, buy what you love, regardless of its real value. Bring your own expert with you, if you are truly serious, or hire one in Hong Kong. A magazine called *Orientations* is available in Hong Kong—it is good background reading on the scene and prices. There are also a number of big-time auctions in Hong Kong; both **Sotheby's** and **Christie's** have offices here. Auctions are held in either spring or fall.

If you think you are serious about something, but can't sleep at night because you're not certain if it's real, get a second opinion. Many dealers on Hollywood Road will appraise an item (from another source) for you on a flat-fee basis.

It also pays to get an education before you go shopping. There are excellent museum collections in Hong Kong; the world's leading collection of Oriental art is in the British Museum in London.

Bear in mind that the truly wonderful pieces are usually put away. Most dealers have warehouses or back rooms where they keep their best wares and are open to the public only by appointment. This weeds out the less-serious browsers. Read *Orientations* for news on the latest players or ask at **Honeychurch** or **Charlotte Horstmann** for suggestions on whom to call for an appointment or two.

LUEN CHAI CURIOS STORE
22 Upper Lascar Row, Hong Kong; 142 Hollywood Rd., Hong Kong (MTR: Central or Sheung Wan).

These are curios like I'm Minnie Mouse—this Cat Street dealer has scrolls, antique porcelain, and exhibition space to show contemporary Chinese painting. Located near the Man Mo end of the antiques shopping street, this store is in an area concentrated with shops that are borderline tourist traps, so it becomes impossible to tell the real from the fake and the good from the too-good-to-be-true.

HANART GALLERY
Central Building, Pedder St. also TZ at Old Bank of China Building, 5th floor (MTR: Central).

One of the most famous galleries in the world for scrolls. Their exhibition space often represents modern Chinese art. This is the place to go—their reputation is outstanding. Hanart also has galleries in New York and Taipei. See listing below for Harold Wong; you may need an appointment. Hanart TZ is a special show space.

HONEYCHURCH ANTIQUES
29 Hollywood Rd. (MTR: Central).

Honeychurch Antiques has been home base on Hollywood Road since the beginning of the *Born to Shop* series, so forgive me if I guide you here; but I know you will be well taken care of by American expat owners Glenn and Lucille.

Honeychurch is located in the beginning part of the antiques run on Hollywood Road, which makes it a convenient first stop. The Vessas have held court for over 25 years; they know everything and everyone; stop by and ask whatever pops into your mind . . . but don't ask if you can call home.

The store carries a wide variety of merchandise; eclectic is the best summary. The look is sort of Oriental Country; there are goods from Japan and other exotic locations besides your basic Chinese antiques. Last visit, I fell in love with a Russian tea strainer.

Try both floors in the main shop and then a warehouse floor next door (ask to be taken over), with larger pieces of furniture and a few other goodies. Yes, they have blue-and-white; yes, they'll let you smell the opium pipes.

CHARLOTTE HORSTMANN & GERALD GODFREY LTD.
Harbour City/Ocean Terminal, Canton Rd., Kowloon (MTR: TST).

One of the most popular and well-respected antiques shops in Hong Kong, Charlotte Horstmann & Gerald Godfrey offer a wide range in museum-class Asian antiques and possibly hold the town's oldest rep among Americans.

There are pieces from Korea, Burma, China, Japan, Indonesia, and India. Choices include Noh masks, Chinese scrolls, Ming tapestries, Tang horses, and period furniture made of sandalwood, rosewood, and blackwood. I've also spied some fancy yet inexpensive pieces here that aren't technically antiques. It's worth a look, but may not be your cup of *cha.* If not, this is sure to be: Charlotte Horstmann has a warehouse that looks like a movie set. Seek here and ye shall find. Or fax ahead, 852-7230-9412.

P.C. LU & SONS LTD.
Harbour City/Ocean Terminal, The Silk Road,
Canton Rd., Kowloon (MTR: TST).

A fine antiques dealer with showrooms in the major hotels, P. C. Lu's family has been in the business for four generations and runs one of the finest resources for antique ivory and jade, porcelain, and decorative work. The three sons, who now run the business, work closely together. Stop in at any of the galleries and browse or get a look when you're prowling The Silk Road (see page 138).

PLUM BLOSSOM INTERNATIONAL LTD.
51 Garden Rd., 17th floor, Coda Plaza, Central
(MTR: Central).

They moved—they expanded—they are players. While I am not terribly interested in contemporary Chinese painting, I have seen work at Plum Blossom that I like. If you agree with me, you may want to spend some time getting to know contemporary Chinese work since it is a genre that is getting increasingly hot among collectors.

Plum Blossom is also one of the best sources in town for antique textile arts, one of my most passionate loves. You can find everything from uncut robes to ready-made carpets to embroidered fragments to Tibetan carpets. This is the kind of place you can look to for guidance in the area of expensive items that will accrue in value.

SCHOENI
27 Hollywood Rd. (MTR: Central).

You have officially begun to "do" Hollywood Road when you stop in here, at one of Hong Kong's toniest dealers. Art and objets d'art from all over the

Orient, so that only a portion of the selection is Chinese, but all of it is serious and expensive.

TAI SING CO.
122 Hollywood Rd. (MTR: Central).

A leading dealer in important Han, Tang, and Sung porcelains, as well as imperial porcelain (which is outrageously expensive), since 1957. They also sell Chinese export porcelain (which while less expensive is still only for the serious collector).

The Silk Road

The Silk Road is an extremely clever marketing ploy to lead tourists to a portion of the mall in Ocean Terminal that is more or less devoted to antiques shops. Nonetheless, there are shops you will enjoy poking into, and the mall is easy enough to get to. The Silk Road portion is marked clearly; you can enter from the Omni Hong Kong Hotel and not have to wander the endless corridors of shopping mall. Pass the coffee shop, then take the escalators straight up to the third floor. If you expect little, you will be pleased. (Confucius says.) Expect too much, and you will be disappointed. Note that **Charlotte Horstmann's gallery** is right here, although it isn't part of The Silk Road promotional setup.

Private Dealers

For those who wish to deal exclusively with private dealers, I can recommend the following without hesitation:

GRACE WU BRUCE
☎ *852-2523-0840; fax 852-2521-2641.*

HAROLD WONG (HANART GALLERY LTD.)
☎ *852-2868-1811; fax 852-2868-1896.*

TONG-XIN HUI
☎ *852-2523-3013.*

BEAUTY SALONS

There are really only three salons I can recommend. If you find others whose results you like, please tell me about them. As everyone knows, good salons should not be kept secret!

HAIR IMAGE
The Regent Hotel (ground floor),
18 Salisbury Rd., Kowloon (MTR: TST).

Located in The Regent Hotel shopping arcade (but not owned by The Regent), this western-style, up-scale salon has a mixture of local and visiting clientele. If there's a big ball or local do, it may be hard to get an appointment. A wash and blow-dry cost $HK 200; I tip $HK 50.

Open 7 days a week; Monday through Saturday 9:30am–7:30pm; Sundays and public holidays, 9:30am–6:30pm. Call for an appointment: ☎ 852-2721-4431 or fax 852-2721-5836.

LA CHIC
Kowloon Hotel, (basement), 19–21 Nathan Rd.,
Kowloon (MTR: TST).

Because of the location of this salon, you won't happen upon it by accident, but it's a good little find and quite convenient. For an appointment call ☎ 852-2721-4666.

LE SALON
13 Duddell St., Central (MTR: Central).

All the ladies who lunch, local and expat, swear by this resource. The most in-demand stylist is Kim Robinson, who takes bookings several months in advance, they say, and costs a whopping $400 for the works—as much as any American or British superstar snipper. Other stylists are less! To book, ☎ 852-2524-7153.

CAMERAS

. . . .

Buying a camera in Hong Kong is confusing unless you are quite knowledgeable about equipment and comparable prices. Every year there are new top-of-the-line models available in every brand, and they're all for sale in Hong Kong along with not-so-new models. Most shopkeepers will tout what they have in stock and not necessarily what you need. Most dealers will try to trade you up from what you came in to buy to what they think you can afford.

I have spent a lot of time not only on Nathan Road but on the phone to various friends around the U.S. Before I arrived in Hong Kong, I had in hand a half dozen of those full-page camera advertisements that run in every big city newspaper on Sundays.

You may be shocked to discover (I was) that Dallas has the best prices of all the major U.S. cities and better prices than one can find in Hong Kong.

I was pricing simple point-and-shoot cameras by brand-makers. It was relatively easy to match up brand and style numbers among the U.S. newspapers; it was much harder to find a match in Hong Kong. Here's the heartbreaking results in a nutshell:

- I paid $99 for a Fuji point-and-shoot at my neighborhood camera store.
- I could have gotten the exact same camera for $88 in Dallas, Texas.
- When I eventually found the same camera in Hong Kong—which took forever—the asking price was $144.
- Had I bargained on this camera and come away with what I thought was a deal, I still would have overpaid.

Since Ian Cook has been a *Time-Life* photographer for 30 years, I sent him out to hunt down both used and new cameras. His report:

- Avoid the dealers on Nathan Road. Period. They're more expensive than they need to be, and they will cheat you whenever possible. Price cameras from shops in Western, Central (there's a few on Stanley Street), and along Kimberley Road in Kowloon. Kimberley Road is right off Nathan Road, no trouble at all to find, and the shop owners are much more professional.
- Bring prices and serial numbers from home; a newspaper clipping with advertised prices is also a good idea.
- Ask if you can test cameras before you purchase them. There is a **Canon showroom** in the **Silvercord Building** where you can test various models. You must supply your own film.
- Once you are quite sure of what you want, price shop. Try several different stores and bargain as if you were going to buy. Don't buy until you have spent several days getting used to Hong Kong and to the way the camera stores do business. Be prepared to spend a lot of time at this; it's not enough to just "dash in"; work several districts of town and keep a chart or pages in your notebook or Filofax on each possibility.

After you have decided where you are going to buy, insist on the following:

- Each piece of equipment needs its own (worldwide) warranty. The serial number of the piece must be clearly marked on the card, along with the agent's stamp and a complete address of where you purchased the item.
- Make sure you are not being charged for extras that should have been included in the original purchase. For example, camera cases usually come with the camera. You should not pay extra for a case.
- Watch your purchase being packed, and check each item as it goes into its box. Don't trust the store owner to pack and deliver your purchase to

the hotel. When you get back, you might discover that a few small items somehow got lost.

- Keep your receipts separate. Customs most likely will not want to open and go through all of your equipment if your receipts are clear and in order.
- For the name of an authorized importing agent for a name-brand camera, call the **Consumer Council** ☎ 852-2736-3322.

Used Cameras

There's an entire arcade of camera dealers who specialize in used equipment on Champagne Court in Kowloon. Some items here are so new, dealers from Nathan Road come here and buy, then pass these items off as new at manufacturer's prices. Ian has made several trips here on each visit to Hong Kong and has had varied results. When he priced camera bodies, he found them outrageously high. Yet certain lenses were a steal, especially compared with London prices, which, on camera equipment, are higher than New York's.

🛍 DAVID CHAN COMPANY
Champagne Court (Shop 15), 16 Kimberley Rd., Kowloon (MTR: TST).

The HKTA found this resource for Ian, and he has done a fair amount of business with them. Luck is a major factor here, as they must have what you are looking for in stock, and you must be pleased with the condition. They sell used modern and antique models as well as film and camera supplies. Film prices are 20% less than on Nathan Road.

KIMBERLEY CAMERA CO. LTD.
Champagne Court (Shop 2), 16 Kimberley Rd., Kowloon (MTR: TST); 48 Stanley St. (MTR: Central).

Resource for new and used models; locations on both sides of the harbor. Bigger and more touristy than David Chan.

LI BROTHERS
Champagne Court (Shop 13), 16 Kimberley Rd., Kowloon (MTR: TST).

This resource has most things put away and sells supplies in bulk. They are happy to deal with pros.

CASHMERE

. . . .

The killer problem with buying cashmere is that you are asked to judge quality without having a lot to go on because you can only tell "cheap" cashmere when you have it side by side with "good" cashmere.

Cashmere from the Orient is not of the same quality as that which comes out of Scotland or Italy, not because of the quality of the goats but because of how it is combed and milled. Meanwhile, there's a lot going on with the philosophy of price points— a sweater may be inexpensively priced because it is cheap stuff or priced to compete with the better cashmeres, even though it's still cheap stuff. Obviously, there's a lot of room for error. To make matters worse, the market is being used to dump Iranian cashmere, which is of even less quality than Chinese.

You can usually tell the quality in not only the hand but in the way it knits. Price should also be related to the number of ply per skein; 2 is the usual number available in Hong Kong although the ply can range from 1 to 4.

I admit that on one trip I found a bin of cashmere sweaters on Fa Yuen Street; each sweater was priced at $20, and I didn't buy any—even as gifts— because I didn't like the quality. That was an easy had a much harder time in the **Pedder Building** where several cashmere sources sell sweaters for $50–$100 each.

Indeed, you can find cashmere in many of the outlet stores in Pedder Building, in several different stores (five or six of 'em) in **The Pen**, at the **Stanley Market,** and even at the Chinese department stores. Quality will be a big issue here—it affects the hand (feel) as well as the price. Most likely, you can get cashmeres at home for prices similar to those in Hong Kong.

CASHMERE OUTLET
Yeung Yiu Chung No. 6 Industrial Building, 19 Cheung Shun St., Kowloon (MTR: Lai Chi Kok).

This really is an outlet. They sell both cashmere and silk; many styles and colors and yes, some have designer labels. Three-minute walk from MTR station. Open Monday through Friday from 9:30am to 5pm and on Saturday from 9:20am until noon. Closed Sundays.

MAGASCHONI
Pedder Building, 12 Pedder St., room 401, Central (MTR: Central).

This is actually an outlet with suits in the front and cashmeres in a room off to one side. Very, very high-quality cashmeres; one of the best sources in town. Not the least expensive but a true find for those willing to spend on the best. Fashionable styles and cuts, great colors. A winner.

MARCUS INTERNATIONAL
Majestic House, 80 Nathan Rd., 9th floor, Kowloon (MTR: TST).

A mail-order source for Oriental cashmere for the price conscious—almost everything is well under $100! This is not Italian or Scottish cashmere, and if you know the difference, you may not be satisfied here. On the other hand, this is worth a look if you just want simple goods.

MONET KASHMIR
The Peninsula Hotel, mezzanine, Salisbury Rd., Kowloon (MTR: TST).

More European styles.

PEARLS AND CASHMERE
The Peninsula Hotel, Salisbury Rd., Kowloon (MTR: TST).

I like the quality here just fine; the selection of colors is also excellent. Prices are not dirt cheap but are competitive with low-end prices in the U.S. so that you get more quality than usual at this price, which is close to $200 per sweater. Some sweaters are less; there are also other items. The store is absolute heaven; you may never want to leave.

CASSETTES, CDS & CANTO POP

I Love Canto pop. This is bubble gum for the ear, Chinese-style, and blares from speakers at all street markets. Stop by my house and get an earful. Want to know what to buy? Ask anyone in a street market (I buy mine in **Temple Street Night Market**). Don't want to shop in the street? No problem.

HMV
Sands Building, 17 Hankow Rd., Kowloon (MTR: TST); Swire House (MTR: Central).

Her Majesty's teenyboppers have invaded TST and with them, a rather large music shop for all the CDs, cassettes, videos, and Muzak from classical to Canto pop you could possibly want. Seems to be the cheapest place in town, and everyone but everyone hangs here.

CHINA & CRYSTAL
. . . .

The largest china and crystal stores are in or near
the major hotels and shopping centers. They all ship
and take orders from overseas. The only problem
arises when the store is out of stock. You can have
many dinner parties before your missing pieces
arrive. Check on availability before you place your
order.

While you may save on pieces you can carry yourself, once you ship, you wipe out any big savings.

BACCARAT
*The Landmark (Shop G3–4), 16 Des Voeux Rd.
(MTR: Central).*

CRAIG'S
*St. George's Building, 2 Ice House St., next to
the Mandarin Oriental Hotel (MTR: Central);
Harbour City/Ocean Centre (Shop 341), 5 Canton
Rd.; Harbour City/Ocean Terminal (Shop 122A),
Canton Rd., Kowloon (MTR: TST).*

EILEEN KERSHAW
*The Peninsula Hotel, Salisbury Rd., Kowloon
(MTR: TST); The Landmark, 16 Des Voeux Rd.
(MTR: Central).*

HUNTER'S
*The Peninsula Hotel, Salisbury Rd.; Harbour
City/Ocean Terminal, Canton Rd.; Kowloon
Hotel, 19–21 Nathan Rd., Kowloon (MTR: TST).
Repulse Bay Shopping Arcade, 109 Repulse Bay
Rd., (MTR: none). The Mall at Pacific Place
(Shops 308 and 309), 88 Queensway (MTR:
Admiralty).*

LALIQUE
*The Landmark, 16 Des Voeux Rd. (MTR:
Central); The Peninsula Hotel, Salisbury Rd.,
Kowloon (MTR: TST).*

LLADRÓ
*The Peninsula Hotel, Salisbury Rd., Kowloon
(MTR: TST); Alexandra House, Des Voeux Rd.
(MTR: Central).*

MEISSEN
*The Landmark (Shop G22), 16 Des Voeux Rd.
(MTR: Central).*

RAYNAUD (LIMOGES)
*Harbour City/Ocean Terminal (Shop 124),
Canton Rd., Kowloon (MTR: TST); Prince's
Building, Chater Rd. (MTR: Central).*

RICHARD GINORI
*The Mall at Pacific Place (Shop 358),
88 Queensway (MTR: Admiralty).*

ROSENTHAL
Prince's Building, Chater Rd. (MTR: Central).

ROYAL COPENHAGEN
*Prince's Building, Chater Rd. (MTR: Central);
Harbour City/Ocean Terminal, Canton Rd.,
Kowloon (MTR: TST).*

ROYAL DOULTON
*The Mall at Pacific Place (Shop 366),
88 Queensway (MTR: Admiralty).*

WEDGWOOD
*The Landmark (Shop G7A), Gloucester Tower,
16 Des Voeux Rd. (MTR: Central); The Peninsula
Hotel, Salisbury Rd., Kowloon (MTR: TST).*

Chinese China

Chinese porcelain factories are a popular shopper's
attraction; you can see some of the goods in production if you are interested, or you can just shop
until you fill a container.

The factories are not overly easy or convenient to get to, so we suggest that you plan your
day around the visit, leave plenty of time, and

remember that most factories close for lunch, usually between 1pm and 2pm.

All Chinese crafts stores have a selection of china; assume that blue-and-white is fake unless guaranteed otherwise. Do check out the numerous porcelain dives as you parade along Hollywood Road (see page 115). Some shops here do specialize in authentic blue-and-white as well as other wares. Talk to Glenn and Lucille at **Honeychurch** if you need a lesson in buying porcelain.

AH CHOW PORCELAIN
Hong Kong Industrial Centre, Block B, 7th floor, 489–491 Castle Peak Rd., Kowloon (MTR: Lai Chi Kok).

If you are doing an outlet spree in Lai Chi Kok, this is a must; otherwise I'd rather you go to **Wah Tung** (see below), which is much larger. Ah Chow is a small outlet that has been servicing a lot of U.S. and British department stores for years. They have excellent prices; they ship (it takes years to get your order—or it seems like years); they will do a custom order for you. I have bought from this factory and been thrilled with my purchases. I must also admit that I do all my personal buying at Wah Tung; this is a convenience and style issue, I think.

OVERJOY
Kwai Hing Industrial Building (Block B, 1st floor), 10–18 Chun Pin St., Kwai Chung, N.T. (MTR: none, take a taxi).

Located in the heart of Hong Kong's shipping and container district, where there are a few other porcelain showrooms, Overjoy is the single most famous source to those who have been living here for years. Grab a taxi to this industrial area, walk up one flight of stairs; the selection includes both western and Chinese patterns. Shipping rates are posted; delivery to your hotel in Hong Kong is free. There is also a showroom in Wan Chai.

🛍️ WAH TUNG CHINA COMPANY
Grand Marine Industrial Building, 3 Yue Fung St.,
Tin Wan, Aberdeen (MTR: none, take a taxi);
148 Hollywood Rd. {MTR: Sheung Wan);
57 Hollywood Rd. (MTR: Central).

This is the single largest source for Chinese porcelain in Hong Kong. While they have two very nice showrooms on Hollywood Road, I really far prefer the Aberdeen addresses where there are floors of showroom and prices seem to be rather negotiable, depending on how much you buy and how aggressive you feel.

I've bought tons from here and loved every minute of it. I rate this the single best porcelain resource in town. I've bought giant ginger jars that now sit on my mantle; I've bought smalls for home and for gifts.

Before you buy anything at Wah Tung, show your copy of this book and tell them I said to give you a flat discount. I think that will even up the price issue for you. The discount is only offered in Aberdeen.

All three showrooms are crammed packed with new pieces and new antiques; they make no fuss about showing you how they antique pieces. Usually an artisan is working so you can watch. Many U.S. department stores use this as a resource; I think it's a must-do. They will send a van to bring you to Aberdeen if you want (☎ 852-2873-2272). All three shops are open on Sundays 11am–5pm.

CHOPS
. . . .

In China, a *chop* is a form of signature stamp (not made of rubber) on which a symbol for a person's name is carved. The chop is dipped in dry dye (instead of an ink pad) and then placed on paper to create a signature stamp, much like a rubber stamp.

Antique chops are quite pricey, depending on age, importance of the carving, materials used, and maybe even the autograph that is engraved. New chops have little historic importance, but make great gifts. Some come ready-made in a standard set of western names; you can have your own carved.

Although chops vary in size, they are traditionally the size of a chess piece, with a square or round base. Up to four Chinese characters or three western initials can be inscribed on the base.

The quality of a chop varies greatly, based on the ability of the person who does the carving. We have done enough chop shopping to know that the very best place to get a chop, if you crave atmosphere, lies in **Man Wa Lane,** deep inside the Western District. It's also the worst place because it is so confusing—you may never find your way back to the proper vendor when you need to pick up your finished chop.

Every hotel has at least one gift shop that will have your chop engraved. (You must allow at least 24 hours.) Many shops will provide 1-hour service. At **Stanley Market** you can get while-you-wait service from a variety of dealers.

You may buy the chop à la carte or in a set or gift box. The boxed set comes with your chop and the ink pot in a silk (or faux silk) covered box with adorable clasp; expect to pay about $HK 100 for the boxed set in Stanley.

COMPUTERS & SMALL ELECTRONIC DEVICES
· ·

For the most part, I am nervous about buying computers and other electronics in Hong Kong—too much can go wrong.

If you're still interested in at least seeing what's out there, check out **East Asia Computer Plaza,** in the basement of the **Silvercord Building,** 30 Canton Rd., Kowloon. This is the place to go to be safe. Downstairs is computer city. There are authorized dealers here for most of the big names in the computer world.

The big names like Apple, IBM, and NEC are sold at authorized stores in the East Asia Computer Plaza. You can haggle and bargain . . . possibly even make a good deal. Make sure, however, that the machine you buy is wired to work on the voltage where you will be using it. The Hong Kong voltage is 220, while standard voltage in the U.S. is 110. Don't let a salesperson convince you that a converter will do. Computers are much too sensitive, and you don't want to risk losing your program because of a power failure. Also make sure that the equipment you buy will work with the monitor you have at home.

If you are a little more adventurous, take the MTR to Sham Shui Po to visit the **Golden Arcade Shopping Centre**, 44B Fuk Wah St. This area is not known for its tourist appeal; it's filled with street stalls selling blue jeans for $5, T-shirts, bed linens, ducks, and roosters. The street odor is strong. People are jammed into every nook and cranny of the area. In the midst of this craziness is the Golden Arcade Shopping Centre, a supermarket filled with computer hardware, software, and educational material. Much of it is bootlegged.

As you get out of the MTR you will be right there . . . just look up to see the arcade marquee. There is a directory listing all 120 shops, but it really doesn't matter. The only way to shop here is to wander and compare. Each shop has a different type of computer, and many if not most of them are clones.

You have to know your stuff. If you speak Cantonese, it will help as well. But don't be intimidated; even if you don't buy anything, this is the place to go. If you are with men or boys who disdain your desire to shop, send them here for a half day while you take off for outlets unknown. This is such a scene that anyone will enjoy observing it or getting wrapped up in the motion.

Important Note: If you buy, please take the time to open the package and run the program right there in the store. One of our readers found that half the program would not boot. They ran a new copy for him on the spot. This is definitely a bargain-hard shopping environment for smart shoppers only.

COSMETICS & FRAGRANCES

. . . .

Cosmetics and fragrances are now duty free in Hong Kong. While the 25% tax has been rescinded, that doesn't mean fragrance and cosmetics are as inexpensive as in Paris. They may be less than in the U.S. They can also be more.

Furthermore, there are gray market goods out there, so you may not even know what you are buying.

Best buys are in terms of availability, not price— check out scents that have been introduced in Europe, but not in the U.S. Whether you save or not becomes meaningless because you'll be the first on your block to have the new scent. If you care.

We have comparison-shopped all the big department stores—British, Japanese, Chinese, you name it—and we find that they all have pretty much the same prices. The duty-free shop at the airport is expensive and offers no wait-til-the-airport bargains that I can discern.

Take Note: Many big-name cosmetics companies manufacture for the Far East in and around Hong Kong; often they will have a product with the same name as the product you use at home, but it will be slightly different. They may also have a product or shade that you will have never heard of and will never find again anywhere else in the world.

THE BODY SHOP
The Landmark, Gloucester Tower, 16 Des Voeux Rd. (MTR: Central); The Mall at Pacific Place, 88 Queensway (MTR: Admiralty).

I do love this English natural cosmetics line, but the prices are high in Hong Kong. Certainly items cost less in the U.K., but if you're American, you'll find it's a toss-up. No bargains, but a standard to live by if you are in need. All the products come in biodegradable containers and are made from natural ingredients. There is a complete line of cosmetics as well as soaps with scents like sandalwood and jasmine. Treat yourself to a bottle of Peppermint Foot Massage Creme after a hard day of bargain hunting. There are branch stores absolutely everywhere.

DFS
Harbour City/Ocean Terminal, Canton Rd., Kowloon (MTR: TST).

The initials stand for Duty-Free Shoppers (International). These guys own the airport, a lot of Hong Kong, and a good portion of TST, and also the world. The stores are enormous and give you the same thrill as shopping at an airport, without the anxiety. Enormous selection of everything including (but not limited to) perfumes, makeup, beauty treatments, and more. There are big stores here and there around town, including one in Tsim Sha Tsui on Hankow Road (**Hankow Centre**) and one in Tsim Sha Tsui East at the **ChinaChem Golden Plaza;** but there are at least a half dozen other locations around town, including one at the **Convention Centre** if that's where you hang out . . . and **The Peak!**

SaSa Cosmetic Company
25 Granville Rd.; Nathan Rd., Kowloon (MTR: TST).

SaSa has emerged as one of the leading discounters in Hong Kong with branch stores all over and a huge rep among not only locals but people in the beauty industry on the international front.

Many of their goods come directly from the sources in the U.S., which makes them much cheaper on a local front. But not cheaper than at home, if you are American. So shop carefully. Also note that some items are closeouts and discontinued lines.

SaSa on Granville Road is a medium-sized, drugstore type of place that is mobbed with locals who have never seen such a huge selection of American and European brands of cosmetics and health/beauty aids. There are many items you won't see in America and many that could have been relocated right from your hometown drugstore—at higher prices, of course. Revlon nail polish costs $HK 21, which sounds like a bargain until you convert and discover it's exactly the same price as at home ($3.). They don't carry Chanel makeup, but they've got tons of everything else. Have a ball.

SHU UEMURA
The Landmark, 16 Des Voeux Rd.
(MTR: Central); Pacific Place, 88 Queensway
(MTR: Admiralty).

Nobody does better colors in eye shadow. Makeup junkies shouldn't miss the opportunity to buy from the Japanese maven of cosmetics and color. Most good Japanese department stores also carry the line. It is available in the U.S., but is hard to find since the New York store closed. There's a store in Paris, but none in London. Load up now. Get a load of the testing center, and try on everything to find the colors that suit you best.

WATSON'S, THE CHEMIST
24–28 Queen's Rd. (MTR: Central).
And in many other locations.

There's a Watson's on almost every big busy block and mall in Hong Kong; I happen to end up at the one around the corner from the **Pedder Building** because it's convenient. There's one in **Prince's Building** and one on **Main Street in Stanley** and one in the center of **Nathan Road** just before the mosque.

Watson's is actually a drugstore cum general store that sells many things with emphasis on makeup and fragrance. I can spend hours browsing in a good one, and do note that each one is not the same so you may want to visit a few of them.

DEPARTMENT STORES

As in any large city, especially one with a diverse population, there are many department stores designed to serve the local population. In a melting pot like Hong Kong, there are different stores for every segment of the population: British department stores, Chinese department stores, and even Japanese department stores. If only for academic reasons, try to see at least one of each. Each is appealing it its own way.

British Department Stores

It seems perfectly normal for there to be British department stores in a former British Crown Colony—especially one that was set up for the sole purpose of trade—but amazingly, there are still no branches of Harrods or Liberty. What is here is still worth checking out, though.

LANE CRAWFORD
70 Queen's Rd. (MTR: Central); The Mall at Pacific Place, 88 Queensway (MTR: Admiralty).

Lane Crawford is the most prestigious western-style department store in Hong Kong and a jewel to those who work and live here, but who crave the elegance of Old-World charm in a retail setting. Lane Crawford is not huge by American standards, but it's comfortable and you'll find all the familiar brands of quality merchandise. It is not really there for tourists, but it does offer the guarantee that you are not getting fakes, seconds, or inferior merchandise.

Snobs often like to buy their jewelry and their lifestyle here.

Lane Crawford was created as a full-service English department store for the people who live here. It doesn't have the food halls of Harrods or the selection of suitable work clothes for younger women of Selfridge's, but it does offer cradle-to-grave services along with the merchandise. The name has snob appeal in Hong Kong, similar to that of Neiman Marcus in the U.S.

Their sales are equally famous.

MARKS & SPENCER
Harbour City Ocean Galleries, 25–27 Canton Rd., Kowloon (MTR: TST); Pacific Place, Central (MTR: Admiralty); The Landmark, 16 Des Voeux Rd. (MTR: Central); Cityplaza III, 1111 King's Rd., Quarry Bay (MTR: Taikoo Shing).

Marks & Sparks, as it is fondly called in Britain, has come to Hong Kong, and in a big way. Every place you turn (especially in the malls), you spot a new one. Now even **The Landmark** has one. Hooray!—a chance to buy more St. Michael's underwear.

Now then, as much as we love M&S, we admit that there are no great Hong Kong bargains here. Being in the store, especially the grocery department, is just like being in England. Except the prices are higher. What you are paying for is the M&S reputation for quality and value; we are not talking factory-outlet prices.

If you shop the Hong Kong outlets or street markets, you'll do better than M&S prices on regular ready-to-wear. Locals depend on M&S; tourists shouldn't really have to.

Please note that in some malls the various M&S departments appear to be in different boutiques or on different levels of the mall so you don't get a sense of shopping the whole store or of being in a department store.

Chinese Department Stores

Welcome to the real Hong Kong and the kind of department store shopping I like best. If you aren't in a street market, you should be in at least one Chinese department store. Of course, to truly experience Hong Kong retail you have to do both. But, if time won't allow, do a department store and pick an authentic—not westernized—one.

Note that there are western-style, Chinese–owned department stores. You may try these on for size if you want to warm up, but these are not the stores I mean when I insist that you go to a Chinese department store. I really want you to go to a place like **Yue Hwa** or **Chung Kiu.** In 1 hour you will have seen the best of Hong Kong's shopping.

There are several Chinese department stores in Hong Kong, but few of them are glamorous. They are a real experience for the traveler, are a fine source of visual treats, and very often have some bargains. They are a great place to shop for souvenirs, silks, arts and crafts items, teas, and traditional medicinal products.

CHINESE ARTS & CRAFTS STORES (H.K.) LTD.
*The Mall at Pacific Place, 88 Queensway
(MTR: Admiralty); Star House, Canton Rd.,
Kowloon (next to Star Ferry); Shell House,
Queen's Rd., Hong Kong, (MTR: Central);
China Resources Building, 26 Harbour Rd.,
Hong Kong (MTR: Wan Chai).*

Each shop is slightly different, but most of the merchandise is the same. *One Warning:* The shops are meant to bring cash into the Communist Chinese government. To make the most, the most is asked. These stores happen to be very expensive for what they are selling. By American standards, the prices are good, although the David Tang look-alike merchandise is just as expensive as his! Ouch!

The silk fabric (yard goods) department is fun, although the prices are cheaper in Jardine's or The

Lanes. I love the porcelain, baskets, and tablecloths. I've been told this is a reputable place to buy jade. There's no imitation passed off as real here. Be warned, however: Real jade is quite pricey.

The store will ship for you; sales help have been very pleasant to me—unusual for some Chinese stores. A good place for souvenirs. This is the most western of the various Chinese department stores. Hours in all stores are basically Monday to Saturday from 10am to 6:30pm; Sunday hours vary with the location. The Wan Chai branch is convenient to the Convention Centre. Other branch stores may exist; they just keep popping up all over.

SINCERE
83 Argyle St., Kowloon (MTR: Mong Kok); 173 Des Voeux Rd. (MTR: Central or Sheung Wan).

A department store with a local reputation, Sincere doesn't appeal to tourists very much because it feels junky and crowded. The big news is that Sincere is actively going after the new Chinese money and is opening stores in Shanghai and possibly in economic zones like Guangzhou and Shenzhen. Remember this name.

WING ON
361 Nathan Rd., Kowloon (MTR: Yau Ma Tei); 26 Des Voeux Rd. (MTR: Central); 62 Mody Rd., Tsim Sha Tsui East, Kowloon (MTR: none); Riviera Plaza, 28 Wing Shun St., Tsuen Wan, N.T. (MTR: Tsuen Wan).

Wing On is not much of a resource for tourists, yet it sometimes has western-style merchandise at a savings over the U.S. price. Many prices are lower than at **Stanley Market.** We're not talking Calvin Klein, but you can find some inexpensive work clothes here. Large-size Americans need not apply. Avoid weekend shopping. It's very crowded at all branches. I only send you to Wing On for academic purposes.

This also is not what I mean when I insist you visit a real Chinese department store.

YUE HWA CHINESE PRODUCTS EMPORIUM
Main store: 301–309 Nathan Rd., Yau Ma Tei, Kowloon (MTR: Jordan Rd.); Park Lane Shopper's Blvd., 143–161 Nathan Rd., Kowloon (MTR: TST).

This is a real Chinese department store, with many convenient branches. Unfortunately, the newer the store, the more western it is, which is not my favorite style for a real Chinese department store. Buy from the "Great Wall of China" as I call their china department; get silk pjs; get silk by the yard.

The main store is rather jam-packed and junky and absolutely divine. If this is too hard for your system to digest, the newer Park Lane store is almost as nice as Macy's. Ignore the western goods and buy Chinese. They mail to the U.S. Hours are daily from 9:30 or 10am to 8 or 9pm.

Japanese Department Stores

Japanese department stores must be considered the eighth wonder of the world. They are so total, so complete, so very staggering in their stock that they're somewhat overwhelming. Visitors to Japan often go nowhere else but department stores. Visitors to Hong Kong should take some time to take in a few of these stores, just to see what they are like, even if you do not plan to buy anything.

Basically, Japanese department stores in foreign countries serve Japanese expats. The Japanese department stores in London sell the same things Harrods does. The ones in Hong Kong sell a little of everything; they are particularly known for their inventive gift items and for their food halls.

If you expect just Japanese merchandise, you are very wrong. Every big-name French and Italian designer is represented in the bigger Japanese department stores. Fabulous Japanese cosmetics are sold in quantity, but the selection of all types of products is maximal. On one of my recent trips to **Seibu,** I discovered an Australian line (Red Earth) that I never could have found in the U.S. or Europe.

To be true to the whole picture, you're single best bet is Seibu in **Pacific Place.** When it first arrived, the store was considered too expensive; it has now taken root and has even replaced **Lane Crawford** as the big daddy upscale department store of choice.

Prices in Japanese department stores tend to be high so I don't buy a lot, but I just rush through salivating as I go.

One Final word to Claustrophobics: Don't go during rush hours. Stores are open until 9 or 10pm, so relax and enjoy yourself away from the maddening crowd.

DAIMARU
Fashion Sq., Paterson St. (MTR: Causeway Bay).

Closed on Wednesday in the traditional Japanese habit of closing 1 day a week, Daimaru is okay, but pales when compared to the competition. Asian pop music blares; major designer goods are abundant. Prices are not bargain-basement, but are no higher than at other Japanese department stores.

Daimaru is divided into two large department stores, one for fashions and one for housewares and furniture. The stores feel much more Japanese than the other department stores. This is a good "real-people" resource if you live in Hong Kong.

Inexpensive Japanese (a fashion style you will grow to appreciate when you see it) is cute and fun—great for teens. There are watches and pearls here, but the selection and quality are not as snazzy as at **Mitsukoshi.** Daimaru is more middle class than some of the other stores. Hours are 10:30am to 9:30pm.

ISETAN
Sheraton Hotel, Salisbury Rd., Kowloon (MTR: TST).

Isetan is more young-at-heart than the other Japanese department stores. It's also a bit hard to shop, due to the crowding of merchandise and the weird shape of the store itself. It's a smallish store, across the street from The Regent; it only offers a small hint of Japanese taste. This store also has several basement levels. Fun for teens; convenient enough to your basic Kowloon shopping spree that you can pop in for a few minutes. Hours are daily from 10am to 9pm.

MATSUZAKAYA
Paterson St. (MTR: Causeway Bay).

This department store feels a lot like Sears but has pockets of designer clothes here and there. If you crave Godiva chocolates, you can buy them here. The ground floor has cosmetics, perfumes, handbags, and accessories; the first floor is ladies' and children's ready-to-wear; the second floor is men's and sports; and the third floor is housewares, stationery, and toys.

The overall quality is everyday Hong Kong, which might not be your look back in the U.S. I'm not wild for the store, except for its good cosmetics department and those marvelous Godiva chocolates.

Hours are daily from 10:30am to 9:30pm; closed on Thursday.

MITSUKOSHI
*Hennessy Centre, 500 Hennessy Rd.
(MTR: Causeway Bay).*

In case you aren't up on the ranking of *depatos*, Mitsukoshi is a legend in its own time. While it carries tons of designer goodies, it's a high-end name that isn't as luxurious as Seibu. Mitsukoshi is more like Bloomingdale's when Bloomingdale's was good.

The store is located in Causeway Bay and takes up most of the ground floor of the Hennessy Centre; it is one of the largest and fanciest of the ese department stores in Causeway Bay. Fine watches, pearls, leather handbags, and some designer labels dot the ground-floor display cases. Prices here are standard Japanese prices, which means there are no bargains.

As you descend into the heart of the store, each floor gets less and less American. The lower-level fashions downstairs are geared more for Hong Kong tastes and budgets. As you go down, the lights get brighter and the music seems louder. Don't go if you have a headache.

Mitsukoshi has designer clothes and accessories— Gucci, Lanvin, Christian Dior, Guy Laroche, Chloé, Mila Schön, and more. The housewares department is great fun; there is also a grocery store on B3.

Hours are Sunday, Monday, and Wednesday through Friday from 10am to 9pm and Saturday until 9:30pm; closed Tuesday.

SEIBU

The Mall at Pacific Place, 88 Queensway (MTR: Admiralty).

I walked through Japan murmuring "Seibu, I love you." Take a few minutes in this branch store—one of the anchors of Pacific Place Mall—and you, too, will say the same. Seibu considers itself a cut above the other Japanese department stores in town; it considers **Lane Crawford** the competition, instead of the other Japanese department stores. Frankly, I think it's *more* expensive than Lane Crawford and certainly more with-it.

If you are at all interested in the creative aspects of retail, wander this store just to stare and maybe take notes. There are no bargains, but there is power in the beauty of the choices. I fell in love with everything from hair ornaments to plastic containers. Go, wander, enjoy, have fun; buy. There is nothing like this back home, unless your home is Tokyo. Open daily.

Sogo
Lockhart Rd. (MTR: Causeway Bay).

Sogo is right over the Causeway Bay MTR station, which makes it very convenient. (Or, if you are driving, there is free parking for 2 hours at Windsor House.) It's open late, so you can get in some night-time shopping with pleasure. All the big designers are represented here; this is the best of the bunch here.

Hours are daily from 10:30am to 10pm.

Yaohan
*Whampoa Gardens (ground floor), Kowloon
(MTR: none, take a bus from Star Ferry);
New Town Plaza, 18 Sha Tin Centre Rd.,
Sha Tin (KCR to Sha Tin).*

While I am loath to send you to out-of-the-way locations, it just may be that Yaohan is worth the effort. This Japanese department store has recently expanded to Hong Kong with stores in both Whampoa Gardens and Sha Tin. They are best known for their food departments and, trust me, this place is a sight to see.

I'm not sure what you'll do with all the items you'll be tempted to buy here, but any serious foodie should consider this a must. A stop at Yaohan is also important for those who want to study the Chinese yuppie scene and see what's going on in the New Territories. The mall in Sha Tin is just a mall, true, but it's a study in hot new local trends and manners. Open 7 days a week.

More branches are expected. Watch this space.

DESIGNER GOODS
. . . .

Hong Kong gets more and more designer shops every day; I cannot come to town without being annoyed that so many new shops have opened. Who in the world is shopping at these places? Did any of us come to Hong Kong to buy big-name designer clothes at regular retail prices? I mean, *really*.

Every now and then you can get a break on designer goods, but not often. Some Chanel items (such as makeup) are cheaper. Most items are not cheaper than at home. Therefore, if you are interested in a certain designer line, I suggest you shop the line at home and come to Hong Kong with notes in hand. Don't be surprised if designer prices are totally out of line; Ferragamo may just give you heart failure.

It is possible that you will find designer lines in Hong Kong that have not yet come to the U.S., so you can be the first on your block to wear a certain style. For the most part, however, I'd much rather you were out on the streets, in the markets, eating dim sum with your fingers, or going to Macau than shopping the high-end, fancy, drop-dead-chic stores in hermetically sealed malls and stalls. Of course, I know some of you will ignore my advice and head for the high-end fashion. You know what to expect from each of your favorite designers, so you don't need me to describe the ware in their shops. Following is a directory of where to find the biggies. End of speech.

American Big Names

DIANE FREIS
Harbour City/Ocean Terminal, Canton Rd., Kowloon (MTR: TST).

DONNA KARAN
The Regent Hotel, 18 Salisbury Rd., Kowloon (MTR: TST).

ESPRIT
88 Hing Fat St. (MTR: Causeway Bay); Auto Plaza, 65 Mody Rd., Tsim Sha Tsui East, Kowloon (MTR: TST); Park Lane Shopper's Blvd., Nathan Rd., Kowloon (MTR: TST); Cityplaza II, 1111 King's Rd., Quarry Bay (MTR: Taikoo Shing).

LIZ CLAIBORNE
Times Square (MTR: Causeway Bay).

PALOMA PICASSO
The Landmark (Shop G44), 16 Des Voeux Rd.
(MTR: Central).

RALPH LAUREN
Ralph Lauren/Polo, Central Building, 19–23
Queen's Rd. (MTR: Central); The Peninsula
Hotel, Salisbury Rd., Kowloon (MTR: TST).

TIFFANY & CO.
The Peninsula Hotel, Salisbury Rd., Kowloon
(MTR: TST); The Landmark, 16 Des Voeux Rd.
(MTR: Central).

TOYS R US
Harbour City/Ocean Terminal, Canton Rd.,
Kowloon (MTR: TST).

Asian Big Names

ISSEY MIYAKE
Swire House, Connaught Rd. (MTR: Central).

ISSEY MIYAKE PERMANENTE
The Landmark, 16 Des Voeux Rd.
(MTR: Central).

JIM THOMPSON
The Peninsula Hotel, Salisbury Rd., Kowloon
(MTR: TST).

KAI YIN LO
The Peninsula Hotel, Salisbury Rd., Kowloon
(MTR: TST); Ocean Terminal, Deck 1, Shop
120–D, Canton Rd., Kowloon (MTR: TST);
The Mandarin Oriental Hotel (mezzanine),
5 Connaught Rd. (MTR: Central); The Mall at
Pacific Place, 88 Queensway (MTR: Admiralty).

MATSUDA
Swire House, Connaught Rd.
(MTR: Central).

British & Continental Big Names

This small alphabet of designer soup is designed to give you an idea of where the players play; they frequently do the cha-cha or simply open yet another branch store, so there may be more branches available to you than are listed here. If you are using only one address for one specific shop, please verify with your hotel concierge or the telephone book before you venture forth.

ALFRED DUNHILL
The Peninsula Hotel, Salisbury Rd., Kowloon (MTR: TST); Hyatt Regency Hong Kong, 67 Nathan Rd., Kowloon (MTR: TST); Prince's Building, 5 Ice House St. (MTR: Central); The Mall at Pacific Place (level 3), 88 Queensway (MTR: Admiralty).

BALLANTYNE
The Landmark, Gloucester Tower, 16 Des Voeux Rd. (MTR: Central); The Mall at Pacific Place, 88 Queensway (MTR: Admiralty).

BALLY
The Peninsula Hotel, Salisbury Rd., Kowloon (MTR: TST); The Landmark, Gloucester Tower, 16 Des Voeux Rd. (MTR: Central).

BELTRAMI
The Landmark (Shop 109), 16 Des Voeux Rd. (MTR: Central); The Peninsula Hotel (basement), Salisbury Rd., Kowloon (MTR: TST).

BENETTON
The Mall at Pacific Place (level 1), 88 Queensway (MTR: Admiralty); Cityplaza II, 1111 King's Rd., Quarry Bay (MTR: Taikoo Shing); Harbour City/ Ocean Centre (Shop 003), 5 Canton Rd., Kowloon (MTR: TST); Harbour City/Ocean Terminal (Shop 217–20), Canton Rd., Kowloon (MTR: TST) and many, many more.

BOTTEGA VENETA
Swire House (ground floor), Connaught Rd.
(MTR: Central).

BRUNO MAGLI
Central Building (ground floor), Pedder St.
(MTR: Central); The Regent Hotel, 18 Salisbury
Rd., Kowloon (MTR: TST); Harbour City/Ocean
Terminal (Shop 233), Canton Rd., Kowloon
(MTR: TST); China Hong Kong City, Canton Rd.,
Kowloon (MTR: TST).

BULGARI
The Landmark, 16 Des Voeux Rd.
(MTR: Central); The Peninsula Hotel,
Salisbury Rd., Kowloon (MTR: TST).

BURBERRYS
The Landmark, 16 Des Voeux Rd. (MTR:
Central).

BYBLOS
Harbour City/Ocean Terminal (Shop 201),
Canton Rd., Kowloon (MTR: TST).

CACHAREL
The Landmark, 16 Des Voeux Rd.
(MTR: Central); Harbour City/Ocean Centre,
5 Canton Rd., Kowloon (MTR: TST).

CARTIER
Prince's Building (ground floor), Chater Rd.
(MTR: Central); The Mall at Pacific Place
(3rd floor), 88 Queensway (MTR: Admiralty);
The Peninsula Hotel, Salisbury Rd., Kowloon
(MTR: TST); The Regent Hotel, 18 Salisbury
(MTR: TST).

CÉLINE
The Landmark, 16 Des Voeux Rd.
(MTR: Central); The Peninsula Hotel,
Salisbury Road, Kowloon
(MTR: TST).

CERRUTTI 1881
*Harbour City/Ocean Centre, 5 Canton Rd.,
Kowloon (MTR: TST); The Peninsula Hotel
(basement), Salisbury Rd., Kowloon (MTR: TST);
The Mall at Pacific Place (Shop 367),
88 Queensway (MTR: Admiralty); Prince's
Building, 3A (MTR: Central); The Landmark
(B19), 16 Des Voeux Rd. (MTR: Central);
Repulse Bay Shopping Arcade, 109 Repulse Bay
Rd. (MTR: none).*

CHANEL
*Prince's Building, Chater Rd. (MTR: Central);
The Peninsula Hotel, Salisbury Rd., Kowloon
(MTR: TST); The Regent Hotel, 18 Salisbury Rd.,
Kowloon (MTR: TST).*

CHRISTIAN DIOR
*The Landmark, Edinburgh Tower, 16 Des Voeux
Rd. (MTR: Central); The Peninsula Hotel,
Salisbury Rd., Kowloon (MTR: TST).*

CHRISTIAN DIOR MONSIEUR
Prince's Building, Chater Rd. (MTR: Central).

COURRÈGES
*The Landmark, Gloucester Tower, 16 Des Voeux
Rd. (MTR: Central); Harbour City/Ocean Centre
(Shop 207), 5 Canton Rd., Kowloon (MTR: TST).*

DAKS
*Prince's Building, Chater Rd. (MTR: Central);
The Peninsula Hotel, Salisbury Rd., Kowloon
(MTR: TST).*

DOLCE & GABBANA
*Harbour City/Ocean Centre (ground floor),
5 Canton Rd., Kowloon (MTR: TST); The World
of Joyce, The Galleria, 9 Queen's Rd.
(MTR: Central).*

EMPORIO ARMANI
*Harbour City/Ocean Centre, 5 Canton Rd.,
Kowloon (MTR: TST); 16 Queen's Rd.
(MTR: Central).*

ERMENEGILDO ZEGNA
The Mall at Pacific Place 2 (Shop 355),
88 Queensway (MTR: Admiralty); The Peninsula
Hotel, Salisbury Rd., Kowloon (MTR: TST);
Ocean Terminal, Deck 2, Canton Rd., Kowloon
(MTR: TST).

ESCADA
Central Building, Pedder St. (MTR: Central);
The Peninsula Hotel, Salisbury Rd., Kowloon
(MTR: TST); Kowloon Hotel, 19–21 Nathan Rd.
Kowloon (MTR: TST); China Hong Kong City,
Canton Rd., Kowloon (MTR: TST).

ÉTIENNE AIGNER
The Mall at Pacific Place (Shop 338),
88 Queensway (MTR: Admiralty); Alexandra
House, Des Voeux Rd. (MTR: Central);
The Landmark, 16 Des Voeux Rd.
(MTR: Central); The Regent Hotel,
18 Salisbury Rd., Kowloon (MTR: TST);
Hyatt Regency Hong Kong, 67 Nathan Rd.,
Kowloon (MTR: TST).

ETRO
The Peninsula Hotel (basement), Salisbury Rd.,
Kowloon (MTR: TST).

FENDI
Harbour City/Ocean Centre, 5 Canton Rd.,
Kowloon (MTR: TST); The Mandarin Oriental
Hotel, 5 Connaught Rd. (MTR: Central).

FERRAGAMO
Harbour City/Ocean Terminal, Canton Rd.,
Kowloon (MTR: TST); The Regent Hotel,
18 Salisbury Rd., Kowloon (MTR: TST);
The Peninsula Hotel, Salisbury Rd., Kowloon
(MTR: TST); The Mandarin Oriental Hotel,
5 Connaught Rd. (MTR: Central).

GIANFRANCO FERRE
Pacific Place 2, 88 Queensway
(MTR: Admiralty).

GENNY
*The Peninsula Hotel, Salisbury Rd., Kowloon
(MTR: TST); The Landmark (Shop 232),
16 Des Voeux Rd. (MTR: Central).*

GIANNI VERSACE
*MTR: TST); The Landmark (For Men, Shop G19;
For Ladies, Shop 14A), 16 Des Voeux Rd.
(MTR: Central); The Peninsula Hotel, Salisbury
Rd., Kowloon (MTR: TST).*

GIEVES & HAWKES
*The Peninsula Hotel, Salisbury Rd., Kowloon
(MTR: TST); Harbour City/Ocean Terminal,
Canton Rd., Kowloon (MTR: TST); Prince's
Building, Chater Rd. (MTR: Central); Repulse
Bay Shopping Arcade, 109 Repulse Bay Rd.
(MTR: none).*

GIORGIO ARMANI
*The Landmark, Gloucester Tower, 16 Des Voeux
Rd. (MTR: Central); The Mandarin Oriental
Hotel, 5 Connaught Rd. (MTR: Central);
Regent Shopping Mall, Salisbury Rd., Kowloon
(MTR: TST).*

GIVENCHY
*The Landmark, Gloucester Tower, 16 Des Voeux
Rd. (MTR: Central).*

GOLDPFEIL
*Swire House (Shop 19), Connaught Rd. (MTR:
Central); The Peninsula Hotel, Salisbury Rd.,
Kowloon (MTR: TST); China Hong Kong City,
Canton Rd., Kowloon (MTR: TST).*

GUCCI
*The Landmark, Gloucester Tower, 16 Des Voeux
Rd. (MTR: Central); The Peninsula Hotel,
Salisbury Rd., Kowloon (MTR: TST); Repulse
Bay Shopping Arcade, 109 Repulse Bay Rd.
(MTR: none).*

GUY LAROCHE
The Landmark (Shop 102B), 16 Des Voeux Rd.
(MTR: Central).

HARVEY NICHOLS
The Landmark (Shop 218), 16 Des Voeux Rd.
(MTR: Central).

HENRY COTTON'S
The Regent Hotel, 18 Salisbury Rd., Kowloon
(MTR: TST).

HERMÈS
The Galleria, (ground floor), 9 Queen's Rd.
(MTR: Central); The Mall at Pacific Place
(level 3), 88 Queensway (MTR: Admiralty);
The Peninsula Hotel, Salisbury Rd., Kowloon
(MTR: TST).

ICEBERG
The Landmark (Shop 236), 16 Des Voeux Rd.
(MTR: Central).

IKEA
Sun Plaza Arcade, 28 Canton Rd., Kowloon
(MTR: TST).

JAEGER
The Regent Hotel, 18 Salisbury Rd., Kowloon
(MTR: TST).

JEAN-PAUL GAULTIER
Prince's Building, Chater Rd. (MTR: Central);
Harbour City/Ocean Centre, 5 Canton Rd.,
Kowloon (MTR: TST).

JIL SANDER
The Regent Hotel, 18 Salisbury Rd., Kowloon
(MTR: TST).

KARL LAGERFELD
The Landmark, Edinburgh Tower, 16 Des Voeux
Rd. (MTR: Central).

KENZO

The Landmark, 16 Des Voeux Rd.
(MTR: Central); The Peninsula Hotel,
Salisbury Rd., Kowloon (MTR: TST).

KRIZIA

The Landmark (Shop 237), 16 Des Voeux Rd.
(MTR: Central); Hankow Centre (Shop G7),
15 Hankow Rd., Kowloon (MTR: TST).

LANVIN

The Landmark, Gloucester Tower, 16 Des Voeux
Rd. (MTR: Central); The Regent Hotel,
18 Salisbury Rd., Kowloon (MTR: TST);
Hyatt Regency Hong Kong, 67 Nathan Rd.,
Kowloon (MTR: TST).

LÉONARD

The Peninsula Hotel, Salisbury Rd., Kowloon
(MTR: TST); The Landmark (ground floor),
16 Des Voeux Rd. (MTR: Central).

LOEWE

The Landmark, 16 Des Voeux Rd. (MTR:
Central); Repulse Bay Shopping Arcade, 109
Repulse Bay Rd. (MTR: none); The Peninsula
Hotel, Salisbury Rd., Kowloon (MTR: TST).

LONGCHAMP

The Peninsula Hotel, Salisbury Rd., Kowloon
(MTR: TST); The Regent Hotel, 18 Salisbury Rd.,
Kowloon (MTR: TST).

LOUIS VUITTON

The Landmark, Gloucester Tower, 16 Des Voeux
Rd. (MTR: Central); The Peninsula Hotel,
Salisbury Rd., Kowloon (MTR: TST); Repulse
Bay Shopping Arcade, 109 Repulse Bay Rd.
(MTR: none); The Regent Hotel, 18 Salisbury
Rd., Kowloon (MTR: TST).

MOSCHINO

Swire House, Connaught Rd. (MTR: Central);
The Regent Hotel, 18 Salisbury Rd., Kowloon
(MTR: TST).

NINA RICCI
*China Hong Kong City, Canton Rd., Kowloon
(MTR: TST); The Peninsula Hotel, Salisbury Rd.,
Kowloon (MTR: TST); The Regent Hotel,
18 Salisbury Rd., Kowloon (MTR: TST);
The Mandarin Oriental Hotel, 5 Connaught Rd.
(MTR: Central).*

PAUL SMITH
*Harbour City/Ocean Centre (Shop 005), Canton
Rd. (ground floor), Kowloon (MTR: TST).*

THIERRY MUGLER
*The Landmark (Shop 242), 16 Des Voeux Rd.
(MTR: Central).*

TRUSSARDI
The Landmark, Central (MTR: Central).

VALENTINO
*The Landmark (MTR: Central); The Regent
Hotel, 18 Salisbury Rd., Kowloon (MTR: TST).*

VAN CLEEF & ARPELS
*The Landmark (atrium), 16 Des Voeux Rd.
(MTR: Central); The Peninsula Hotel, Salisbury
Rd. Kowloon (MTR: TST).*

VERSACE VERSUS
The Landmark (MTR: Central).

Up-and-Coming Talent

More and more young designers are finding that
Hong Kong is a fine place to be discovered. Although
many of the young designers in town are not yet
represented in boutiques, they are busy designing
private-label goods for large stores. You may have
never heard their names, but you may dig their
designs.

Find the latest and wildest designs by these hot
young talents in the shops that line **Kimberley Road**
and **Austin Avenue**. These two streets, in the north-
ern end of Tsim Sha Tsui, have become the SoHo of

Hong Kong. The decor of the shops is avant-garde; the prices are affordable. Start at the corner of Austin and Nathan roads, walking east. Austin Road turns a corner and becomes Austin Avenue, which will turn again and become Kimberley Road, heading back toward Nathan Road.

EMBROIDERY & WHITEWORK

For centuries, the Chinese have been famous for their embroidery. There are several styles to choose from: pieces with colored silk threads, pieces with white cotton thread, and pieces with white thread used on white linen or cotton, which is called whitework.

Antique embroidered goods are quite valuable and are more likely to be found on Hollywood Road, at **Charlotte Horstmann** (see page 136) or in antique stores where slippers, collars, and possibly even robes are sold. New versions of tablecloths, napkins, place mats, sweaters, jackets, and fabric purses are all sold with embroidery. In terms of quality, you'll do better with antique handwork or newly made whitework.

Whitework with cutouts is called *drawnwork*. The best drawn embroidery is supposed to come from Swatow in China. A great deal also comes out of Shanghai and may cost the same in Hong Kong as it does in your hometown.

Take the time to learn how the look of hand embroidery differs from the look of machine embroidery. The goods coming out of Shanghai are new and machine-made. In fact, most of the shop goods are machine-made. Hand embroidery is very expensive. If you want finely crafted pieces, try:

THE CHINESE BAZAAR
Prince's Building, Chater Rd. (MTR: Central).

This store offers a good selection in table linens, napkins, coasters, and children's clothing. They have been in business since 1905.

HANDART EMBROIDERIES
Tung Fai Building, 4th floor, 27 Cameron Rd.,
Kowloon (MTR: TST).

This shop offers a particularly good selection of bed
linens, place mats, and doilies. They specialize in
Battenberg lace, which is popular all over Hong
Kong, but they also sell more traditional Asian
products and some souvenirs.

LACE LANE
Omni Hong Kong Hotel, Shop 211,
3 Canton Rd., Kowloon (MTR: TST).

My pick for selection and service. The hand-smocked
dresses for little girls are especially wonderful. They
will special-order for you and will ship to the U.S. I
found linen of a quality here that I couldn't find
anywhere else in town.

WAH SING LACE COMPANY
7 On Lan St. (MTR: Central).

On Lan Street is a short block full of wholesalers
and manufacturers located up from Central near
Wyndham Road. Not all may offer retail, but this is
a good lane for finding bargains. Wah Sing manufactures and does export, in case you want to buy
lots.

Please note that good drawnwork is getting
harder and harder to find. Young people don't want
to do it (because it wrecks the eyes), and shipment
and business procedures from China are dicey, so
orders don't come in when anticipated. If you find
the real thing, expect to pay dearly for it. Once you
have seen finely made, hand-bound cutwork or
drawnwork, you will laugh at what is generally sold
in markets, Chinese department stores, and crafts
stores. You may find mass-produced whitework in
the U.S. for less than it costs in Hong Kong.

It's very hard to quote prices and remain accu-
rate as the world turns, but I admit that, in almost

all cases, prices for whitework and embroidery in Hong Kong are expensive, especially when compared to the quality I was offered. Expect to pay about $25 to $35 for a set of four place mats with napkins. The higher price will bring you greater detail and a finer stitch.

FABRICS & NOTIONS

As one of the ready-to-wear manufacturing capitals of the world, Hong Kong has more fabrics and notions than just about any other city we've seen. Prices for even the most luscious Chinese or Japanese silks are reasonable, although Chinese silk is much less expensive than Japanese. (Japanese silks are much more intricately printed; the Chinese rarely run multiple screens on their silks.) There are also distinctive Thai silks available, less expensive in Thailand but if you aren't going to Thailand, make hay while the sun shines.

There are two basic fabrics-and-notions neighborhoods with a growing newcomer in the **Sham Shui Po area. Western Market** also has dealers.

Jardine's Bazaar When you go to Jardine's Bazaar, weave in and around all the little streets behind the market itself; you'll find numerous fabrics, notions, and yarn shops with incredibly low prices.

Wing On Street Old China Hands may remember that this was Cloth Alley—no more. It has been torn down to make room for progress. Many of the cloth dealers of Wing On Street have moved to **Western Market** (page 232); I don't really think you want to make the trip here just for fabric. But if you're in the area anyway, by all means, stop by.

The Lanes They do indeed sell fabric off the bolt from The Lanes. If you're interested, **Li Yuen West** is your street. You won't find designer fabrics here, but there are many fashion and novelty prints along with an assortment of dress-up looks. I've bought poly-chiffon for about $6 a yard, which is slightly less than it costs at home, but not significantly.

Other good sources for fabrics:

- **Tailors:** You can buy fabrics from most tailors; the really fine tailors bring in the best goods from Europe.

  Bespoke tailors always have a large selection of fabrics for men's suits and shirts, but you cannot buy these goods off the bolt unless you are a regular customer. There are usually fine Italian, French, and English wools for women but there is never the same selection for women as for men. For the truly fashion-conscious woman, it might be easier to bring fabrics from home.

- **Chinese department stores:** A wide variety of types of silk are sold off the bolt in the various Chinese stores. Raw silk is available at most Chinese department stores and costs about $15 a yard. This is comparable to the U.S. price, but the color selection may be better in Hong Kong. I have seen raw silk go on sale in Hong Kong for $8 a yard.

  There's also sand-washed silk, washable silk, regular old silk, etc. Prices are usually based on the quality of the fabric and the screens, and the color range.

  Brides and debs, note: White-and-cream raw silk gowns are "in"; you can indeed have a gown made in Hong Kong if you want a simple style. But keep it tailored or you may be sorry.

FOLK ART

. . . .

Hunting down bargains in arts, crafts, and antiques is one of our favorite shopping adventures in Hong Kong. Our definition of arts and crafts is broad enough to include handwork of any kind, from hand-carved teaware to cloisonné that has been done within the last 100 years. We include pottery that is original or copies of originals, ivory carvings, jade carvings, handmade dolls, and paper cuts.

The Hong Kong Tourist Association publishes a list of factories that produce brassware, carpets, carved furniture, Chinese lanterns, pewter and china, and are open to the public.

AMAZING GRACE ELEPHANT COMPANY

Harbour City/Ocean Terminal (Shop 348), Canton Rd., Kowloon (MTR: TST); New Town Plaza (Shop 526), Sha Tin, N.T. (MTR: none); Excelsior Hotel, 281 Gloucester Rd. (MTR: Causeway Bay).

Amazing Grace carries handcrafted items from all over Asia. In particular we like the Taiwanese temple carvings. You can also buy silk pillow covers, brass carts, bowls, candlesticks, incense burners, jewelry, Korean chests, paper carvings, fans, dolls, bird cages, mirror frames, tea sets, and more. This shop has a broad appeal and can be a good source for small, inexpensive gift items. Branch stores are as far away as Sha Tin or as near as the Excelsior Hotel in Causeway Bay. This is sort of the local version of Pier 1.

The warehouse/outlet, in the New Territories, is open to the public. If you are doing serious shopping, it might be worth the drive. You cannot get there any other way but by car, so take that into consideration. We suggest you stop in the Harbour City/Ocean Terminal shop and get directions.

You can also take the KCR to Sha Tin—there's an Amazing Grace at the big mall there—and make a day out of it. Locals use Amazing Grace for inexpensive goods to do up their homes; I think you can buy a lot of this stuff at home, and it's not worth a lot of your attention. But that's just my opinion.

BANYAN TREE LTD.

Harbour City/Ocean Galleries, 25–27 Canton Rd., Kowloon (MTR: TST); Prince's Building, Chater Rd. (MTR: Central).

Banyan Tree is a mass-market kind of handcrafts shop that sells rattan furniture, fabrics, figurines, lamps, porcelains, rugs, screens, and hundreds of other items for the home on both a retail and wholesale basis. They have a large exporting business, and can deliver anything you buy to your hometown. We would trust Banyan Tree to pack and ship anything. This is another version, with a slight Martha Stewart bent, in the Pier 1 mold.

MOUNTAIN FOLKCRAFT
12–15 Wo On Lane (MTR: Central).

One of my favorite shops for handcrafted items, Mountain Folkcraft carries a little bit of everything in a small amount of space. It's also got a rather folksy location in an alley with a tiny temple at the corner. This is a much more authentic environment than Amazing Grace, or just about anybody else, although the crafts come from all over Asia and include: batik fabric, boxes, chests, puppets, baskets, toys, and pottery. The location is right behind Wellington Street and actually is easy to find.

TAI PING CARPETS
Hutchison House, 10 Harcourt Rd. (MTR: Central); Wing On Plaza, Mody Rd., Kowloon (MTR: TST). Factory Shop: Tai Ping Industrial Park, Ting Kok Rd., Lot No. 1687, Tai Po Market, N.T. (MTR: none).

One of the major craft industries in China is carpet making. Carpets are still made by hand, and many take years to complete. Tai Ping is one of the leading manufacturers and importers. You can visit their retail shop and order a custom carpet (takes 6 to 12 weeks), or check out the factory shop on Monday and Thursday from 2 to 4pm. In Hong Kong call ☎ 852-2656-5161, ext. 211, to arrange a visit.

YUE KEE CURIO COMPANY
Harbour City/Omni The Hong Kong Hotel Arcade, 2 Canton Rd., Kowloon (MTR: TST).

Yue Kee has many options in fine-art curios, including carvings, wall pieces, floor pieces, screens, and statues. There are also Chinese vases in every size. The shop is very crowded, and we don't suggest that you bring children or large shopping bags. It will take some time to make your mind up here. Yue Kee also has antiques.

IMITATION DESIGNER HANDBAGS

ASHNEIL
Far East Mansion (1st floor), 5–6 Middle Rd., Kowloon (MTR: TST).

The neighborhood is convenient enough, but slightly offbeat; the building is actually frightening. Never mind. When you get inside Ashneil and see the Judith Leiber look-alike merchandise, you will be happy you came here.

If the address isn't familiar, this street is right off Nathan Road a half block from The Regent and right behind The Sheraton. Easy as pie when you don't panic and remember to look left for the way up.

FINE 'N RHINE
15 Mody Rd. (1st floor), Kowloon (MTR: TST).

You won't believe this, but in the space of 1 week I got two different unsolicited letters from readers, both recommending this source. This happens to be around the corner from Far East Mansion and the other "Judith Leiber" source; it is not in Tsim Sha Tsui East, which is what I thought at first. Mody Road is the main drag in Tsim Sha Tsui East, but it begins right at Nathan Road. This address is in the first block right near the Holiday Inn Golden Mile.

Look for Lieber-style copies in both tiny animal-shaped evening bags with rhinestones and gem insets and the leather bags in traditional Leiber shapes and styles. There are also Chanel styles as well.

Note: They don't open until 10:30am each morning; they close at 4pm on Saturday and are not open on Sunday.

SAM WO
Li Yuen St. West (MTR: Central).

The deal is strange because Sam's merchandise appears to be the same as everyone else's, and his prices are much higher. Then you examine two pieces and see the difference—Sam's quality is much more like the real item.

Furthermore, if you have the time and the inclination, you can tell Sam what you are looking for and see if he can get it for you. Sometimes it's been put away in a safe place.

JEWELRY & GEMSTONES

Hong Kong trades every variety and quality of gemstone. It is the fifth-largest diamond-cutting center in the world. The money changing hands in this industry totals billions of dollars per year.

The good news about buying gemstones in Hong Kong is that you can bring them (unset) back to the U.S. for a negligible duty (or for no duty at all). The bad news is that finding good stones requires a Ph.D. in gemology.

The jewelry and gemstone businesses are separate and converge only at the wholesale level, where you will never be admitted without a bona fide dealer. If you are serious about buying stones, you should be introduced to the wholesale dealers. This requires personal contact from a dealer here or from a friend who is Chinese and living in Hong Kong. It is a very tight business. Don't expect to just walk into a shop off the street and see the best stones or get the best prices.

There is risk in every purchase, but if you are dealing with a reputable jeweler that risk is minimized. Reputation is everything. If you are looking for good pearls, diamonds, opals, jade, or ivory, educate yourself first. Take the time to learn before you leap.

Please note that I have divided these resources into five different categories: "Expensive Jewelry" and "Not-So-Expensive Jewelry" (for listings of fine jewelers who carry both jewelry and gemstones) and "Diamonds," "Opals," and "Pearls," with information (and, in the case of pearls, additional store listings) for shoppers who are only interested in a particular gem.

Jewelry

Jewelry is the word I use to describe decorative baubles made of gold and either precious or semi-precious stones. There are almost as many jewelry shops in Hong Kong as there are tailors. As you walk down almost any street in Hong Kong, your eyes are constantly drawn to windows full of magnificent pins, rings, and earrings.

Much of the jewelry in Hong Kong is made with 18K gold, which is popular in Asia because it costs more and, therefore, denotes status if you can afford to buy it. Jewelers accustomed to dealing with overseas clients keep pieces on hand in both 14K and 18K, and discuss this fact up-front. Decide which you prefer before you begin serious negotiations on a piece. I usually choose 14K because it is less expensive than 18K. Gold will be marked with either a K label or, alternately, "375" (9K), "585" (14K), or "750" (18K).

One of the best buys in the jewelry field is in custom-made pieces. If you have a favorite Tiffany, Harry Winston, or Van Cleef & Arpels catalog, take it with you. A good jeweler can translate any basic design into something just for you—at half the cost.

Jewelry can obviously be bought in branch stores of internationally famous jewelers such as **Cartier**, **Van Cleef & Arpels**, etc. These businesses have set prices, which may be geared for the businessperson or Japanese customer who is willing to pay top dollar: Price at home first. If you've come to Hong Kong with plans to save money on jewelry, you probably are not looking to do business with the branch stores.

Also remember **Lane Crawford:** It's expensive, but it has a fine reputation and a guarantee on whatever you buy.

- Look at many things in the shop, both expensive and inexpensive. This allows you to assess the range, the workmanship, and possibly how fair the pricing system is and if there's any give from the jeweler. You never know what the jeweler will use as a promotion piece in order to get you going as a client.
- Ask questions. If the jeweler is not willing to spend time with you, leave.
- Negotiate prices on a few items before you get down to business on the one that you really want. If the jeweler knows that you are looking for a good price at the beginning, the process will happen faster.
- Ask if you can get an outside appraisal of the piece of jewelry that you are considering. If the jeweler hesitates, question why.
- Remember that you will pay duty on set versus unset stones coming into the U.S. Use this as a negotiating tool.
- Always get a written certification of the gold content of your piece of jewelry. This is important for insurance and customs.
- Also get a receipt from the store, quoting the exact price that you paid. Don't leave it up to U.S. customs to evaluate your goods.
- If you choose to have the jewelry sent to you, confirm that it will be insured, and for how much.
- If you are buying a piece of jewelry with large stones, have a separate appraisal done on them. It should include a photograph and a detailed description of each stone.

Expensive Jewelry

GEMSLAND
The Mandarin Oriental Hotel, 5 Connaught Rd.
(MTR: Central).

Years ago my partner Judith got this source from a
friend of hers; she had several pieces made and then
later, I did too. I simply haven't used other jewelers
for custom work and indeed, truth be told, have
very little "good" jewelry, anyway.

Richard Chen and his mother Helen run this family business; they carry many classic ready-made
pieces suitable for international clientele, or he will
custom make your order in 5 to 7 days. It's hard to
give you an idea of price since that really depends
on what you have made; in two cases I brought unset
gemstones with me and had them made into finished pieces for $250–$300 per item in 14K gold.

I've gotten happy letters from readers who also
have been pleased; one reader did write that the store
would not take a personal check. If you are planning on a big purchase, you may want to arrange an
appointment ahead of time and check on their payment policies.

HARRY'S JEWELRY LTD.
34 Cameron Rd., 7B, Kowloon (MTR: TST).

This hot tip comes from Arthur and Ellen Wagner,
whom I met on *Sea Goddess*; they say ask for Harry
and say Arthur sent you. They bought pieces for
themselves—rings, bracelets, precious stones, you
name it—and were thrilled with this source which
they claim is a true insider's secret. Since I don't
normally go around buying this sort of stuff on any
grand scale, I bow to Arthur and Ellen . . . and Harry.

JEWELS BY JUDY
Nan Fung Centre, 264–298 Castle Peak Rd.,
Tsuen Wan (MTR: Tsuen Wan).

A producer at *Good Morning America* I know swears by Judy Cabot. While she primarily carries pearls, she can also obtain other gemstones, tennis bracelets, gold chains, and more. Fax for an appointment, 852-2367-9266. She will come to your hotel if you find a trip to the outer reaches doesn't work for you. No drop-ins, please, there is little stock on hand for security purposes. Call ☎ 852-2366-3906, Monday through Friday from 10am to 5pm.

KAI YIN LO
The Peninsula Hotel, Salisbury Rd., Kowloon (MTR: TST); The Mandarin Oriental Hotel (mezzanine), 5 Connaught Rd. (MTR: Central); The Mall at Pacific Place, 88 Queensway (MTR: Admiralty).

Hong Kong's best with an ethnic flavor that's both serious and fun. Her designs using gold and semi-precious gemstones are unique in Hong Kong and sold worldwide. You will save money by buying in Hong Kong. Several branch stores.

KEVIN
Holiday Inn Golden Mile, 50 Nathan Rd., Kowloon (MTR: TST).

This shop on the Golden Mile has some very unusual and creative pieces of jewelry. Not the usual stuff you see in the hotel arcade shops. For the person who wears the jewelry and doesn't let the jewelry wear her.

RONALD ABRAM
Prince's Building (Shop 128), Chater Rd. (MTR: Central).

Rare jewels for the connoisseur; prices to match.

THE SHOWROOM
Central Building, 12th floor, Pedder St. (MTR: Central).

I run with an expatriate crowd in Hong Kong that seems to do everything in groups; everyone knows everyone and shares the same resources. Many of those resources have become regulars in these pages. According to my sources, the place for jewelry these days is a small place simply called The Showroom where a woman named Claire Wadsworth holds court. Good work at excellent prices is the general opinion, backed up by many I trust.

Not-So-Expensive Jewelry

🛍 PAN AM PEARLS
9 Lock Rd., Kowloon (MTR: TST).

I swear by this shop but do wish to note a letter I received a few years ago from a reader who experienced confusion between the price she was quoted and her bill. As long as you pay attention in your dealings, you can come away as happy as I have.

This is where I buy my faux pearls. I have been here numerous times and had a variety of experiences: One or two times the help was not very friendly and would not give me very good service. (Don't go on a Sunday for that reason.) Other times, they couldn't be nicer—and I could bargain and buy and get a gift with purchase (an enamel ring worth exactly $HK 10).

I have seen fluctuations in quality according to stock. I have yet to match the quality of my double-strand, 8mm set that cost me $40 3 years ago. However, all the faux pearls I've bought here are about the best I've seen at these prices, and I still think this is one of my single best sources in Hong Kong.

A strand of pearls runs about $20; they will string together several strands into a single necklace with a new clasp as you wait. Baroque pearls are also available.

This is right near the Hyatt Regency Hong Kong, so don't let the address throw you. It is upstairs; take the stairs if the elevator looks too rickety for your taste. They also sell some souvenir-type gifts. Be sure to ask for a silk pouch for each item you buy.

TANG'S
Sheraton Hotel (shop D–4), Kowloon
(MTR: TST).

This resource actually belongs in its own price category, "Moderately Priced Jewelry." Tang's specializes in pearls and semiprecious stones in the form of multistrand chokers. Since these are not usually outrageously priced, I have included them in this more affordable section, but this is not inexpensively priced merchandise.

This listing originally came from a reader who says that only Gump's in the U.S. rivals Tang's and that Gump's prices are, need we tell you this?, four or five times higher. The store is located on the first level above the hotel lobby; watch this space for their new address after the Sheraton bites the dust.

Diamonds

Diamonds come into Hong Kong duty free from around the world. It is one of the world's largest diamond-trading areas. If you wish to buy diamonds, check with the Hong Kong Tourist Association, which publishes a list of some 200 jewelers they recommend. Also contact the **Diamond Importers Association Of Hong Kong Ltd.,** Diamond Exchange Building (Room 401), 8–10 Duddell St., Hong Kong, for their list of authorized agents. The Diamond Importers Association also publishes a variety of educational leaflets that you can send for ahead of your trip. Or call ☎ 852-2523-5497 when you are in Hong Kong.

When looking for diamonds, judge their value by the four Cs: cut, clarity, color, and carat. The cut of the diamond is determined by your personal choice. No one cut is more valuable than others, although the round cut is the most classic and salable because it allows for the most brilliance and fire. Clarity in a diamond is judged by absence of inclusions, then number, size, and position of existing inclusions. A "flawless" diamond is unusual.

Color is an important factor in the value of the stone. A perfect blue-white stone is the most valuable. The more intense the color, the higher the price. Colorless diamonds are rare.

Carat is the weight of the stone. One carat equals $1^1/_5$ gram. Price goes up as carat weight increases. There are 100 points per carat. A 4.02 carat stone would weigh 4 carats 2 points. A flawless stone larger than 1 carat is considered of investment quality because of its rarity.

Before you buy any stone, get an independent appraisal done by the **Gemological Lab of Hong Kong,** Luk Hoi Tong Building, 31 Queen's Rd., Central, Hong Kong. It usually takes 5 working days to certify a diamond. It's worth the time to make sure that you don't get caught buying a cubic zirconia at a diamond price.

Should you prefer cubic zirconia to diamonds, **Blunco** is a well-known source in Hong Kong—see them at Hanley House, Flat B (13th floor), 68–80 Canton Rd., Kowloon.

Opals

I have only one suggestion when it comes to buying opals: Buyer beware. Opals are mined in Australia, among other places, and brought to Hong Kong to be cut, polished, and shipped out again. Considering this, it is surprising that there are not more opal stores. You will see opals in fine jewelry stores, but you will not see many. One company in particular, **Opal Mine,** has cornered the tourist opal trade. They have set up one shop in Burlington Arcade, 92–94 Nathan Rd., Kowloon, that is a re-creation of an opal mine, with illustrations and samples of what to look for and what not to look for. It is informative and fun, especially if you are with children. The mine opens up into the (surprise!) retail store with opal choices galore. There are big stones and little stones, set stones and unset stones. All the opals are guaranteed to be authentic and not tampered with in any way. Prices are high, and the sales pitch is strong, but for small pieces, there are many choices. Comparison-shop elsewhere before coming, and then bargain once you are there. Remember, it is easy to be duped when it comes to opals.

Pearls

I find buying pearls extremely tricky and almost shout, "Be careful!" anytime anyone asks my opinion as to where to go or whether there are bargains to be had in Hong Kong.

If you are searching for pearls and pearls alone, you will have many options. Every jewelry store has them in the window. The question is: Whom do you trust?

You see, the value of a really good pearl is based on size and color and evenness . . . but more importantly is based on the number of layers of nacre. The untrained eye cannot see the layers of nacre and cannot guess if there's only a layer or two that will quickly wear off with use. That's why you pay money and go to a reputable jeweler.

The bigger jewelry shops are a safe bet for buying quality pearls. The price tag will be higher than on the street, but you have some assurance that, should you have a problem with your second appraisal back home, they will make amends.

Expect to pay about $1,000 for a strand of serious pearls; $3,000 is not an outrageous price for an incredible strand of pearls from a place like **Trio**. You will get few bargains in the $500–$750 range; these are the pearls that could wear thin so it's not worth the gamble.

Remember that part of the value of the pearls is based on color and that different cultures prize different colors; also because there are so many skin tones in America's melting pot—various women may prefer differing shades of pearls to complement their skin tone. I happen to like my pearls on the pink side; most prefer their pearls very white. The English like their pearls to be creamy.

Size of the pearl and length of the strand are other factors in price; if the strand has graduated pearls in varying sizes it will probably cost less than a strand with pearls of all the same size. To check on the uniformity of the size of the pearls, roll the strand with your palms and fingertips along the black velvet mat provided by the jeweler. You'll feel every bump and inconsistency as you roll those pearly whites back and forth.

The clasp is usually sold separately from the pearls for two reasons:

- Pearls without a clasp enter the U.S. with less duty, making this an attractive product to many Americans;
- The clasp is essentially a piece of jewelry and can cost as much or more than the pearls, depending on size and the inclusion of gemstones.

Negotiating for the clasp, or the change of clasps on any given strand of pearls, should be a separate piece of business from buying the strand or strands of pearls but should be included in your general knowledge so that you understand you are dealing with what are really two different elements here.

To help you get ready for your pearl purchase, you may want to call or write **Tiffany & Co.,** which publishes a free brochure on buying pearls, ☎ 800-526-0649.

You might also want to use Tiffany for your own personal pricing system—you don't want to pay Tiffany prices in Hong Kong for inferior goods. Also note that in resale value, name brand jewlery has a higher resale.

Let's not get carried away; we're here for the pearls of Asia. I, on the other hand, buy fake ones. I gave my real ones to my niece the day she was born. Yet, I interviewed Ivana Trump once and asked her what her single most important investment fashion accessory was and she said immediately, "My pearls; I never take them off." It must be a lifestyle thing.

GEMSLAND
The Mandarin Oriental Hotel, 5 Connaught Rd. (MTR: Central).

Richard Chen or his mother, Helen, are happy to spend hours rolling pearls to find the best ones. We even know people who mail-ordered pearls and were happy with the quality.

JEWELS BY JUDY
Room 834, Nan Fung Centre, 264–298 Castle Peak Rd. New Territories/Kowloon (MTR: Tsuen Wan).

One of *Good Morning America's* producers came to Hong Kong with this source because of a family connection; on his first visit, he bought a strand of serious pearls and was thrilled with them. They appraised much, much higher than what he paid for them. They were not inexpensive, but he feels that he got marvelous quality and price.

🛍 K. S. SZE & SONS
The Mandarin Oriental Hotel, 5 Connaught Rd. (MTR: Central).

This showroom is so swank it might make you nervous to enter, although it looks fancier from the windows than it is inside. It is a few doors from **Gemsland.** While they also sell diamonds and gemstones, they are well known for the quality of their pearls and the fairness of their prices.

RIO PEARLS
39 Mody Rd., 3rd floor, Front Block, Kowloon
(MTR: TST).

Recommended by a reader who was impressed with
the shop, the brochure they print, the fact that they
will pick you up if you need a ride . . . and impressed with the items she bought. All the pearls are
graded by the Japanese government.

TRIO PEARL
The Peninsula Hotel, Salisbury Rd., Kowloon
(MTR: TST).

One of the best places to go to in Hong Kong is
Trio, whose reputation for high prices and even
higher quality is well known. Whether you plan to
buy here or not, make this your first stop if only to
get an education. You will have to do it discreetly,
on your own, however.

On my last visit here, I found two things remarkable: The sales help weren't terribly attentive once I
made it clear I only wanted to look at single-strand,
unclasped, 8mm pearls in a 16-inch strand. While I
wasn't ignored, they made it clear that they were
more interested in larger purchasers.

The second most remarkable thing was the quality of what I saw. I saw pearls for $3,000 a strand
that I will simply never get over as long as I live.
They were luminescent.

LEATHER GOODS
. . . .

All of these sources are for elegant, big-name leather
goods, none of which are easy to find in the U.S.

COMTESSE
The Landmark, 16 Des Voeux Rd. (MTR:
Central); The Peninsula Hotel, Salisbury Rd.,
Kowloon (MTR: TST).

Leather goods handmade in Germany and considered a major status symbol by both Europeans and Japanese. If you believe in a very expensive bag that makes a statement, and your goal is to have something different from everyone else's, this store is a must. The line is also sold at **Duty Free Shoppers.**

LANCEL
Harbour City/Ocean Terminal, Canton Rd., Kowloon (MTR: TST).

A big name in France, known for well-made handbags and leather goods that often have the heavy stitching of the chic country look. Their collection of bags with white stitching on dark leather is timeless. Sold in several Japanese department stores because of the appeal to that market, but also in their own shops, which are either in hotel arcades or in the giant Harbour City malls.

LOEWE
The Landmark, 16 Des Voeux Rd. (MTR: Central); The Peninsula Hotel, Salisbury Rd., Kowloon (MTR: TST); The Regent Hotel, 18 Salisbury Rd., Kowloon (MTR: TST).

They are standing three deep at the counters, and they are not American.

LONGCHAMP
The Regent Hotel, 18 Salisbury Rd., Kowloon (MTR: TST); The Peninsula Hotel, Salisbury Rd., Kowloon (MTR: TST).

French leather goods that aren't overdone in the U.S., but are a huge status symbol in parts of Asia. Their refined sporty elegance gets a lot of attention.

MEN'S SHIRTS: MADE-TO-MEASURE

Having a shirt made is not quite the science that having a suit made is, but there is a big difference between a well-made shirt and a poorly made one. Furthermore, men with hard-to-fit figures will always look better in custom-made shirts. A made-to-measure shirt allows you to combine fit, fabric, and quality. And you get a monogram at no extra cost.

There are a lot of choices to be made: the fit of the body, the type of collar and cuffs, the fabric, and the possible use of contrast fabric. Prices usually depend on the fabrications: 100% cotton fabric costs more than a poly blend; Sea Island cotton costs more than regular cotton. Expect to pay about $75 for a Sea Island custom-made cotton shirt, although such a shirt can cost more, depending on the maker.

Many shirt houses have a minimum order on shirts; most tailors make shirts as well as suits. If you are buying the shirt and the suit from the same tailor, there is usually no minimum order on shirts. Most shirt houses make pajamas and boxer shorts as well as shirts.

All the men in my family (including Ian) have their custom shirts made at **W. W. Chan,** as it is tremendously easier to order shirts and suits at the same time and from the same quality maker. Ian has both dress shirts and work shirts made; the work shirts have a second pocket and place with a tab for a pen.

There are other choices, however.

ASCOT CHANG CO. LTD.
*The Peninsula Hotel, Salisbury Rd., Kowloon
(MTR: TST); The Regent Hotel, 18 Salisbury Rd.,
Kowloon (MTR: TST); Prince's Building,
Chater Rd. (MTR: Central).*

Perhaps the best known of the internationally famous shirt dealers, Ascot Chang advertises heavily in the U.S. and stresses their quality and devotion to fit. This shirt maker has many branches in Hong Kong and Kowloon. The shops are filled with wonderful fabrics imported from Switzerland and France. Prices are competitive with **David's** (see below); they offer mail order once your measurements have been taken. Shirts run between $40–$125, depending upon the fabric and style. Top of the line. They have a shop in Manhattan.

DAVID'S SHIRTS
Victoria Hotel (unit 201), Shun Tak Centre (MTR: Sheung Wan); The Mandarin Oriental Hotel, 5 Connaught Rd. (MTR: Central); Wing Lee Building (ground floor), 33 Kimberley Rd., Kowloon (MTR: TST).

David's is the other most popular and famous of the custom shirt shops in Hong Kong. (They also have a branch in New York City.) The main shop in Hong Kong is in Kowloon, on Kimberley Road. But there are more conveniently placed branch shops, mostly in hotels like The Regent or The Mandarin Oriental. David's is less glitzy than **Ascot Chang,** but just as famous to those in the know.

For custom shirts, two fittings are necessary—one for the measurements and then one with the garment. David's will copy any favorite shirt you may have. Just bring it with you and plan to leave it. They also have a framed illustration of collar and cuff styles you can choose from. Mail order is not only possible but common with repeat customers. If you cannot get to Hong Kong, ask for a current swatch and price list. Return a shirt that fits you perfectly and a check, along with fabric and collar/cuff choices. Approximately 4 to 6 weeks later a box of new shirts will arrive.

MEN'S SUITS: MADE-TO-MEASURE

Probably the most famous Hong Kong fantasy is that made-to-measure suits grow on trees or that they are easily and inexpensively obtained with a snap of the fingers and a few hundred dollars. Not!

Yes, there are still tourist joints and rip-off tailors who will make you a suit, with two pairs of trousers, for $250. Maybe even less. But I have to lay it on the line, guys: The suit you get for $250 does not look like the suit you get for $650, and you don't really want the suit for $250. At least, I can't take responsibility for what you will look like in a $250 Hong Kong–made suit. However, I guarantee you'll look like a million bucks if you go to one of Hong Kong's better tailors and spend what it takes for Savile Row quality.

True, you can go to any American discounter or outlet mall and buy an off-the-rack suit for $250, maybe less. Ian bought two suits for $99 each at a blowout sale at Filene's Basement. They're great cheap suits. (Made in Mexico, by the way.) But they are cheap suits and cannot be compared in fit, fabric, life span, or appearance to a more expensive suit. Ian happens to be a 40R and easy-to-fit, and he looks good in everything. If a bespoke suit looks so enormously different on him, imagine how much better the man with the less-than-perfect figure will look.

Remember the first law of Hong Kong custom-made suits: A bargain is not a bargain if it doesn't fit. Furthermore, the whole point of a bespoke suit is psychological—you must feel (and look) like a king in it. Its impact derives from the fact that it was made for your body, that it moves with your body as no off-the-rack garment can.

I've gotten a few angry letters from readers who were not happy with the famous (or infamous) cheapie Hong Kong tailors suggested in past editions. So I've modified my plan. It's simple: If you want a truly fine bespoke suit, Hong Kong can give you British quality at a Hong Kong price. If you cannot afford to trade up to a quality suit, please do not waste your money on an inferior product.

• Start your search for a tailor the minute you arrive. Leave yourself time for three fittings while in Hong Kong. The first will be for measurements and choice of fabrics; the second fitting will be a partially finished suit with only one sleeve in place; the third will be to detail the finished garment, if it is not perfect. Good tailors usually have everything wrapped up by the third fitting.

- If at all possible, choose your tailor before you leave home and fax ahead for an appointment so you can meet shortly after arrival in Hong Kong. After you check in to your hotel, the tailor should be your first stop. While it is not difficult to get across the harbor in Hong Kong, you may want to choose your hotel based on the convenience to your tailor. We make more trips to **W. W. Chan** than any other address in Hong Kong or Kowloon; it helps to be staying nearby.

- Most tailors carry a full line of imported fabrics from Italy, England, and France. If your tailor is not one of the Big Three, ask whether the thread they use is imported also. If it is not, ask to see the quality, and test it for durability. Remember all those horror stories you have heard about suits falling apart? It wasn't the fabric; it was the thread. You do not need to worry about quality at the Big Three tailors.

- Again, if you aren't certain of your tailor's quality, check the lining fabrics. The better tailors have beautiful choices, some imported and some not, but all in good taste. Be sure to specify a fully lined jacket. No fine tailor would consider giving you anything but the best lining.

- If you still have questions about the quality of your tailor, check the inner-facing material to make sure it is stiff enough to hold the shape of the suit.

- Check the quality of the shoulder pads, the buttons, and the buttonholes. A tailor could save a lot of money by using inferior goods. A bad tailor cannot make a good buttonhole. The mark of an excellent tailor is the fact that the handmade buttonholes actually work.

- Well-made suits from a Hong Kong tailor are no longer as inexpensive as they used to be. Gentlemen who came to Hong Kong in the 1960s paid $99 for a suit; that is no longer the going price— even from a cheapie tailor. Imported fabrics run about $20 to $80 per yard, and an average-sized suit will take 3½ yards. The silk/wool blends and cashmeres cost more. The finished price for a top quality, killer suit will run in the area of $500– $800. You could do better in some cases with an off-the-rack suit in the U.S., but the quality would not be the same. Ask for tailoring prices with and without the material. In some cases you might wish to supply your own.

- The shop will want a 50% deposit to start the work. You may be able to pay with a check in U.S. dollars or pounds sterling. Ask ahead of time.

- If you are having the tailor ship the suits to you, remember to figure in the customs charges and shipping. On average, it costs $20 per suit to air-freight them to you. Shirts can be shipped for $30 per dozen. U.S. customs charges about $75 in duty on a single new suit. Once you have established an account with a tailor or a shirt maker and he or she has your measurements on file, you can simply get the fabric swatches sent to you for the new season and do your shopping through the mail—or in a local hotel.

- Check to see if the tailor you have chosen makes trips to the U.S. to visit customers. Chances are, if you live in a major city (New York, Washington D.C., San Francisco, Los Angeles, or Chicago), he or she will. Most of the tailors we recommend either come in person once a year or send a representative with fabric books and order forms. At that time, new measurements can be taken in case you have lost or gained weight.

- The tailors we recommend have been tried and tested. There are many other tailors in Hong Kong. There is at least one in every hotel shopping arcade. There are even tailors who set up booths at the various night markets. Unless you have a personal recommendation, let the buyer beware.

The Big Three: Hong Kong's Finest Tailors

A-MAN HING CHEONG CO. LTD.
The Mandarin Oriental Hotel, 5 Connaught Rd.
(MTR: Central).

Fondly referred to as "Ah-men," this tailor shop in the Mandarin Oriental Hotel turns out quite a few garments for the rich-tourist-and-businessman trade and, therefore, has become very adept at relating to the European-cut suit. They don't even blink twice when you ask for an extra pair of trousers. They just smile and ask for more money. The prices here are on the higher side, with a suit costing about $650. However, the quality is excellent, and that is what you are paying for. Anyone can buy off-the-rack. This is a Savile Row–quality suit.

A-Man will also do custom shirts for approximately $50–$150. If you wish to cable them, their cable name is "Luckylucky." You will feel lucky lucky when you get home and enjoy your new bespoke clothing. ☎ 852-2522-3336; fax 852-2523-4707.

H. BAROMON LTD.
Swire House, Connaught Rd. (MTR: Central).

Tycoon alert: This is a No. 8 warning! If you wonder where the real financial heavyweights have their clothing made, wonder no more. H. Baromon has been in the business for 40 years, serving the elite. His reputation is so above the rest of the world, we are surprised his shop hasn't been moved to Savile Row. When you go to choose suit fabric from H. Baromon, you receive a little booklet containing a photo of the shop, a brief description of the H. Baromon philosophy, a page where you can paste your sample cutting, a memo page for notes, a dollar conversion chart, and a very nice map to help you find your way back.

A made-to-order suit takes at least 7 days. The average suit price is well over $750. Shirts average $100. H. Baromon does not send representatives to the U.S.

W. W. CHAN & SONS TAILOR LTD.
Burlington House (2nd floor), 92–94 Nathan Rd., Kowloon (MTR: TST).

My personal choice for myself, my husband, my son, and for Ian is W. W. Chan. Note that this is the only tailor in the Big Three that has a division that makes women's clothing (**Irene's Fashions**, see page 214).

Peter Chan carries on a family business, which he has built and expanded over the years. He is the only Big Three tailor with offices in Kowloon. *Please Note:* Peter runs the business—which has expanded into China—and does not personally fit suits.

The average price for a suit is $500–$650; the mink/cashmere blends do run up the price.

The W. W. Chan showroom is decidedly more relaxed than the other two big-time contenders. The showroom itself is neat, clean, modern, and even spacious, which is hard to find in Hong Kong. But the location in Kowloon and the approach to the actual showroom are not so swank; businessmen who are used to wall-to-wall carpet may need a moment to adjust, until they are inside the showroom (which has wall-to-wall carpet).

The showroom is wood-paneled and divided into two parts; one-half is primarily for men, although there are more men's fabrics on the side that appears to be for women. The walls are divided into bins, which house zillions of bolts of fabric, most of which come from Europe. More booklets and fabric swatches lie around. When we are picking fabric for suits, we always try to provide a hint at what we want (gray flannel, for instance) because the task of just looking at all the possibilities can be daunting.

The quality of the Chan product is equal to its first-rate reputation; customers here tend to be those who demand the best and like to find it for themselves. The Bijan crowd may prefer **H. Baromon;** the British tycoons may be happier in Central. The people who come to W. W. Chan feel like they are members of a club. I've actually made friends with other customers who were having fittings; there is a constant flow of airline pilots and businessmen coming through the door. Single women may want to hang out just to meet men.

The company sends out tailors twice a year; you may request their U.S. schedule and make an appointment to be fitted Stateside. Fax: 852-2368-2194.

Other Expensive & Well-Regarded Tailors

GIEVES & HAWKES
Prince's Building, Chater Rd. (MTR: Central);
The Peninsula Hotel, Salisbury Rd., Kowloon
(MTR: TST).

Talk about bringing coals to Newcastle—this always gives me a kick: Here you have one of the most famous Savile Row tailors opening shop in Hong Kong, the city where tailors commit their lives to bettering Savile Row. Gieves & Hawkes does a very good business with those who do not trust a Chinese tailor (silly chaps) and who want the status associated with one of London's veddy, veddy best. They also appeal to status-conscious travelers from other countries who want a London label.

JIMMY CHEN
The Landmark, Edinburgh Tower, 16 Des Voeux
Rd. (MTR: Central); The Peninsula Hotel,
Salisbury Rd., Kowloon (MTR: TST); Harbour
City/Omni The Hong Kong Hotel, Canton Rd.,
Kowloon (MTR: TST).

Jimmy Chen has a good reputation and nice shops in the city's best tourist locations. His shop is especially known for making a little of everything: suits, shirts, men's clothes, and women's clothes. He also makes cotton summer suits for men, which many other tailors refuse to do. Prices are equal to those charged by the Big Three.

Less-Expensive Men's Tailors

I'm seriously down on inexpensive tailors because I've seen work that makes me wince, especially compared to the Big Three. Since not everyone has $500 or more for a suit, there should be alternatives, right? These come from reader suggestions; I have not used them personally.

DE LUXE TAILOR
Yip Fung Building (Room 708), 2–18 D'Aguilar St. (MTR: Central).

This is from Barbara Basler, writing for *The New York Times,* claiming well-made suits at a good, although not low, price ($350–$400).

WILLIAM CHENG
Han Hing Mansion, 38 Hankow Rd., Kowloon (MTR: TST).

Reader Muriel Mitzman from New York wrote to recommend this tailor, whom she found refreshing after visiting the infamous Sam (who is no longer in these pages). She and her husband bought suits and shirts and were happy with make, fit, and price.

SHOES
. . . .

If you are a shoe fanatic, read carefully, because there's no business like shoe business in Hong Kong.

First things first: In Hong Kong, shoes are usually sized in the European manner. There are few, if any, women's shoes above a size 40 (U.S. 9^1/$_2$). American and European women with large feet spend a lot of their time in Hong Kong complaining about the difficulties in finding shoes. If you wear a large size, and are in an emergency situation, the good news is that the **Marks & Spencer** department stores carry large-sized shoes (up to size 10 or 10^1/$_2$). These are private-label, not designer, styles, but they are good, "sensible" English shoes and are reasonably priced at around $50 a pair.

I remain disappointed in the shoes available on Leighton Road in Happy Valley. The shoes are manufactured in Hong Kong and then printed with Italian labels. Expect that they will not last that long. However, at these prices you might not care how long they last. For the most part, these are inexpensive copies of fashion styles. They sell for about $40–$60 a pair.

There are many European shoe boutiques in Hong Kong, and many of them have quality goods at prices about 20% lower than in the U.S. **Charles Jourdan** has an extensive stock at savings against U.S. prices. **Gucci** is more expensive; **Bally** is about the same. **Ferragamo** is much more expensive. Go figure.

You may find inexpensive fashion shoes and running shoes in **Stanley Market,** indeed in most street markets.

I've investigated having shoes made and found it's cheaper to buy a ready-made shoe and not gamble. There are customers who are thrilled with made-to-measure shoes from Hong Kong. I take my big feet to Ferragamo and pay retail. But nothing goes wrong. The latest rumors are that the made-to-measure shoe business is dying in Hong Kong because the last makers have all gone to Japan, where they make more money. It is possible that having shoes made here is no longer as smart as it once was.

Custom–shoe shops usually look like holes in the wall, junked up with dusty shoes. Even the fanciest ones in the fanciest hotels don't look like John Lobb in London. If you really want shoes made, ignore the surroundings and walk in. The shoes you see displayed are samples of what can be made. Some people come to Hong Kong with shoes and ask to have them copied. Others decide once they are there, and have no idea what they want. All of the custom shops have similar policies:

- Once you have decided on a style, a canvas will be made of your foot. This will then be turned into a mold from which the shoe will be made. If the shoemaker you have chosen simply takes measurements, leave. This is not what you are paying for. You won't be happy with the results.
- Unless you specifically ask to pick out your skins, the shoemaker will do it for you. I suggest you pick your own and mark the backs so that no one else will use them. In the case of leather, ask to see the hides and examine the quality. Be able to verify that the skins you selected were indeed used.
- Many kinds of leather or skin are used in making exotic shoes and boots. The following cannot legally be shipped into the U.S.: kangaroo, elephant, shark, antelope, gnu, sea lion, lizard, sea turtle, or alligator. Crocodile shoes must enter the U.S. with proper certification.
- The shoemaker usually has a base price list from which he or she works. A basic pair of men's Cordovans cost $150, say. Then you add the extras. This is especially true of boots, where you might decide to have fur lining ($20), zipper sides ($5), or double leather soles ($4). If a man's foot is bigger than $12\frac{1}{2}$, a special price will be quoted.
- If you are having shoes shipped to you, allow for shipping charges. Surface mail postage for shoes or a handbag should cost $15. Air mail for the same will be $20–$30.
- The shoemaker will want a deposit (at least one-third, possibly one-half) or full payment before he or she starts to make the shoes. This is often negotiable, depending upon the store.

- If at all possible, pick up your shoes yourself. If they are uncomfortable, it is easier to remedy the problem while you are there.
- It takes 5 days to make up a pair of shoes.
- Prices vary from $20–$100 on the same shoe style from shop to shop. Some shops will bargain; others will not.
- Made-to-measure shoes are usually more expensive than U.S. designer or top-of-the-line brand shoes.

So if you're out doing the town, you may want to try some of these sources:

LEE KEE SHOES AND BOOTS
65 Peking Rd., Kowloon (MTR: TST).

Another big name, especially for men's shoes. I've seen nice shoes from this source, but my last visit didn't impress me.

LILY SHOES
The Peninsula Hotel, Salisbury Rd., Kowloon (MTR: TST); Kowloon Hotel, 19–21 Nathan Rd., Kowloon (MTR: TST).

Lily has a huge reputation among westerners, probably because one of their shops is in the ever-convenient Peninsula Hotel. Prices are high for Hong Kong, but moderate when compared to the rest of the world. (A Chanel-style handbag: $175 from Lily, $795 from Chanel.) They will make women's shoes for about $200 a pair. The store in the Kowloon Hotel Shopping Arcade is always empty and will bargain with you; the one in the Peninsula is mobbed and not too big on customer service. Frankly, they both leave me cold. Others have been thrilled.

MAYER SHOE COMPANY
The Mandarin Oriental Hotel, 5 Connaught Rd., Central (MTR: Central).

European-styled shoes and handbags sold in such a pleasant atmosphere, without hype, that it is a delight to shop here. They understand the Ralph Lauren school of elegance perfectly. They have shoes in stock or will make a pair for you. Your choice.

They also make a very nice Kelley bag; it's not cheap but it's better than Hermès prices. Expect to pay around $300.

SHOEMAN LAU
Hyatt Regency Hotel, 67 Nathan Rd., Kowloon (MTR: TST).

The best bet for men's made-to-measure shoes, with an international reputation to match. Prices have tripled in the last few years, watch it!

VIDEO CAMERAS

Since Ian doesn't know anything about video cameras, I was on my own here. The frightening thing about the hunt is that I used the same method as for the Fuji point-and-shoot, only this time I found a real bargain. I was offered a Sony camcorder with the best price in the U.S. being about $500; Hong Kong price (asking price) was $440. I found this so frightening I could only stutter. For days, many of us talked about going back to buy this camera, but we never did. I think it's healthy to be afraid of these video shops. I paid more in the U.S., but feel confident—that's worth money.

VIDEO GAMES

Technologically speaking, the things a not-too-plugged-in parent needs to know are: **Game Boy** game cassettes are international in form, and they fit the U.S. and Asian machines interchangeably. **Nintendo,** on the other hand, has a Japanese system and an American system, as well as a laser disc

system and other new technologies. Most of the
Nintendo game cartridges sold in Hong Kong are
for the Japanese system. However, you can buy a
plastic converter for about $8–$10. You only need
one converter, although we have heard of some cases
when the converter simply didn't work. So to be
safe, we bought three; they all worked. Sega fits with
a different converter as well.

While local talent has not figured out how to
bootleg American–style games, there are plenty of
inexpensive Japanese versions on sale.

Most camera and/or small electronics stores sell
video games. Japanese department stores have huge
selections of games (your kids do not care if the instructions are written in Japanese), but prices tend
to be slightly higher than at camera shops. Japanese
department stores do sell all versions of the games,
including the newer laser disc system.

If you are looking to buy game programs for a
PC, shop very carefully. I priced "Where in the World
Is Carmen San Diego?" and found Hong Kong to
be more expensive than home. Prices may be competitive to London.

Peter Chan's best source for video games is:
Masskey Development Ltd., Golden Arcade Shop-
ping Centre, 152 Fuk Wah St., Sham Shui Po,
Kowloon (MTR: Sham Shui Po).

On a much smaller scale, in the realm of touristy
shops that also sell video games, I've done well at
Ricky Lau, Haiphong Alley, Kowloon. For Nintendo
games (Japanese-style) I pay $25, tops.

WATCHES

There are plenty of watches for sale in Hong Kong,
real and fake. Or as they say on the street, "Copy
watch, lady?" The trick is finding the right watch
at the right price. You can pay anything from $50
to $10,000 and still not know what you have
bought. Furthermore, the savings seem to be on very

high-end merchandise, so yes, you can save $3,000 on a $15,000 Rolex but, really, did you want a $15,000 Rolex in the first place?

Did you perhaps want a $10 Rolex? If so, you can think again—those famous "copy watches" that they tout on Nathan Road are relatively expensive; the asking price will be between $100 and $150. I bought a fake Rolex on Canal Street in Manhattan for $10; I've never seen anything like it price or quality-wise in Hong Kong. I gave it as a joke present to a friend who was going to Russia, so I'm not sure if it's still ticking or not. Or if he is.

If you are in the market for an international brand of watch, you are wisest to go to one of the authorized dealers for that brand. They are all listed in the phone book as well as through the Hong Kong Tourist Association. All of the companies expect to lower their prices by 10%. You might expect to get an even better discount if you pay in cash.

If you are looking to buy a watch, but don't care if it's a name brand, there are some things to be aware of before you buy:

- Check to see that the whole watch and not just the movement was made by the manufacturer. A common practice in Hong Kong is to sell a Swiss watch face and movement with a Hong Kong–made bracelet. The bracelet is probably silver with a gold plating. This can work to your advantage if you do not want to spend $5,000 for a solid-gold watch but want the look. A reputable dealer will tell you that this is what you are buying, and price the watch accordingly. These watches can cost anywhere from $150 to $400.
- Check the serial number on the inside movement with the serial number of your guarantee. If you do not receive a worldwide guarantee, don't buy the watch.
- If you are buying from a name-brand dealer, do the same careful checking as if you were buying from a small no-name shop on the street. We know

of someone who bought a name-brand watch from a reputable dealer, got the watch home, and had problems. When she went to the U.S. dealer for that name, they told her that yes, indeed, she had bought one of their name watches, but the movement was 5 years old. She had bought a current body with a used movement!

- If it's not necessary that you find a name-brand watch, and you are simply looking for something unusual and fun, try the following:

City Chain   This is a popular chain that carries Seiko, Bulova, and Zenith among their name brands. They also carry fashion watches like Smash (a takeoff of Swatch). There's a branch of this huge chain in every mall and shopping district.

Swatch Shop   502 Hennessy Rd. (ground floor), Hong Kong (MTR: Causeway Bay). Swatch is a big seller in Hong Kong. Prices are no cheaper than in the U.S., but you might see some different styles.

For a list of authorized sole agents of big-time watchmakers and their phone numbers, see the back pages of the free HKTA booklet on shopping.

WEDDING GOWNS

In the last year, three different women have asked me where to have a wedding gown made in Hong Kong. I even had a fax sent directly to me on the set of *Good Morning America* from Katherine Larkin of Dallas who wanted me to phone her with my picks.

Unfortunately, I haven't got a slew of tricks up my sleeve. In fact, if you want a fairy tale, princess bride kind of dress straight off the cover of *Bride's* magazine, don't have it made in Hong Kong. Chances are, they can't get it right.

If, however, you want a very tailored wedding gown or suit and you have pictures and patterns and we're not talking about working with knits or lotsa lace, you might want to try it. But, frankly, I wouldn't unless you were talking a very simple suit that just happens to be white.

It's my experience that Hong Kong tailors make perfectly fine tailored suits, but they fall apart when it comes to froufrou and serious drape or couture.

But here's a thought for you: My sister found a white dinner suit that she adored; it was sort of a Joan Collins Cannes Film Festival job with a shawl collar fitted jacket and short miniskirt. My sister bought the suit, trashed the miniskirt, and had a long skirt made by her tailor in Hong Kong. In her case, she was able to get a match on the fabric—it was plain old Thai silk. Again, the skirt she had made was very tailored. And, I can honestly say it was beautiful! While this is not everyone's idea of the perfect wedding outfit, if it strikes your fancy, you can have it made for you in Hong Kong.

WOMEN'S CLOTHING: MADE-TO-MEASURE

Men have been having suits made in Hong Kong for years, but women are still learning the ropes. Finding a tailor who can properly drape fabric on a womanly western figure takes a lot of doing.

I started going to **W. W. Chan** for the simple reason that Peter Chan makes my husband's clothes. But there is method to my madness; I didn't just pick an agreeable face from our circle of friends. The three best men's tailors in Hong Kong (see page 199) are so defined because they have their own workshops; only Chan makes women's clothing. After my first suit, I was addicted; now I have most of my good clothes made by Danny Chen at W. W. Chan.

There are scads of tailors in town who will take on curvy clients; possibly some of them can tailor a suit to your liking. You can find tailors less expensive than the Big Three. But for women who want the best, only W. W. Chan will make you a suit that fits like couture.

When you pick a tailor in Hong Kong, know the rules of the game: Absolutely every handmade garment in Hong Kong with the exception of those from the Big Three is contracted out as piecework. In piecework, seamstresses and tailors are paid by the piece, not by the hour. It behooves them to finish quickly. They do not have time to press individual seams, to move slowly, to do painstaking work.

The Big Three pay their tailors by the hour and will accept only the best because their clients insist on it. Work is not farmed out; each item is made on the premises. A French atelier or Savile Row shop would not be any more professional. The quality of the garments from these workrooms is superior on every piece cut.

Prices on men's and women's clothing differ at W. W. Chan. You are charged a flat rate for the making of the garment (no matter what size or how complicated); you pay for the fabric by the yard (or provide your own). A woman's suit totals about $500, depending on the fabric. French wools (the same ones used at Chanel) bring the cost up. A dress costs about $170 for labor alone; a jacket, $175.

I recently got a letter from a reader who went to **Irene Fashions**—the women's tailor at W. W. Chan—and was quoted a price of $800 for the suit she wanted made. She was upset with the walk up the staircase to W. W. Chan, the casual attitude at the shop, and the price. She chose another tailor and got what she wanted for much less money. The point here is simple: You can indeed get what you want for less money at any number of tailors. But you will not get the same quality of workmanship. The Big Three tailors are only for those who are willing to spend top dollar to get top quality. Your lifestyle and taste level may not demand this kind of workmanship.

While three fittings are recommended, especially for a first-timer, these guys can get it more or less perfect after the first measurements are taken.

I would have had some women's clothing made at other tailors, but the truth is, I was frightened off in the research stage, and I'm so happy with W. W. Chan that I can't stand the thought of possibly wasting my money. The two other tailors I tried to use did not pass muster after I inspected recently finished garments on their new owners. I was impressed by **Mode Elegante** (see below), which is a firm used by several women I know. I have not had anything made there.

- If you know you want to use Danny Chen, it's best to write, call, or fax ahead for an appointment. If you aren't headed for Hong Kong, ask about being fitted in the U.S., since Mr. Chen travels to major cities once a year. Men can book with Peter Chan. Contact **W. W. Chan & Sons Tailor Ltd.,** Burlington Arcade (second floor), 92–94 Nathan Rd., Kowloon, Hong Kong. ☎ 852-2366-9738 or fax 852-2368-2194. You can always drop in, of course, but if your time is limited or you need to work at odd hours, an appointment is smart.

- If your mind is not made up as to which tailor you want to use, spend your first day in Hong Kong visiting shops, looking at the samples, asking questions, and feeling goods. Because you should schedule three fittings, you'll need at least 3 days to have a garment made; 5 days is preferable. Try to see clothes being fitted on other people, which isn't as hard as it sounds. You don't have to climb into the dressing room, but watch the public waiting area and observe the fit between garment and owner. A well-made garment is worthless if it doesn't flatter the wearer.

- Tailors make tailored clothing best. Don't ask them to make a knit bodysuit or a Diane Freis–style dress with flounces and crystal pleating.

Danny Chen will make a bodysuit with finished facing (you must provide the knit; there is none in Hong Kong) at the same charge as a blouse ($75 for labor), but he prefers not to.

- All tailors sell fabric by the yard; the better the tailor, the better the quality and selection of his or her goods. Be advised that tailors are geared for men's suits and not women's clothing, so fabric choices for ladies can be limited.

- If you bring fabric with you, make sure you have enough. (See our chart below.) If you bring a fabric with nap, a large pattern or a plaid, or if you are larger than size 14, bring more yardage. If you are buying fabric in Hong Kong, it is easiest if you buy from your tailor, but by no means essential. If you bring a pattern with you, look at the fabric chart on the back and figure accordingly. You may want to buy an extra yard, just in case. I looked at the wrong line on a pattern once and had to have a completely different outfit made since I'd goofed and had few choices left.

- Bring your own buttons and trim if you want top-of-the-line polish to your suit. Every tailor in town can make a Chanel-style suit, but none look as classy as the real thing, for lack of proper buttons and trims.

- Have all measurements taken so that you may reorder or have additional items made at a later date without a return trip to Hong Kong. My first suit was a jacket and skirt; I didn't want trousers, so we didn't even do those measurements. A year later, when I wanted trousers, it was not so easy. If the measurements existed, I would have been able to fax in an order and have it shipped to me without much ado. Mail delivery from Hong Kong happens to be safe and efficient. Most tailors use air freight, which costs about $50.

- If you care enough to use a master like Danny Chen, have enough sense to listen to what he has to say. He'll make whatever you insist that he make, but if you're smart, you'll listen to him

Peter Chan's Fabrications

Fabric Width	Garment	Yardage
44"	long-sleeved dress	4½ yards
44"	blouse	2½ to 3 yards
54"–60"	trousers/woolen	1½ yards
54"–60"	blazer	2 yards
54"–60"	pleated skirt w/ jacket	3 to 4½ yards
60" knit	long-sleeved bodysuit	2 yards

before you make a costly mistake. "Suits that look bad have only two problems," he says. "Wrong fabric or wrong style for body." Also listen carefully to what Danny doesn't say. Recently he said to me, "What do you think of your buttons?" What he was really saying is that he thought the buttons I brought with me were wrong for the suit, and he wanted me to reconsider. He's a real diplomat, so consider every word.

Women's Tailors

IRENE'S FASHIONS
Burlington Arcade (2nd floor),
92–94 Nathan Rd., Kowloon (MTR: TST).

In Hong Kong, a city where locals often think Americans are inscrutable, you'll find some unusual marketing practices. Thus it is that W. W. Chan, known as a men's tailor, has a women's division in the same shop, but this tailor has a secondary name (Irene's Fashions), so that customers will know there is a women's tailor on hand. Clothes made at Irene's are made on the premises, which means this is the only one of the Big Three to make women's clothing. Don't mind if some of the women's samples hanging around are a bit dowdy; for the low-down on having something made here see below.

Since I've now been having my clothes made here for several years, I've a few practices that have worked well: I keep a standard Vogue pattern in Hong Kong. This is a pattern for a dress that covers all my figure flaws and works for all occasions, even sitting on an airplane for 20 hours. I can ask Danny to modify the sleeve or the cut of the skirt or whatever in order to change the dress around a bit (I have six versions of this one dress), but he and I are always speaking the same language since he keeps the pattern.

I've also had coats made: Danny fit me for several different lengths and keeps them on file. That way you can order a coat depending on style plus need. Once you are fitted for a coat, take the time to see where other lengths will hit on your body frame so that you are prepared a few years down the road.

If your weight fluctuates, as mine does, have the tailor keep fat and thin measurements. You can fax information—I'm up or down 5 pounds, etc. Also have standard styles that will fit under all conditions. My perfect dress has an elastic waist, so I needn't worry about my weight changes too much.

Most Important: Give a project plenty of time. The more you put in, the more you communicate, the better your finished garment. You can't go wrong with Danny.

MODE ELEGANTE
The Peninsula Hotel, Salisbury Rd., Kowloon (MTR: TST).

Of all of the zillions of tailors I went to in search of women's clothing, this was the only one that had samples that were not only stunning, but were true fashion and not pale imitations. While I did not have anything made, I was impressed. Furthermore, several of my Hong Kong lady friends—all business-women—use this source.

Chapter Ten

· · · · · · ·

MARKETS & MALLS

DOUBLE HAPPINESS
· ·

Double Happiness is a common Chinese wish, often inscribed on beads and pottery, even written
across trams. In fact, last time I was in Hong Kong,
as I got into the bus on the tarmac at the airport
upon arrival, I looked up and saw an enormous bill-
board inscribed: "Double Happiness."

For those who can shop in both malls and markets, you, too, will achieve Double Happiness. If
your time in Hong Kong (especially your shopping
time) is limited, you're going to have to make some
choices.

Shoppers in Hong Kong have a very serious reality to face up to very quickly. You may even be forced
to make this decision *before* you get to Hong Kong,
when you are planning your daily schedule of
sightseeing. The question at hand: To mall or not to
mall?

Hong Kong is famous for its malls; these lavish
pieces of real estate and architecture do indeed represent a very specific slice of the local shopping scene.
Perhaps you cannot understand the whole shopping
scene without looking at some of these malls.

But the truth is, the malls have the fanciest shops
and the fanciest shops have the highest prices. I don't
come to Hong Kong to spend money; I want to save.

The more I come to Hong Kong, the less I am attracted to the malls. Don't get me wrong, these malls are fabulous. But there's so much of the real Hong Kong to see out in the streets that I am drawn to the markets, not the malls. I spent several hours on my last trip trying to find some wonder in Ocean Terminal but could not.

With luck, you'll be able to see and enjoy the good malls, to decide for yourself which style of shopping you prefer. With luck, and enough time, you'll find Double Happiness.

MARKET HEAVEN

. . . .

Hong Kong is truly market heaven. There are fruit and vegetable markets; general merchandise markets; jade markets; thieves', ladies' and men's markets. There are market lanes and market areas. There is even a market city (**Stanley**).

Markets are a way of life in Hong Kong, and I love them. When I was depressed about all the modern changes in Hong Kong and the lack of low prices on many items, I fled to the markets and found them unchanged. Thank heavens!

Markets are also a very real slice of life. Some are not pretty or fancy. If you have a squeamish stomach, avoid the food markets that sell live chickens or ducks and slaughter them on the spot. Steer clear of wriggly snakes and lizards staked out on cardboard.

But it is the way of life in Hong Kong. Open-air food markets like **Jardine's Bazaar** are a little easier to take than indoor ones, like **Central Market,** where the sights and smells are intense. You should have no trouble with fruits and veggies; indoor markets are the ones that normally house the livestock.

Merchandise markets are busy and hectic. There are no spacious aisles or racks of organized clothing. Some markets exist only during certain hours of the day or night. At a pre-appointed time, people appear from nowhere, pushing carts laden with merchandise. They set up shop along the street, selling their goods until the crowds start to dissipate, at which time they disappear into the night.

Markets have their own rules, just like stores. If you want to be successful at bargaining and come home with good buys, some suggestions:

- Dress simply. The richer you look, the higher the starting price. Most goods on carts do not have price tags. If you have an engagement ring that broadcasts *rich American,* turn it around, or leave it in the hotel safe. We like to wear blue jeans and T-shirts to the market. We still look like visitors, but no one can tell what our budget is.
- Check with your hotel concierge about the neighborhood where the market is located. It may not be considered safe for a woman to go there alone, or after dark. I don't want to sound chauvinistic or paranoid, but crime in market areas can be higher than in tourist areas, especially at the night markets. Arrange your handbag or money carrying situation to be as crime-proof as possible.
- It's also difficult to bargain and then offer a large bill and ask for change. As a bargaining point, be able to say you only have so much cash on hand.
- Branded merchandise sold on the street can be hot or counterfeit.
- Sizes may not be true to the tags.
- Never trust anyone who does business from the street to mail anything for you.
- Don't give your hotel address to anyone who wants to bring you some other samples the next day.
- Make sure you are buying something you can legally bring back to the States. Don't buy ivory; all varieties are illegal to import. Don't buy tortoise shell; it will be impounded by customs.
- Don't think less of yourself if you end up paying the asking price. After all, when that steal of the

century is only $10, why haggle if yo
the mood?

Most markets have no specific street address, but
are known by the streets that are boundaries or in-
tersect in the middle of the market area. The majority of cab drivers know where the markets are by
name. However, it is always a good precaution to
have your concierge write the name of the market
and location in Chinese before you leave. You probably won't need it, but it can't hurt. Buses, trolleys,
and the MTR usually service the markets as well.
Take a hotel business card with you, so you'll have
the address in Chinese in case you need directions
back home.

STANLEY
· ·

STANLEY MARKET
*Stanley Main St., Stanley Village, Hong Kong
(MTR: none, take bus no. 6 from Exchange Sq.
in Central).*

Stanley Market is world renowned. Some call it
famous; I call it infamous. Any tourist coming to
Hong Kong knows about Stanley. Shopping legends
abound about fabulous bargains on designer clothing. Some people love Stanley; I find that they are
mostly first-timers. As an Old China Hand, I have
to tell you in all honesty, I wept on my last trip to
Stanley. It was crassly touristy; there was nothing I
even wanted to buy. I found no retail stock and no
fake designer merchandise (Oh woe!). All I found
were tourist goods—white linens, Chinese pajamas,
knickknacks, and cheapie gift items. Not bad if you
want that sort of thing, but I wanted deals!

If you want to still go to Stanley, know it for
what it is. Stanley is merely a tourist trap—but it's
not intimidating or frightening, and it feels less foreign than a Chinese street market. Furthermore,
Stanley is located in a beautiful part of Hong Kong

Island. The drive here is one of the best things about the adventure. When you go around the curve at Repulse Bay and you see the inlet beaches and the sun gleaming off the water, your heart will simply miss a beat.

If you are traveling with children, Stanley is great entertainment for them. It's safe, it seems exotic (to them), they can wander a little but not get lost, and there is merchandise for sale that interests them—including souvenirs, toys, and running shoes. Ditto for the husbands—there is enough men's merchandise from $3 ties to $100 leather bomber jackets to $15 copied Swiss Army watches to engraved chops and lessons in Chinese calligraphy—that even the nonshopping man can be content for an hour or two. Which is all you really need here.

If you have the time, go on the bus and return by taxi (since you will have a lot of packages). You can go with your car and driver and make a stop at **Repulse Bay** to see the elegant shopping there in the mini-mall (109 Repulse Bay Rd.); you may also want to go for a swim in the lovely little bay right before you get to Stanley. There is a public beach. If all you care about is the shopping, don't arrive before 9:30 or 10am, as the vendors don't really set up too early.

Start your tour of Stanley Market at **Watson's**—this is a western-style chemist shop right at the beginning of the market village—and use it as a landmark in case you get separated from friends or family. (It also has rest rooms.) From Watson's, walk straight down Stanley New Street toward the water, and when you reach the main street of the market, choose left or right. I usually go left first, and explore the main market street, then the alleys that lead up the hill. The restaurants are located in this area. If you really are in a hurry, there are fast-food stands in the market as well.

When you retrace your steps along the main street and continue on the other side of Stanley New Street, you will have a beautiful view of the beach and can stop to take pictures. The main street is where you can expect to find your more substantial purchases. These shops are housed in buildings and have been in the same location for years. Many of them take credit cards and traveler's checks. If not, there are two banks on Main Street.

If you haven't bought too much to carry and are taking the bus home, the stop is across the main road at the top of the market. Ask for directions. You can get off at Admiralty to connect to the MTR. Market hours are 7 days a week from 10am to 7pm.

KOWLOON

· ·

LADIES' MARKET (MONG KOK MARKET)
Argyle St. and Nathan Rd. (MTR: Mong Kok).

Thankfully this market has not changed—it was a welcome treat after a few days in Hong Kong to know exactly where to come for fun junk and designer fakes. My European friends, who are gaga for anything Ralph Lauren and actually pay a hundred dollars for a polo Polo shirt, were elated with $4 fakes from the market. In fact, I filled a suitcase with goodies from a one night shopathon here.

The market sets up a short distance away from the Mong Kok MTR station; it begins around 4pm and goes into the evening, until about 10pm or so. It is a very typical Hong Kong street market, not as extravagant as **Temple Street** but almost a textbook example of what's available. It does begin in late afternoon but really gets going after work. Watch your handbag.

The streets have the feeling of a carnival, with lots of people parading by the stands, stopping to examine shirts, socks, sewing sets, buttons, and bras. There are some toys and sunglasses, but mostly lots of trinkets, shirts, socks, and everyday goods and the usual ringing alarm clocks, fake designer goods, electrical doodads that flash and whirr; no live snakes, however.

are comparing markets and making choices
now there is more to buy here than at Temple Street;
Temple Street is more classic as a piece of theater
than as a shopping mall. The Ladies Market is the
choice if you want bins piled high with fake Ralph
Lauren/Polo shirts, naughty underwear, blinking and
bleeping electronics, T-shirts, and bootleg CDs.

To get to the Ladies Market: take the MTR from
Central, Admiralty, or Tsim Sha Tsui to Mong Kok.
Exit in the direction of the Sincere department store.
Cross Sai Yeung Choi and turn right on Tung Choi.
This is where the market begins. Walk on Tung Choi
until it dead-ends into Dundas. If you turn right and
cross Sai Yeung Choi again, you will be on Nathan
Road. The Mong Kok station will be to your right
and Yau Ma Tei to your left. There will be more
action on the other side of the station as well, toward Mong Kok Street.

KOWLOON CITY MARKET
Lion Rock Rd. (MTR: TST, then take a taxi).

This one is a bit far out, but is especially entertain-
ing because this is where the young locals like to
hang out. Merchandise is a little more with-it; there's
more fun in the air. This is one of the few markets
where you'll find china sold. There are lots of blue
jeans, factory-outlet rejects, and fashions from young
Japanese and Chinese designers. This market only
operates during the day; do not forget to make a
detour to the **DD Warehouse** nearby (see page 257).

TEMPLE STREET MARKET (KOWLOON NIGHT MARKET/ THIEVES' MARKET)
Temple St. and Jordan Rd., Kowloon
(MTR: Jordan Rd.).

If you are only going to one market in Hong Kong,
this is the one. It's a night market. You can go out
for dinner where ever you like and come here after-
ward. There's action until 11pm and sometimes later
(on Saturday nights). You can also eat in the street

as this is one of the homes of the *dai pai dong*—the street vendor selling dinner from a cart. I don't dare eat in the streets, but it is an option.

This is the market where the Chinese opera singers are; this is where you can have your fortune told by a bird! Shopping is secondary to all the other action.

The market can be extremely crowded, with people pushing and shoving to get past, especially on weekends. If you are nervous in crowds, don't go. If you do go, don't carry a lot of cash. Dress down; don't carry a purse.

Getting to this market is very simple, but entering the market at exactly the right place in order to start off with the opera singers takes a little know-how. I just heard from a reader who couldn't find the action, so pay attention.

Take the MTR to the Jordan Road station. Exit onto Nathan Road toward **Yue Hwa Chinese Products Emporium.** You will see Yue Hwa; you can't miss it. Stay on the Yue Hwa side of the street which, if the harbor is to your back, is the left-hand side of the street. You will be walking north on Nathan Road for about 2 or 3 blocks.

Keep looking to your left. You are looking for a tiny entranceway, a small alley crammed with people. This is where the opera singers do their thing on little patios. When you spot the alley, turn left into the crowd. Opera singers will be on your right and left, but mostly on your right. This alley is only about 50 yards long. When you emerge from the alley you will be on Temple Street and at the corner of a real temple, hence the name of the market.

Walk straight forward 1 block, so that you have the sidewalk that borders the grounds of the temple yard on your right side. On this sidewalk you'll see a long row of fortune-tellers, each with his own gimmick. One or two may speak English. Ian and I went with Peter and Louisa Chan one time, and Peter was able to translate my fortune for me. I wouldn't have missed it for the world.

Peter explains that this is not a joke, and you must take it very seriously. To joke or be a smart-ass would be very rude. I found a fortune-teller with a cage filled with birds. I picked the bird I wanted. Said bird then hopped out of the cage toward a row of cards laid on the pavement. He hopped around a bit, then pecked a card into his beak. He gave the card to the fortune-teller. (The bird was rewarded with a snack.) The fortune-teller then told my future in Chinese, and Peter translated. It was a very good fortune (thanks to Peter or the bird, or both) and the entire experience began the night with just the right note of magic.

We have been back to the Temple Street Market on our own and found it just as much fun, but we had no one to translate the bird words to us. So we just went shopping.

The shopping is the typical street-market fare: first a block of carts and stalls, then many, many blocks of stalls lining Reclamation Street. You can do a similar market on Sundays during the day.

When you get to Reclamation Street, note that there are stores along the sidewalk and many of them have bargains, too. Like Levi's for $10; running shoes (no-name brands) for $25. The stalls in the main thrust of the market all seem to be selling the same things after a while: imitation Hermès and Picasso scarves, alarm clocks that beep and peep, belts, socks, T-shirts with characters from video games, chinos, and every now and then jade or jadelike things.

JADE MARKET
Kansu and Battery sts. (MTR: Jordan Rd.
or take a taxi).

This market is also high on my Don't Miss It list—the Jade Market is located very close to the **Temple Street Market;** while the markets are entirely different affairs, you will find some similarities. But they are held at different times of the day, so you won't get much crossover unless you go for a Sunday day market on Reclamation Street.

You can take a taxi to the Jade Market or get there by walking along Nathan Road until you get to Temple Street. But then you would miss all the fun of the fabulous street market on Reclamation Street that's held on Sundays. In fact, Sunday mornings were made for Jade.

The Jade Market is a day market where you will find your best buys on those little green (or violet or pink) stones that everyone will expect you to bring home. The scene varies according to the day, time, and season. One time we went, and it was so crowded we could hardly squeeze our way in to look; another time, we were the only ones there. We can't guarantee what you will find, but we do know that you won't be disappointed if you are looking for variety and a chance to hone your bargaining skills.

The market is located in two free-standing tents under the overfly of the highway at Kansu and Battery streets. I can't say if one tent is better than the other; what happens is that you use up so much energy in the first tent that by the time you get to the second one, you will have lost a lot of your enthusiasm for jade. This is all a matter of what feels good to you and what you are looking for.

I personally don't buy much green "jade," so I look for dealers in old jade—which is brown or amber or dark red—and in other colored trinkets. Ian likes carved stone animals. We both like big ethnic pieces that make a dramatic fashion statement, rather than the touristy junk that passes for souvenirs. Your eye will take you to the booths that sell what most appeals to you, and since there are a total of about 500 vendors in the two tents, you'll have no trouble spending your budget. At the end of our spree, we had each bought so much that we were forced to pool our final resources to keep shopping and then got out with only enough for lunch.

But we bought some great things. We're just not certain how much we paid for them or who owes who what. That's a problem in places like this.

The Jade Market is an official market organized by the Hong Kong and Kowloon Jade Merchants Workers' and Hawkers' Union Association. Each merchant inside the fence is licensed to sell jade and should display his license above his stall. It is a good idea when buying to note the number next to your purchase, just in case you have a problem later on and the jade turns out to be plastic.

If you are hoping to buy quality jade, there are a few things to check. In fact, there's a lot to check.

Make sure that the color is pure and strong. Quality jade is white, not green; there is good green jade, of course, but if you only go by how bright the green is, you can get taken. All that green stuff on the floor and in the bins and baskets surrounding you? It's nephrite, a cheap type of jade.

A few jaded tips:

- There should be no hint of black (unless the jade is black) or yellow. If the color is translucent, that is a good sign of value. Make sure that the color is as even as possible. A carving will have variations, but a jade circle should not. Also, check for fault lines. A good piece of jade will not have them. If any of the above faults appear in the piece of jade you are buying, bargain accordingly. (See page 100 for more information on jade.) Don't hesitate to point out flaws when bargaining.
- For heavens sake, don't even start bargaining until you really get your bearings and have learned your way around asking prices at the various dealers.

  I bought a jade frog at the Jade Market of only so-so quality, but I was in a hurry. I later found a far superior frog, same size, in Stanley for half the price that I paid after bargaining in the Jade Market. And that was asking price in Stanley; I didn't even want to bargain because I was so angry with myself.

Getting taken might be half the fun, but don't lose your head.

As you walk into the market, stop and get your bearings. The area is laid out in rows of tables and stalls, back-to-back in the middle and around the perimeter. We like to do one walk-through before we get serious. There is more for sale than just jade, so keep your eyes open for other good buys.

The jade merchants have very similar merchandise; it's just a matter of how much you want to spend and which one will make you the best deal. I find a table I like and then try to bargain hard. You could spend a day here, but you'd be exhausted.

If you are not willing to bargain here, don't buy. The merchants in the Jade Market expect to lower their price by 20% to 40%, depending on your bargaining skill and their need. We have always had our best luck by pulling out a single bill and saying, "This is all we have left." If the shopkeeper says no, we walk away and try again elsewhere.

We also do the "you don't need it" routine. I act like the interested party; Ian plays the part of the husband who tells his wife to forget it. I say I have to shop fast before he gets angry at me and make a low offer; Ian glares at me. Don't knock it; it works.

Please note that we bought a big, heavy necklace of amber-colored beads with the 12 animals of the Chinese zodiac carved into 12 different beads. We paid $100. Two days later I spotted the same necklace at the Chinese Arts & Crafts store in Star House for $500.

I think the most fun is to be had while seated on the floor or on a tiny plastic stool while playing around with tons of "jade" rings and doodads, all priced accordingly from $1 ($HK 7) on up. Is it real jade? Well, it's real nephrite, which is a type of jade but its a type that's not worth very much.

Who cares?

To get there from the street market, exit the MTR at Jordan Road and turn right. Walk along Jordan Road for 2 blocks until you get to Shanghai Street, turn left onto Nanking, and then turn right onto Reclamation Street. Follow it, right through the market, to Kansu Street. You'll see the overfly of the highway and know you are approaching the Jade Market. When you leave the Jade Market, drop down a block and hit Temple Street, so you can visit the temple in the park. Light joss sticks and think of me.

Market hours are 10am to 3pm, although many of the vendors close up shop at 2pm. Go early rather than late.

BIRD MARKET

Yuen Po Street Bird Garden, located next to the Mong Kok stadium. (MTR: Prince Edward).

The good news is that there still is a Bird Market, and it is a special place. The bad news is that its been relocated because the real estate in Mong Kok where it used to be located became too valuable. This is a standard Hong Kong story.

The Bird Market is one of those marvelous Hong Kong sights, which is so astounding that you almost can't describe it; you have to experience it. It's really just an alley that sells birds and bird supplies. The sound of the chirping is overwhelming. I just want to know if the noise is made by birds chirping or grasshoppers chirping. Grasshoppers are what these birds eat.

The vendors sell bird supplies (obviously this includes grasshoppers); you will be surprised at how many bird cages you suddenly want to buy. The new site is brand new, created in the poured concrete pagoda style of architecture with green tile rooftops. There are fewer vendors and prices are higher. It cannot be considered a tourist trap, however, because while tourists come to stare or take pictures, they don't buy enough to pay the Hong Kong–style rents.

CAUSEWAY BAY

. . . .

JARDINE'S BAZAAR
(MTR: Causeway Bay).

If you stay in Causeway Bay, you have a foot up on
the rest of the world when it comes to Jardine's Bazaar, Jardine's Lookout (a hillside residential area),
and the web of streets between the two. This is what
we came to China for. This is the little street market
in the back alley that weaves through a hole in the
world no one knew was even there.

The first half of the market is full of fruit, vegetables, and other foodstuffs. At midpoint Jardine's
becomes a dry-goods market and sells the same stuff
you'll find everywhere. Jardine's is also in a home-
sewing neighborhood, so you may enjoy wandering
around looking at fabrics and notions, which are
upstairs.

In truth, by the time you get to the dry goods,
the market is rather ordinary. It's the fruits and
veggies that I love so much—so colorful and exotic
and yes, you can find them at other street markets, but there's something about this narrow and
tiny bend in the road that makes it all the more
appealing.

To get there: Leave MTR Causeway Bay station.
You will come out under the Japanese department
store Sogo and weave right then left then right at
the veggies. You can't miss it.

CENTRAL

. . . .

CENTRAL MARKET
Queen's Rd. (MTR: Central).

The major food and produce markets for Hong Kong
Island are located in specific areas. Central Market
serves the area of Central. As you get even remotely
close to Central Market on a sunny summer day,
you can sniff your way there.

It's a four-story warehouse, and the ventilation is not terrific. The market sells every variety of fresh produce and meat that you might imagine. There are three levels of gleaming vegetables and fruit, clucking chickens, and quacking ducks in cages waiting to be picked for dinner.

This is not a pretty tourist sight for children or the weak of heart or stomach.

CAT STREET MARKET
Cat St., just below Hollywood Rd.
(MTR: Central).

Cat Street Market is Hong Kong's answer to a flea market: Used merchandise of the tag sale variety is sold from blankets and a few stalls on a 2-block street of pedestrian pavement just below Hollywood Road.

Some dealers specialize: One guy sells only used typewriters and used sewing machines. Others move around—the man with the Chairman Mao buttons was in one place in May and in a different one in November. A few dealers sell the kind of old jade I like; one vendor has old Chinese sunglasses from the 1930s that are truly sensational, but not worth the $HK 100 asking price. The shops behind and around the market specialize in formal antiques; some of these stores are reputable and even famous.

After you pass the **Man Mo Temple** on Hollywood Road, turn right onto Ladder Street. Walk down Ladder Street just a few steps and you'll see the blankets almost immediately. Turn left onto Cat Street, which is a pedestrian-only alley. There is an official **Cat Street Market Building** behind the street vendors, where you can buy furniture and antiques. The market operates during normal business hours.

The Lanes

The Lanes, two alleys crammed with booths, are in Central and are within walking distance of each other. They are also near many other places in

Central, so it's likely you will pass them in your daily travels.

Li Yuen Street East

If you're looking for an inexpensive look-alike designer handbag, Li Yuen Street East is just the place. There are not a lot of inexpensive, high-quality leather goods available in Hong Kong, and while Li Yuen Street East is not Neiman Marcus, it is the location of choice for locals who need handbags or briefcases. Expect to pay between $40 and $50 for a nice leather handbag of the current fashion rage, or of the Hermès flavor. If you look hard, you can even find a nice Chanel–style bag. It won't have the CCs, but the styling and design will be exact. Assorted versions of the Louis Vuitton–colored leather tote bags are also a viable choice. Li Yuen Street East is also famous for its knitting shops, fabric stores, notions, and padded brassieres.

Li Yuen Street West

Perhaps you want one of those satin-quilted happy coats or vests that you associate with a trip to China. Li Yuen Street West is crammed with them. Be sure to try them on, as the shoulders sometimes run small. Whatever you didn't see on Li Yuen Street East will be on Li Yuen Street West. To get to these two streets, follow the signs as you exit the Central MTR stop.

Pottinger Street

After a big lunch, give your leg muscles a workout and make the steep climb up Pottinger Street. There's nothing unusual for sale here, merely notions. But they are about 20% cheaper here than in a regular Hong Kong department store. If you buy jade circles for gifts, you can buy polyester or silk cord in rainbow colors on Pottinger Street. Hang the cord through the circle, and you have a beautiful necklace. One meter of cord per necklace will be perfect.

WESTERN

· ·

WESTERN MARKET
Des Voeux Rd., Western (MTR: Sheung Wan).

Once upon a time Western Market was in the same shape as Central Market—possibly worse. Then along came a developer with some sort of western travel experience who has obviously seen American malls and developments like Faneuil Hall in Boston and Covent Garden in London. While the Hong Kong thing to do would be to tear down the building and build a modern gleaming high-rise, good sense prevailed and this colonial structure was restored and preserved and turned into a festival marketplace.

I have very mixed feelings about it because the space seems so American and not very Chinese at all. But there are a few wonderful dealers there, many of them handcraft-oriented. There's a branch of **Fook Ming Tong,** the fancy tea brokers; there are toy soldiers and plenty for kids to see and buy.

Many of the cloth merchants who were disenfranchised when Cloth Alley was destroyed have taken space on the second floor of Western Market. On the third floor there is a nice Chinese restaurant.

Flags fly, banners flap, people shop. There's a lot of energy in the space and a number of unique stalls that sell merchandise I haven't seen anywhere else in town.

Man Wa Lane

If you are looking for fun, Chinese atmosphere, and maybe some business cards in Chinese, don't miss Man Wa Lane. Man Wa Lane is headquarters of the chop business. But whether you are looking for chops or not, you should see this small, neat street, which spans about 3 blocks and has a few other stalls that sell general merchandise. If you do buy something from one of the shops and have to return for it, make sure you get a piece of paper with the shop address in both English and Chinese. The stalls do not have numbers but symbols, and they're all in Chinese. We tell you from embarrassed experience: You will never find your way back to a given stall unless you have the address in Chinese. Man Wa Lane is halfway between Central and Western, leaning more toward Western. Catch it as you walk back from Western (and the **Western Market**) toward Central.

NEW TERRITORIES

LUEN WO MARKET
Luen Wo, N.T. (taxi to KCR, KCR to Fanling, bus no. 78 or taxi to Luen Wo).

The market at Luen Wo, also in the New Territories, is a very authentic local food market. It is not enormously different from markets you can see in town, so the trip may not be worth your time. On the other hand, if you plan a day in the New Territories, you can get in a lot of experiences and a few rides on the KCR.

Take a taxi from Kowloon to the KCR station, which is in Hung Hom. It's a huge modern train station. Buy a ticket to Fanling, which will cost a few dollars. Trains are modern commuter-style trains. Exit at Fanling and grab bus no. 78 (clearly marked at its stand) or take a taxi to Luen Wo. The taxi will cost about $HK 10, so you can splurge on this one.

The market fills 1 square city block. The people who are shopping are far more rural-looking than those you might find in downtown Central, but the goods for sale are not that different. You go here for the total experience, for the fact that it's real. The Luen Wo Market makes for a nice Sunday excursion.

SHOPPING CENTERS R US

Rumor has it that the shopping mall was invented in Hong Kong by a brilliant British tycoon who knew that all tourists want to go shopping and that rain prevents them from doing some of that shopping. Indeed, once you set foot in any of the plethora of shopping centers and buildings, you will not know—or care—if it is day or night, light or dark, winter or summer, rainy or dry outside.

Hong Kong is totally overrun with shopping centers. It's like a contagious disease spreading to all architects, who now feel compelled to equip a hotel or an office building with three floors of retail shops before they get to the actual offices. Somewhere, somehow, they find tenants for all those shops.

THE CENTERS OF CENTRAL

With the pressure on in Hong Kong, and Pacific Place blooming into a major force in mall history, some of the older buildings have banded together for advertising and promotional purposes. I'm speaking specifically of what is advertised as the "Centres of Central"; this is an organization of the main buildings in Central that house shopping malls. Their ads can be confusing; there is no one big mall called Centres of Central. The individual member buildings are detailed in the section below. Unless otherwise noted, the MTR stop at Central will get you close to any of these shopping centers.

THE LANDMARK
16 Des Voeux Rd. (MTR: Central).

The most famous of the Central malls, The Landmark has the reputation and the big names but is having to fight to stay ahead of the game. Many of the big names that started here have remained but have opened other shops around town, so they are no longer exclusively in The Landmark. Surely the mall is a must for visitors, who will be awestruck by the glitz and the fountain and the money it takes to make a place like this work.

The multilevel mall is topped by Gloucester and Edinburgh towers. I often suggest this mall as a jumping-off place for westerners who want to see something but aren't quite ready for Kowloon. After a quick survey, you'll probably find that everything is gorgeous but very expensive and that you are ready to move on. There are a few cafes here for lunch, including **Fountainside.**

Among the upscale and big-name tenants you'll find **Gucci, Ballantyne, Céline, Courrèges, Esprit, Benetton, Lanvin, Valentino, Burberrys, The Body Shop, Kenzo Jungle Jap, Cerrutti 1881, Mandarina Duck, Wedgwood, Bulgari, Meissen, Shu Uemura, Timberland, Louis Vuitton,** and many, many more.

If you are on a quick tour of Hong Kong and must pick and choose each shopping moment, you might want to take a pass. There are few bargains, and the atmosphere is decidedly western.

CENTRAL BUILDING
19–23 Queen's Rd. (MTR: Central).

Next door to, and occasionally adjoining **The Landmark** in some doorways, the Central Building is styled in the same tradition, but without the fountains. In fact, it's hard to tell where one center stops and the other starts. The newness of the stores in the Central Building make it feel as if new life had been breathed into The Landmark. The space is not as large and, therefore, not as overwhelming; it's sort of the appetizer before the main course. More big names are here, of course, including **Basile, Charles Jourdan, Prada, S. T. Dupont, Pierre Balmain, Bruno Magli, Junko Shimado, Maud Frizon Club,** and **Lacoste.**

Again, it's another plush western-style mall.

PRINCE'S BUILDING
Chater Rd. (MTR: Central).

This office building with five levels of shopping has so many big names now that it competes with **The Landmark** and the **Central Building,** both of which are across the street. The Prince's Building is easy to shop because it is perfectly square! It connects by bridge to the Mandarin Oriental Hotel (don't miss shopping there, either) and may be more fun than The Landmark for you. It is not mind-boggling like The Landmark, so you can shop and enjoy yourself. Among the many upscale tenants are **Diane Freis, Cartier, Fogal, Royal Copenhagen, Chanel, Ascot Chang,** and **Bree** (Italian natural leather handbags). Then there's the useful category, such as trusty old **Watson's,** the drugstore that sells everything.

I confess that when I am walking from the Star Ferry into Central, I usually take a path that takes me out of the tunnel and alongside the Prince's Building, so that a Chanel shop just happens to be on my right-hand side and my feet just happen to walk in the door without thinking about it.

THE GALLERIA AT 9 QUEEN'S
9 Queen's Rd. (MTR: Central).

Why does the Galleria announce itself with its address? Because it's the new and very hot kid on the block. This is a small, luxe, luxe, luxe mall that is owned by Joyce Ma, who is my hero. Joyce, a famous character in fashion and retailing in Hong Kong, owns most of the big-name designer stores in Hong Kong anyway, so a mall of her own makes perfect sense.

There are numerous **Joyce Boutiques** in the building as well as branches of famous name shops such as **Hermès, Alexandre De Paris** (the hairdresser who owns a few accessories shops that sell hairbands for $50 each), etc. There are a few tony restaurants/snack bars here, so that it makes for a very upscale pit stop. Don't miss it; even if you buy nothing, you need to understand what Joyce has done to Hong Kong and vice versa.

Swire House
Connaught Rd. (MTR: Central).

I don't think Swire House makes much of a mall, but you can't beat the location in Central, between the Mandarin Oriental Hotel and The Landmark. The lobby floor does still have several big-name shops and a few of the winners you may be looking for, like **Bottega Veneta, Daks, Issey Miyake, Moschino, Kenzo Paris,** and **Fila.** The building has entrances on Connaught Road Central, Pedder Street, and Chater Road.

Pedder Building
12 Pedder St. (MR: Central).

Well, the Pedder Building is looking cleaner and safer these days, but it's still not swank. Although it's across the street from **The Landmark,** it offers the opposite in shopping appeal—outlet stores on one side and the famed **Shanghai Tang** on the street level.

Pedder Building can be stifling if you go in summer when the air is heavy and your feet are heavy and your shopping bags are heavy, and the stores here are not too enlightening. But I digress.

First, the facts:

The Pedder Building couldn't have a better location in all of Central.

Also, the Pedder Building has several factory-outlet stores in it (see page 250). *Note:* There are several shops that are fancy, expensive, and not at all outlets—beware. Shanghai Tang's certainly isn't an outlet—don't hold that against it!

Complain as I may about the uneven quality of the shops in the Pedder Building, I want to make it clear that I had no trouble buying a knit dress for $20 and feeling good about it. When I hit the stores that were packed with last year's Chanel markdowns, I thought I would flip. (I restrained myself.)

The building has had a huge turnover in tenants, but it's perfect for one-stop shopping.

KOWLOON SHOPPING BUILDINGS

NEW WORLD CENTRE
18–24 Salisbury Rd., Kowloon (MTR: TST).

Despite my love affair with The Regent Hotel, I am far from wild for the New World Centre. Even though the two properties are attached at the hip, they certainly aren't Siamese twins.

I guess I don't like New World Centre because it's so clean.

The New World Centre is yet another massive, multilevel, spic-and-span, concrete-and-cold-floor shopping center filled with little shops, 1-hour photo stands, and ice-cream vendors. It has one of the best air-conditioning systems in Hong Kong (important in summer), as well as a cute Japanese department store (**Tokyu**—open 10am to 9pm; closed Thursday) on the street level. There's a branch of **Episode** and a few other nice places, but really, don't waste your time on my account.

Now then, not to muddy the waters, but if I get confused on this perhaps you will, too. On the other side of the harbor, on Victoria Island, there is a big business tower called **New World Tower**. It is not a shopping mall but on the ground floor is the biggest (and best) branch of **American Express**.

SILVERCORD BUILDING
30 Canton Rd., Kowloon (MTR: TST).

Located at the upper end of Tsim Sha Tsui, across from Harbour City, right there on beautiful downtown Canton Road, the Silvercord Building is best remembered for its sublevel computer shopping.

If you're interested in computers, fax machines, or other high-tech electronic goodies, head straight to the basement, where the **East Asia Computer Plaza** shops are located. It's a great place to begin your research before buying electronics.

Upper-level shops in the Silvercord are rather average.

STAR HOUSE
Canton Rd., Kowloon (MTR: TST).

Star House is the first building you come to on your left as you exit the Star Ferry. It's got a **McDonald's,** a **Fotomax** for 1-hour film processing, and a number of stores. You will also see a large branch of **Chinese Arts & Crafts** store.

HOTEL ARCADES & MALLS
. . . .

There are several reasons for the popularity of hotel arcades in Hong Kong. They're dry in rain; they're cool in summer (like shopping malls); they're handy for the tourist who will spend according to convenience; and, most important, they receive the benefits of trust. Shoppers have come to judge the shops in a hotel to be as reliable as the hotel itself. Thus the fanciest, most deluxe hotels have the most trustworthy shops. Shoppers believe there is a direct correlation between the quality of the store and the quality of the hotel.

Certainly the shops in **the Peninsula, the Mandarin Oriental,** and **The Regent** are the most expensive and most exclusive. But that doesn't mean there's anything wrong with the shops in the **Holiday Inn.** And get a look at what's going on underneath the **Kowloon Hotel:** You'll find some big names for a hotel that no one has ever heard of. (It's part of the Peninsula Group, which explains everything.)

Some hotel arcades offer a handful of shops. Others have three levels of stores and hundreds of choices. Often, a hotel arcade connects to a main shopping center. From the **Omni Prince Hotel** at the far end of Harbour City, you can walk through a shopping arcade to connect to the **Omni Marco Polo Hotel,** and then go into another shopping center and keep on connecting for a few miles to several hotels and thousands of stores, end up at **The Omni Hong Kong Hotel** . . . and step right onto the Star Ferry.

These are my favorite hotel shopping arcades in both Central and Kowloon; you must also consider that if you stay in any of the big three hotels above Pacific Place that you have an entire mall in your lobby. These hotels do have a smattering of their own stores inside the actual lobby as well.

THE MANDARIN ORIENTAL HOTEL
5 Connaught Rd. (MTR: Central).

The glitziest stores in town fight to get space in the Mandarin Oriental Hotel, not only because the hotel is so fabulous and its clientele so tony, but because the location is prime. Part of your Central shopping spree must include a visit to the stores, which include **Ferragamo, Kai Yin Lo, Fendi, David's Shirts,** and **Gemsland,** which is the jeweler I happen to use.

THE KOWLOON SHANGRI-LA
Mody Rd., Tsim Sha Tsui East, Kowloon (MTR: TST).

There are only a few stores (discounting the fact that there's a huge mall outside the door), but they are awfully good for hotel stores. Stores are located on the floor above the lobby and offer enough range to get you through a business trip without worrying about getting elsewhere—there's souvenirs in one shop and nice gifts and crafts in another.

THE REGENT HOTEL
18 Salisbury Rd., Kowloon (MTR: TST).

As the hotel arcade/shopping center/mall sweep-stakes heat up, The Regent enters the fray with per-haps the best of the bunch—to date. But stand by, we are awaiting an announcement that more shopping will pave the mall-way from The Regent to The Pen.

Right now, The Regent's mall is light and bright, with higher ceilings than in the basement levels of The Pen, so you don't get so claustrophobic. The usual combination of drugstore and needed stores is here with big names like Giorgio Armani, Donna Karan, Chanel, Joyce, Van Cleef & Arpels, Ascot Chang, Cartier, Basile, Jaeger, Longchamp, etc.

THE PENINSULA HOTEL
Salisbury Rd., Kowloon (MTR: TST).

Small shops fill the eastern and western wings of the hotel, with more on the mezzanine and still more in the basement. Every big name in the world has a shop here. The arcade hosts a number of big-name, high-ticket designers: **The Peninsula Boutique, Kenzo, Lladró, Gieves & Hawkes, Longchamp, Hermès, Polo/Ralph Lauren, Tiffany, Prada, Céline, Beltrami, Genny, Gucci, Matsuda, Léonard, Gianni Versace, Cartier, MCM, Charles Jourdan,** etc.

There are also several cashmere shops and several leather goods shops that make handbags and shoes. If you ever want to go into Kelly-bag overload, step this way. There's a very glitzy and modern pharmacy in the basement loaded with western and Chinese goods and European perfume brands that may or may not come from Europe. Local prescriptions are filled here as well.

KOWLOON HOTEL
19–21 Nathan Rd., Kowloon (MTR: TST).

A small, underground arcade you reach by escalator directly from the street. There are two levels of basement stores, all small but uncrowded. Because of its association with the Peninsula Hotel, the hotel has a classy retail arcade with big-name designer tenants, although I have noticed such a complete turnover that it's anyone's guess as to who will be here when you visit.

HYATT REGENCY HONG KONG
67 Nathan Rd., Kowloon (MTR: TST).

A very fancy hotel in a prime shopping area, with several stores in the middle of the Golden Mile. The street-level back shops are not as nice as the front and basement shops. The real reason to go downstairs is the shoe and leather goods store **Alan Fung,** one of the makers of custom shoes and Kelly–style handbags in sensational colors.

HONG KONG MALLS

· ·

THE MALL AT PACIFIC PLACE
88 Queensway (MTR: Admiralty).

This is the hottest location in town; the one that made everyone do the cha-cha; the one that houses **Seibu** (the best of the Japanese department stores); the one that pushed The Landmark to the limit and put Admiralty on the map for tourists.

If you are staying in one of the many hotels built next to the mall, this place is a natural for you. If you are not staying nearby, you may want to come by if you are in a hurry since you can pack a lot in. I would send you here if only to buy the Red Earth line at **Seibu,** but that's my preference. I'm crazy for their Earth Serum aromatherapy products and can only find them here—this is an Australian line that I've never found elsewhere.

Please note that the official name of this place is the Mall at Pacific Place, but everyone calls it **Pacific Place.** Technically speaking, Pacific Place includes the office tower above the mall and the congregation of fancy hotels grouped around the tower (Marriott, Conrad, Island Shangri-La).

The nicest approach to Pacific Place is from either the Marriott Hotel or the Conrad Hotel, or from your limousine, but of course the MTR will do just fine (Admiralty stop). You can also take a tram to the Queensway stop.

This upscale mall offers a hefty dose of everything you want to see. Most stores are open 10am to 8pm daily, although not every store is open on Sunday, and the stores that do open on Sunday usually open at 1pm.

There are a few gourmet food stores; some antique shops (**C. P. Ching**); some eateries, including an American barbecue restaurant (**Dan Ryan**); and the usual big names like **Dunhill, Boss, Ermenegildo Zegna, Davidoff, Ballantyne, Carlos Falchi, Kai Yin Lo,** and **Marguerite Lee.** There are also more casual chains, such as **The Athlete's Foot, The Body Shop, Marks & Spencer, City Chain** (watches), **Benetton,** etc. The small branch of **Chinese Arts & Crafts** is not up to my standards.

TIMES SQUARE
Hennessy Rd. (MTR: Causeway Bay).

When **Pacific Place** put Admiralty on the map, developers around town must have been foaming at the mouth to find the next hot spot. Causeway Bay came out the winner. Despite the fact that there are a ton of tour group hotels in Causeway Bay, this is not really a key tourist area. And Times Square, the mall, was not built for tourists.

The mall is divided by category of goods, which simplifies life for someone shopping for a specific item or wish list; it combines western chains and big names (**Liz Claiborne** chose this location for her first Hong Kong retail store) with local dealers and small firms.

There are four floors of restaurants; this is a destination and a lifestyle choice—not merely a mall.

PEAK GALLERIA
118 Peak Rd. (take a taxi or the Peak Tram).

There have long been rinky-dink "artists" selling along the pathways across from the Peak Tram; they have been selling Peak Café souvenirs in the cafe for years. But now the Peak is really getting developed—too developed if you ask me.

I hate this mall! There is no reason for you to set foot in it; go to the Peak Café across the way and pretend the mall was never built.

KOWLOON MALLS

. . . .

HARBOUR CITY
Canton Rd., Kowloon (MTR: TST).

The shopping complex that occupies most of Tsim Sha Tsui's western shore is generally known as Harbour City. It includes **Ocean Terminal, Ocean Centre,** and **Ocean Galleries** along with **The Omni Hong Kong Hotel,** the **Omni Marco Polo Hotel,** and the **Omni Prince Hotel.** There are four levels of shopping from end to end, and if you can successfully negotiate your way from one end to the other, you won't even have to come up for air.

The idea of a shopping complex on the waterfront originated with Ocean Terminal, which is the building that juts out into the water alongside the Star Ferry Pier. Ocean Terminal was so successful that Ocean Centre and then Ocean Galleries were developed. It is hard to tell one from the other unless you detect the different patterns in the floor tiles. I find Ocean Terminal to be the least claustrophobic part of the complex because there are windows. Once you get into the bowels of Ocean Centre and Ocean Galleries you need your compass and lots of luck to find your way back out.

Do make a point of finding the area called **The Silk Road,** which is a small gallery of antique shops that's kind of fun to visit (see page 138). After that, I say you're on your own. Every store in Hong Kong has a branch here, but there's no magic to the shopping—it's only a matter of convenience.

HANKOW CENTRE
Hankow Rd., Kowloon (MTR: TST).

This is a quasi-mall, a big city type vertical mini-mall put up in an existing building that has been re-habbed and spiffed up and enjoys a sensational location. Among tenants: DFS, the duty-free people (upstairs) who have just about taken over the entire building, Benetton, and Krizia.

PALACE MALL
12 Salisbury Rd., Kowloon (MTR: TST)

This new mall is underground, so from the street it looks more like a metro station than a mall—nonetheless, the builder has visions of connecting with the malls at **The Pen** and **The Regent**—and maybe digging 'til he gets to China!

Located right on Salisbury Road, the entrance is literally in the ground right next door to The Regent and alongside the **Hong Kong Museum of Art and Space Museum** —look for the white wrought iron and the fancy bus stop, and you've found it.

The mall consists of four levels with two levels of stores—it's about the same size as The Regent Hotel Mall and the Peninsula Hotel arcades; there are underground walkways that connect the stores to **New World Centre** on the far side of The Regent Hotel and the various hotels on that block.

HONG KONG PLACE
Whampoa Gardens, Hung Hom,
(MTR: none, take a bus from the Star Ferry).

If you think Harbour City is a monstrosity, get a load of Hong Kong Place, which is currently the largest mall in Southeast Asia. The two-story mall has 200,000 square feet of space, which means that it's not as big as a giant U.S. regional mall or even the combined three-mall glory of Harbour City. But to locals it's a big deal.

To me? Well, I'm getting to hate Hong Kong malls. I cannot in good conscience tell you to go out of your way to come here. But if it's a rainy day and you're terribly curious, well, okay.

The various levels are named after local streets with implied (but lacking) charm. I recommend the real live Granville Road for shopping, not the part of this mall named Granville Road. But the space seems to appeal to locals rather than tourists anyway.

There is bus service from the Star Ferry, or you can take a taxi here—this is technically Hung Hom, although it is sometimes written as East Kowloon. There is no direct MTR service.

PARK LANE SHOPPER'S BOULEVARD
Nathan Rd., Kowloon (MTR: TST).

This is a strip mall of unique architectural proportions that will certainly catch your eye (and maybe your credit card) as you stroll the infamous Nathan Road. The two-level mall has a park growing on its roof. It's made of white tile, but broken up at intervals with quasi-Japanese *torii* in bright colors. About half of the space is occupied by **Yue Hwa,** a Chinese department store making a rather upscale, modern, and western statement. There's also an **American Express** for changing traveler's checks (go upstairs).

Chapter Eleven

· · · · · · · · ·

FACTORY OUTLETS

EMOTIONAL OUTLETS

· ·

I know, I know . . . in your fantasies of Hong Kong, silk blouses grow on trees and cost only $30 each. I'm sorry to have to be the one to tell you, but it is in fact a complete fantasy. You can get silk blouses for $30 (and less), but you may not like the quality of them. You can also pay over $100—even if you shop in a factory outlet. And yes, I am talking U.S. money here.

Furthermore, a lot of manufacturing has moved out of Hong Kong; the outlets of yesteryear simply aren't here any more. Nor are the bargains. You may do better at the TJ Maxx nearest you, if you are talking cheap silks.

A drop-dead-chic, top-of-the-line quality silk blouse easily costs $100. But you can get by for less. And just as I warn you that it's not like it was in the old days, I'm fading to memories of my last trip when I almost fell into Hong Kong Fever when I discovered a ton of American designer silk blouses in a Pedder Building outlet for $30 each. Yes, Ellen Tracy and the like.

So it's a cruel world out there, changing beneath our feet and making it harder and harder for us. There are still factories, and there are some buys. But there are also a good many fake outlets—a trend in Hong Kong's manufacturing business is to have your own outlet store whether you fill it with bargains or not. And, there are so many out of the way, hole-in-the-wall places stocked with small sizes that you'll want to cry (unless you are a size 4).

If there's a good deal to be had, it will more than likely be advertised in the local paper, the *South China Morning Post*. There is an entire page devoted to this sort of advertising; look here first for news of special sales or bargains.

If you see something in the paper that sparks your interest, go for it. Otherwise, I suggest you pick your outlets carefully because so much time can be spent looking for a bargain that the effort invested begins to outweigh the money saved. As your Indian scout, I can't tell you how many miles I've logged on the prairie of bad buys and lost hopes.

Many outlets aren't as good as they used to be; too many outlets manufacture fake bargains and simply aren't cheap. (You may do better at Loehmann's!)

Ian once bought his wife an Anne Klein II silk blouse for $150. I fail to find a bargain anywhere in that; I'm sure it would cost less at an American discounter. True, it was a gorgeous blouse and the best of many we looked at in several outlets, but it was no "street bargain." I'm sure that, to this day, she thinks he paid $50 for it.

The moral of this story? Know your prices at home before you assume there are savings in outlets; if you are buying a gift for someone, make sure they can understand its true value. Your friends and family at home might not grasp the fact that quality costs a lot of money, even in Hong Kong.

Also take note of addresses. Don't expect to find a great deal in a factory-outlet shop that has a tony address. Outlets attached to real factories still offer the most certain guarantee of authenticity and your best bet for a real bargain.

There are some outlets that are fun; some that are easy to get to; some that are worth doing. We

---

Bargain Bits

Factory Factoids:

- Be sure that you are not planning your factory-outlet visits on a public holiday, and especially not during the Chinese New Year, when everything will be closed up tight.
- Factories and their outlets close during lunch, usually from 1pm to 2pm.
- Go to the bathroom when you eat lunch at a nice, clean restaurant or in a hotel.
- If you can't get enough of the outlets, don't forget that there is a local guide that lists only outlets—it's a really great book.

---

can't tell you to track down all the wild and weird ones, especially because after your trip to the Sek Kong Market in the New Territories you'll be broke anyway. Outlet shopping these days becomes a matter of choices and neighborhoods, time, convenience, and personal shopping style. If you don't like funky shopping, forget most of the outlets. (But not all of them!)

Choose by neighborhood, and you'll never be angry that you schlepped halfway around the world to find a dump. And speaking of neighborhoods, do not trek all the way out to the **Joyce Warehouse** in Aberdeen if you wear a large size, if you are looking for a bargain, or if your time is precious.

Ambience in the outlets varies widely. Some good outlets are in the factories themselves and are exciting to visit. Other outlets are funky but have good-quality merchandise mixed in with seconds. More and more outlets are quite elegant, have large modern showrooms, and accept credit cards; nevertheless, they offer quality merchandise at discount prices.

One thing to remember about shopping in an outlet is that there are no returns or credits. Once you leave the store, the merchandise is yours, even if you find a huge hole in the sleeve when you return to your hotel room. Always check the merchandise for dye lots and damages before you buy it. Always try on an item; verify sizes. Most outlets will have some place for you to try on items. Sizes are not always marked correctly. As with the rest of Hong Kong shopping, the motto is "Buyer Beware." Don't be surprised if some factories sell goods that are over a year old.

OUTLETS BY NEIGHBORHOOD

. . . .
Central

Central is the main retail shopping, banking, and business hub of Hong Kong. The rents are very high. Get the message? Because more and more tourists are looking for factory outlets that are convenient, more and more manufacturers are complying by opening branches in Central. However, you cannot expect to get a fabulous bargain in a shop where the overhead is outrageous. Especially if the floor is clean.

Yet I don't want to pooh-pooh Central for bargains, for fun, and for those with time constraints. If you only have time for one or two outlets, or you are looking for a taste of the scene without wasting too much time, Central is for you. In fact, the Pedder Building was made for you.

I like the Central outlets for convenience. It sure beats an hour on the MTR and getting lost in Kwun Tong. But you will pay the price for this convenience. For many, time is money.

THE PEDDER BUILDING
12 Pedder St. (MTR: Central).

If you can even look past the glamour of **Shanghai Tang,** you'll note that upstairs in the Pedder Building there are some outlet stores. So Pedder becomes a double must-do; Tang's plus bargains. But buyer beware: Many of the shops located within the building are not discounters. Both the ones that claim to be outlets, and the real outlets, still have very high prices. I paid a very high price for a silk blouse at **Anne Klein II;** it was merely 20% less than it cost in Saks Fifth Avenue. (I paid $180.) I just happened to need that blouse to complete a suit I had just ordered. But then, I also bought a silk skirt at Anne Klein for $30, so you never know.

Because places come and go and we all do have different tastes, the best advice I can give you is to start at the top of this building and simply work your way down. Go up in the elevator then continue downward via the staircase. There are stairs on both ends of each hall; do not be frightened—as the building continues to be renovated, it's not as shabby and is perfectly safe.

Among my favorite outlets in the Pedder Building: **Shopper's World Safari, Cachet Lingerie, The Silkwear House, Exhibition Top Cashmere, Ça Va, Mogaschoni, Blanc de Chine,** and **La Place,** which actually has a couple of showrooms—all selling Chanel and other top designer names (I think it's last year's stock).

SHOPPER'S WORLD SAFARI
Pedder Building (room 104), 12 Pedder St. (MTR: Central).

This used to be what a factory outlet should look like. It was one of the first, and may be one of the last. It is small, crowded, and packed with people and merchandise. Men's shirts are in bins along the wall in the back of the shop; the rest is women's sportswear. Last time I was there it was very smart; there were few bargains—but many swear by it as a regular haunt.

Hours at the Pedder Building are Monday through Sunday from 9:30am to 6:30pm.

ANNE KLEIN II
Pedder Building (room 301), 12 Pedder St.
(MTR: Central).

A smart, modern outlet in the Pedder Building that features Anne Klein II with some deals and some nondeals. There are lots of choices to make in lots of colors. Some of the merchandise matches up to what you see in U.S. stores; some of it may be in colors cut especially for the outlet.

There is a sale rack in the rear to the right, sort of hidden from view as you enter. A lot of the clothing is small; there were no size 14s when I asked. Prices may not be any better than at a good sale in the U.S. The selection is clean, bright, and attractive; shopping here is satisfying if you don't mind the high prices. This certainly isn't the down-and-dirty Hong Kong outlet shopping that can be found elsewhere. Hours are Monday through Saturday from 9:30am to 6:30pm. Private dressing rooms; plenty of mirrors.

MOGASCHONI
Pedder Building (room 401), 12 Pedder St.
(MTR: Central).

Formerly known as Wintex, this is one of the tonier outlets in Central, and their cashmeres are sensational in style, color, and price, considering the quality—these are not inexpensive cashmeres, however. I have seen some very famous big-name labels here in the ready-to-wear section.

This is one of those outlets for people who don't like dirty places and insist on high quality. Hours are Monday through Friday from 9am to 6pm and Saturday until 5pm.

ÇA VA
Pedder Building (room 701), 12 Pedder St.
(MTR: Central).

Ça Va carries export merchandise, not seconds. They are rumored to own rights to big-name U.S. merchandise, which they sell here at a discount. Ça Va manufactures a full line of clothing, mostly in silks and gabardines, but it also has cotton-knit clothing and novelty sweaters.

Ça Va is open Monday through Friday from 10:30am to 6pm and Saturday from 10:30am to 5pm.

BLANC DE CHINE
Pedder Building (room 201), 12 Pedder St. (MTR: Central)

This is sort of the poor man's **David Tang** with many traditional style Chinese garments done in fancy enough fabrics to be drop-dead chic and right in style. Prices are not low but are better than at **Shanghai Tang,** and colors are more subtle. They also have some home decorative items and a wonderful throw blanket made of silk that is fabulous for travel, $150.

LA PLACE
Pedder Building, 12 Pedder St. (MTR: Central).

I don't want to sound like an idiot here, but I have never seen anything like this place, La Place. It's like the back room at a department store sale . . . scads of big-time, big-name, knock 'em dead designer clothes—you just can't figure out how old they are or where they came from. There's more Chanel here than in my closet; that's for sure. Chanel shoes, bags, clothes, suits, accessories, Chanel in all sizes, even to fit me! Prices are not cheap (this is *vrai* Chanel) but seem fair, or am I jaded? I toyed with a Chanel coat jacket for $1,000. I didn't do it, but I thought it was fair. Plan to spend several days here.

Other Central Addresses

JENNIE
Well On Commercial Building (4th floor), 60 Wellington St. (MTR: Central).

In a clean, modern building in Central, so it's easy to pop in. It's also easy to skip this one: I was not knocked out, despite Jennie's reputation as one of the best resources in town.

The merchandise includes sweaters, silk blouses, pleated silk skirts, gabardine blazers, and cotton knits of all varieties. The average price of anything is $50 and up. There were no labels that I recognized, but the merchandise was very well made and appeared to be of very high quality. Mostly this outlet was simply too upscale and too fancy for me (can you believe it?)—I could have spent a fortune here easily, but I simply want to pay less.

Hours are Monday through Saturday from 10am to 6pm.

GAT
Cosmos Building, 8–11 Lan Kwai Fong
(7th floor) (MTR: Central).

GAT has several outlets in Hong Kong; this one is on the food street Lan Kwai Fong and is conveniently located for Central shoppers. It's also half a block from **Jennie,** so you can hit two birds with one credit card. GAT appears to be the distributor for the Kenar label. And yes, they have American sizes and a wide range of them for a change.

Hours are Monday through Saturday from 9:30am to 6pm.

ABERDEEN

. . . .

Aberdeen is not the small fishing village you imagine it is—this outlet is not near anything in Aberdeen that I've ever heard of, and my taxi driver actually needed my help in finding it! But, if you insist on covering the waterfront, you heard it here first.

JOYCE WAREHOUSE
Horizon Plaza, 5th floor, 2 Lee Wing St., Ap Lei Chau (this is the district and is imperative to know!), Aberdeen.

Okay, before I get going, some facts:

- The outlet is closed on Mondays but open on Sundays and all other days of the week.
- You will need a taxi and a prayer here.
- They will not call you a taxi at the outlet, or if they do, a taxi will not come. If you don't have your taxi wait for you, you are dependent on the next taxi delivering the next shopper.
- They don't have many big sizes. By big, I mean sizes 10 or 12.
- Clothing for American giants (size 14 and over) is unlikely to be found at all.

Now then, this is an industrial building; it's not hard to find once you find it. If I had it to do over again, I would have my taxi wait for me. But then, I'm a size 12 and couldn't have much fun since nothing in the store fit me. I also thought the prices were high—they're only cheap compared to Joyce regular prices. I'd say this source is for locals, and tourists can give it a miss.

KOWLOON

With the demise of the beloved Sands Building (now a branch of HMV!), there just aren't as many outlets right near the Star Ferry in the heart of TST. The remaining Kowloon outlets are buried off somewhere and may not be worth your trouble, or you can shop with the jobbers on the famous streets of smiles, such as Granville Road and Fa Yuen Street.

Granville Road: My heart beats faster at the very words. Granville Road is not only my first and last stop on any shopping spree to Hong Kong, but it is the barometer of my faith. When I need a pick-me-up, I take myself for a stroll on Granville Road.

I have been on Granville Road when bargains are dried up and when they are flowing; when it's good, this is as close to shopping heaven as you will get. Granville Road is the home to jobbers who have bins and racks filled with American goodies—most are about $10 an item.

I'm not going to name a lot of stores because that's actually more confusing than helpful. Just start at the **McDonald's** 1 block into Granville Road from Nathan Road and walk east until the street ends. Please note that these stores do not take credit cards. Many will take U.S. dollars, but will peg the rate of exchange where they want it, which may be better than you'll get at your hotel, anyway. There is one place to change money toward the end of the stretch across from the Ramada. Bring cash and maybe a trailer.

The last time I was there I saw labels from the Gap, the Limited, Victoria's Secret, Harvé Benard, Eddie Bauer, Banana Republic, and Calvin Klein. I saw this no-name, white linen dress without a belt for $20 that I didn't need but hid anyway and retrieved 2 days later. When I wore it 6 months later in Paris, I saw it for $300 on the Faubourg St. Honoré.

Just go from store to store; don't worry about names and addresses. I always buy from **Value** (no. 32), **Sample Nook** (no. 30), **GX Warehouse** (no. 26), **Factor Fashion Co.** (no. 26A), **Stock Shop** (no. 32A), and **Park Lai Fashions** (no. 46).

To get there: Take the MTR to Tsim Sha Tsui and exit onto Nathan Road, walking north (away from the water). Granville Road is on the right-hand side of the street only, right after the **Burlington Arcade** at no. 92 Nathan Road. The first block is boring, then the fun starts.

Fa Yuen Street

Fa Yuen Street is a less fancy version of Granville Road. It's the best bargain neighborhood in Kowloon for those who like this kind of shopping.

To get there: Take the MTR to Prince Edward and walk south, toward the water, to Fa Yuen Street (use map), or get out at the Mong Kok station, walk north, shop, and end up at the Prince Edward station. The best shopping is a tad closer to the Prince Edward end, but it's 50-50 here.

Kowloon City

Frankly, I don't know that much about Kowloon City. It's the stretch of town before you get to Hung Hom and the outlet buildings, but it, too, is filled with warehouses and outlets, none of which cater to tourists. The only highlight I can note is the **DD Warehouse.**

DD WAREHOUSE
11 Yuk Yat St., To Kwa Wan, Kowloon
(MTR: none, take a taxi).

My darling Jane, who lives in Hong Kong and hates to shop, whispers family secrets in my ear. Luckily, her husband's family is in the garment business, so she passes on some great secrets. Here's another one of her tips. This is the find of the century. DD Warehouse is the outlet for David Sheekwan. And David Sheekwan is one of the hottest designers in town.

The outlet is in a clean, modern building in a factory neighborhood near the airport (take a taxi). It is near Kowloon City, but is technically in an area called To Kwa Wan, which no one (and I mean no one) has ever heard of.

Prices are not street cheap, but neither is the merchandise. The sweater I bought for $40 is my favorite new item this season; it's got a fabulous Euro-Japanese drape and a simple but utterly chic look, just like all the suits and sportswear items here. You can buy an entire wardrobe; there are tons of working woman's suits.

If you choose to get to only one wild and crazy outlet in a semi-far-flung area, this just may be it.

Hours are Monday through Friday from 9:30am to 5:30pm and Saturday from 9:30am to 4:30pm.

Hung Hom

Just past Tsim Sha Tsui and on the way to the airport (in other words, not far) is Hung Hom, the world of factory outlets. Hung Hom is the neighborhood closest to Tsim Sha Tsui and was the first to make factory-outlet shopping an event. **Kaiser Estates Phases I, II,** and **III** are the mainstays of Hung Hom, although there are three other buildings where outlets have popped up as well; many visitors used to make these outlets their first stop in town.

No more. Most of the outlets have closed (except for **Diane Freis**), and I wouldn't mind if you missed this part of town completely.

To get there: Take a taxi from Kowloon. Ask to be let out in front of Kaiser Estates Phase I, as the majority of the shops are located either in Kaiser Estates or in the **Winner Building** across the street. Taxis come and go on a regular basis in front of Kaiser Estates Phase I. Better yet, consider coming with a car and driver.

DIANE FREIS FACTORY OUTLET STORE
Kaiser Estates Phase I (10th floor), 41 Man Yue St., Hung Hom, Kowloon (MTR: none).

Diane Freis no longer sells from her factory in the boonies, which is fortunate for us shoppers, since this clean, spacious outlet is much more convenient. I promise that your heart will stop when you see all the choices.

Most of the clothes are on racks organized by style and price. There are some bins, and there is a dress-up area with hats and some accessories. This is one of the largest outlet stores in Kaiser Estates; it takes credit cards. Dresses are mostly in the $100–$200 range; some of them are more than a year old, but that's the beauty of a Diane design: No one can tell. There are special promotional styles and deals: I bought a dress, with sequins no less, for all of $69.

I must also tell you that sometimes the prices in Loehmann's are better than in Hong Kong, although

I've never seen a match-up. Right before my last trip to Hong Kong, I bought a new outfit to wear to dinner with her; it cost $129 (plus tax), but I thought that was fair enough. Loehmann's doesn't always carry Diane Freis, but you can get lucky in the U.S. as well as in Hong Kong.

Hours are Monday through Saturday from 9:30am to 6:30pm.

Lai Chi Kok

Now we are talking factory town. This feels like the New Territories, but actually it isn't. But it's border-line, and it's on the way to Tsuen Wan, which is indeed N.T.

Lai Chi Kok is just a tad uptown from the basic Kowloon neighborhoods that tourists frequent. It is safe, the MTR access is great (no need to switch trains), and outlets are within walking distance of the MTR station. You don't have to get lost or go any great distance (it's about 10 minutes from Tsim Sha Shui), and all of a sudden, wham, you are in the heart of Hong Kong and the real world. It's a fabulous experience.

Note: When crossing back and forth on Cheung Sha Wan Road and Tung Chau Road, don't be too brave or foolish. The traffic is terrible. Use the lights to cross.

SPLENDID

LeRoy Industrial Building (2nd floor), 15 Cheung Shun St., Kowloon (MTR: Lai Chi Kok).

Splendid is a strong resource for leather garments; note that this is a new address if you have visited before. Same factory, same city, but different outlet, so don't get confused. They have moved the outlet into the main office.

Splendid manufactures upscale leather clothing for European stores. Many lines are made specifi-cally for Germany and Italy. The styling is top-of-the-line. Men's jackets come in every size and many styles. Stock up on leather trousers in various colors.

Now then, let's talk about prices. You've come all this way; it's a very foreign neighborhood; you are expecting a bargain. Well, yes and no. These items would easily retail for $750 and up in New York or London. But prices are in the mid-hundreds here, and I do mean in U.S. dollars. Men's leather jackets cost $250 to $350. That's what they cost. Don't make this trek if you think you're going to get $50 bargains.

Hours are Monday through Saturday from 9:30am to 6pm.

AH CHOW PORCELAIN
Hong Kong Industrial Centre (Block B, 7th floor), 489–491 Castle Peak Rd., Kowloon (MTR: Lai Chi Kok).

Ah Chow is in the opposite direction from the MTR station as Splendid, and since they sell merchandise of a completely different nature, it seems fitting enough.

Ah Chow is a very good porcelain resource. Now then, before you get out your street map and start making tracks, take the time to compare a few things. First off, if you're going to the boonies for porcelain, I like **Wah Tung** better (see page 149). Also, getting here can be a gritty experience—you have to enter through a garage and find the proper lift. You need to have a spirit of adventure and a want to conquer the whole neighborhood. Don't come for this one listing.

That said, I'd like you to know that Ah Chow is indeed great. And worth the trip.

The showroom is crammed with huge jardinieres, waiting to go to a mansion or hotel, and lamps and vases of every size imaginable. Directly ahead from the entry is a room full of sample dishes. If you were a buyer for one of the major department stores, you would go in here and pick one from column A and one from column B. Many of the pieces on the floor have "Sold" signs (in Chinese, of course) on them. We asked; that's how we knew.

If you look at the fine Chinese-style ashtrays, lamps, and ceramic goods in American department stores, you will recognize Ah Chow's merchandise. While they will make any pattern you want, or copy anything you want, it is easier to just pick from the overrun stock sitting around the shop.

I shipped a set of ginger jars, and they arrived in perfect condition—wrapped better than a mummy. The shipping cost more than the jars, but who wants to hand-carry china for 20 hours on a plane? Please note that it took a very, very long time for the jars to arrive and that I have gotten letters from readers who have also complained that shipping seemed to take forever. They were happy with the product but anxious during the wait.

The place is a little bit dusty, but this only adds to the charm. Breakables are piled high—don't bring the children! No credit cards are accepted, but traveler's checks are okay.

Hours are Monday through Saturday from 10am to 7pm.

Chapter Twelve

· · · · · · · · ·

MACAU

WELCOME TO MACAU

· ·

Oy! Macau! A pain, I get a pain right here in my heart when I see what's going on here. God, I hate progress. And Joyce, my icon, my heroine, my favorite retailer in Hong Kong, what have you wrought? An Armani boutique in Macau . . . aiiiiiii!

I welcome you to Macau with enthusiasm but reserve, with pleasure and terror, pathos and delight. I had Macau in my hands, and I saw it slip between my fingers. Aiiiiii.

The new Macau is almost as new as the new Hong Kong, and the old, good, funky stuff is being destroyed as you read. Don't buy my heart at Wounded Knee. Macau will do.

Truth is, I have been to Macau several times, over a period of many years. In the beginning, I was not impressed. I looked around, shopped around, and shrugged my shoulders while singing a chorus of "Is That All There Is?"

I mention this, because it took me a number of years to get to the point I'm at now, where I can suggest that this former Portuguese Colony, which will be returned to the Chinese in 1999, is really worth your time.

I changed my tune when I finally found the wonderful antique neighborhood I had been missing, and when the Hotel Bela Vista opened. Those were the Middle Years. Those beauties still exist, and Macau is very much worth doing, but I have seen a window on time that is slowly fading from view.

Macau is a simple day trip from Hong Kong, or a weekend away, or even a hub city for visits to Hong Kong and other Pearl River Delta cities in China. So, come to Macau for a day, a day and a night; come for a weekend if you insist (although this is not the best time to come), or better yet, come for several days. I know that once you've had a day like my last day in Macau, you'll put this tiny territory on your hit parade and on the list of places to which you must return. I welcome you to an aspect of Hong Kong life that is too special to ignore.

And yes, Macau has opened a brand new spiffy airport, and you can actually come to Macau as a destination and spend a day in Hong Kong! Welcome one and all; any way you want to do it is fine with me—but don't miss out. Macau is waiting for you.

MACAU TRADITIONS

. . . .

Macau has existed in the Hong Kong reality for a series of specific local traditions:

- You go to Macau to have an affair with someone else's spouse.
- You go to Macau to gamble.
- You go to Macau to save money on antiques.

I'm up for at least one of those options (the antiques), and am beginning to understand the other possibilities. I'd rather spend my money on antiques than gambling, but, after inspecting the Hotel Bela Vista, I certainly know the first place I'd go for a fling.

The local tradition is that gambling and affairs are conducted on weekends, so it's better for tourists to avoid Macau at these times whenever possible. Hong Kong crowds consider a trip to Macau in the same vein that westerners consider a weekend in the country. They go to Macau to slow down, to take it easy, to relax. The notion is surely that Macau operates on a different pace than Hong Kong. But if you think you're headed to a sleepy little island, think twice. Macau is beginning to boom; the skyline may soon look like Hong Kong's. Besides, Macau is not an island. It's a peninsula.

It has also been a tradition to come to Macau on the hovercraft or by sea; but, now people can actually fly into Macau as an international destination— the new Macau traditions are truly being written on the wind.

A SHORT HISTORY OF MACAU

Macau is actually making more history now with the new vision of the territory than it has made in years past. Yet it's here that trade with the Far East was originally, well, uh, anchored. The Portuguese got permission to use Macau as their window on the East in 1556. The black ships departed from the harbor here, laden with the exotic trade that made continental Europe stand up and take note of all things Chinese, Japanese, and Asian.

In 1974 there was a coup in Portugal; the new government decided to dump colonies and territories. They tried to give Macau to the Chinese. The Chinese balked. In 1985 they all finally got it together and agreed that Macau would become a special territory (called a Special Administrative Region) for 50 years. The 50 years begin on December 21, 1999. (About 2½ years after the Chinese begin their special relationship with Hong Kong.)

Meanwhile, Macau has always generated its cash flow through gambling—the antiques and forbidden treasures of China slipped quietly across the border when no one was looking. And the husbands and wives slipped between the sheets while everyone was looking, but pretended not to be.

So international tourism was not a big to-do. Until a few years ago when someone realized that the Chinese were indeed moving into Hong Kong in 1997 and Macau in 1999, and it was a good time to woo and win them to the ways of capitalism; wouldn't it be fun to transform Macau? The transformation has been just plain dumbfounding.

In fact, I suggest you get to Macau before they ruin it.

CHANGING TIMES
. . . .

I'm about to say something very two-faced and hypocritical: I adore many of the changes in Hong Kong. I love the architecture and the growth and the fast-paced race with money and destiny. But I am sorry to see Macau headed in the same direction. But here's the catch: I was never in love with the sleepy old colonial Macau (I thought it was a dump), and unlike Hong Kong, Macau is not destroying a wonderful past in order to make room for the future. As long as they don't completely do in the antique district, I'm at peace, and yet, I am also upset . . . I feel *old*.

I also fear for the banyan trees. And I love some of those dumpy buildings. I adore the Apollo Theatre, and I'm not talking about Harlem, my dears. The Apollo is in downtown Macau. What I didn't like about the old Macau was that it wasn't seedy enough to be charming. It just was, and there was no real method to it.

But now I see it disappearing.

Growth in Macau is staggering; each time I visit I am amazed. More changes are planned constantly. Landfills continue to close in the harbor; more hotels are opening, and of course, roads and railroads into China are being built as we speak.

Admire the view from the terrace of the Bela Vista while you can because it's going to go, too—landfill and more buildings are planned. Everything's coming up roses in Macau, high roses. Or is that high-rises?

PHONING MACAU

· ·

If you are indeed in Hong Kong and want to telephone or fax Macau for luncheon reservations or whatever, the area code is 853. The area code for Hong Kong is 852; do not get confused.

A SHORT LESSON IN GEOGRAPHY

· ·

Macau is connected to Hong Kong via a 40-mile sea lane; it's actually 64 kilometers and a million miles away. Macau itself is not an island, but the tip of a peninsula that is directly attached to mainland China, also known as PRC. You can walk to the gate. You cannot walk through the gate without a visa.

If you want to understand where Macau and Hong Kong are in relationship to each other, picture an upside-down letter V or the letter L in Cyrillic. Hong Kong is the lower right point; Macau the lower left. Where they come together, you are firmly in China. If you drew a straight line between Hong Kong and Macau and made a triangle, you'd be drawing across the South China Sea.

So now you know where Carmen San Diego is.

Okay, now for the Macau part. Aside from modern downtown Macau, there are two islands: Taipa (where the new airport is located) and Coloane, which has the beaches and several new hotels that are going for the resort business.

There are bridges to the islands and bridges that loop back toward the main gate and China.

The ferry terminal is not near much of anything, except the Mandarin Oriental. And a lot of landfill.

It may be closer to something else by tomorrow, at the rate they're building.

You will need a bus or taxi to get into town (you can also take a pedicab, if you are game); you will also need a taxi to get to various destinations. You can easily explore the core downtown area by foot, but you'll need wheels to get to downtown from the ferry pier if you arrive from Hong Kong via the sea and Shun Tak . . . or the international airport.

Since we're talking about day-tripping, let's forget about the airport for now.

GETTING TO SHUN TAK CENTRE
. . . .

Shun Tak Centre is the name of the quite modern, two-tower ferry terminal located in the Western District of Hong Kong. The MTR stop is Sheung Wan, which is the end of the line. The building and terminals are located several floors up in the never-ending lobby space; ride several escalators and read a lot of signs. Do not be in a hurry the first time you do this.

GETTING THERE
. . . .

Assuming you are not flying to Macau via the new airport, or crossing the hills from China, you are most likely coming from Hong Kong and most likely from **Shun Tak Centre.** Your choices are simple, one if by air and two if by sea.

Lots of high rollers think it's terribly neat to come to Macau via helicopter. Since I am terrified of the things in the first place, and since I have survived number 8 seas between Hong Kong and Macau and wouldn't like to have been in a chopper at such a time, I can only say *bonne chance,* and have fun. The fare for the chopper is just slightly over $100 on weekdays; it runs more frequently on weekends and holidays, as these are peak travel times. The journey takes 20 minutes. There are several flights a day; eight people fit into the craft. You get tickets at the ferry terminal in Shun Tak Centre (MTR: Sheung Wan); you may also book the ride via any tour organization.

I've always come and gone to Macau via jetfoil. Although there are numerous seafaring vehicles and locals know the difference between a catamaran, a hydrofoil, and a jetfoil, I can only tell you that speed is my choice here, and so I go via jetfoil. I've tried to sample the other methods, but fate was not with me. And I don't plan to be caught dead in a helicopter. So there.

- HYDROFOILS take 75 minutes, but have an open deck.
- HOVER-FERRIES take slightly more than an hour and depart via China Hong Kong City.
- HIGH-SPEED FERRIES take almost 2 hours, so they are misnamed.
- JETCATS take 70 minutes and are similar to JUMBOCATS; they, too, depart China Hong Kong City.
- JETFOILS are made by Boeing, which will bring you great comfort when you begin to panic. The crossing takes an hour. They leave from Shun Tak, they have first-class service in an enclosed upper deck with a no-smoking area and beverage service. This is the most common way to get to Macau.

The fares do change with the times, but the variables include the day of the week, the time of day (night costs more), and the class of service (first costs more). First-class service on a weekday is $HK 126 each way for an adult; departure tax adds another $HK 25 or so. Weekends and holidays are about 10% cheaper on the fare; they do not discount the departure tax. Sorry.

An off point: Weekends on jetfoils are cheaper than weekdays; weekends on hydrofoil (Jetcats) are more expensive than weekdays. Inscrutable all right.

While I do not normally travel first class on European trains, may I now explain to any and all that the ferry to Macau is not a European train. Economy seats are slightly less expensive. Don't do it. Trust me on this.

You may get your tickets up to 28 days in advance, which is nice, so you won't have too much pressure on you once you get to the Shun Tak Centre; this building is a tad confusing and may be all you can handle. TICKETMATE outlets offer tickets; your hotel concierge can get them for you as well.

Now then, this is as good a time as any for a few warnings. Of all the times I have gone to Macau, the crossing has been glorious—the sun sparkles like diamonds across the South China Sea, the hills of China are delicious—the crossing has been a sea breeze. But once, just once, things were less than smooth.

Despite the fact that I checked the weather with the hotel desk, I did not read the *South China Morning Post* before departure. Had I done so, I would have noticed the word "monsoon" and the words "Number 8" along with some swirly circles drawn between China and Hong Kong. You don't have to have a degree in meteorology to know that you do not want to be on the seas during a monsoon, even if the skies are blue and the land is dry. Conditions in the sea between Hong Kong and Macau can be quite different from what's happening on land.

I won't bore you with the unpleasant details, but I will tell you that Ian Cook was afraid. He was more afraid of the whitecaps than I was; this frightened me. I was also frightened by the waves engulfing the jetfoil and all the people around me puking on my silk dress didn't make me feel any better. The luggage was flying, water was sloshing into the sides of the boat, and Ian's eyes were real big. "Hundreds Lost at Sea," he whispered as I reached for my barf bag.

Yes, it was bad luck. We had engine trouble; the jetfoils stopped running after ours left, due to rough seas. It rarely happens, and we came out of it shaken but just fine. But there are a few things to learn:

- Be a sport; pay for a first-class ticket. Our economy seats had us crammed in with hundreds of others, so when the rocking and rolling started, they were thrown on top of us in all their humanity. We also had the waves crashing around us. First-class is elevated; the waves would have never been seen or felt. It's more spacious; we might have turned around and flagged a helicopter to get to Macau. We would have thought of EuroDisney and laughed. A first-class seat usually costs $3 more than an economy seat. You're worth it.

- Read the newspaper before you leave for the ferry terminal. Words such as "monsoon" and "typhoon" should set off warning bells in your brain. What's the dif? A monsoon is periodic wind and very heavy rainfall; a typhoon is a tropical cyclone. The typhoon season occurs during the spring and summer.

- Don't think that the "authorities" are a better judge of the situation than you are. They will eventually stop running boats if things get out of hand, but if you want to be captain of your own fate, you'll get information before you leave town. The radio runs weather reports constantly. Or talk to your concierge. Remember the weather report for Hong Kong is meaningless; you want the report for the South China Sea and the pathway to Macau. It also helps to know precisely where Macau is in relationship to Hong Kong and the China coast, so you can read a map and follow the weather patterns yourself. Guangdong is the name of the coastal province of China next to Macau—if winds are blowing from Guangdong toward Hong Kong and you are riding right smack into them, well, you catch my drift.

If you think these notes are only for the nervous, think twice. Erica's jetfoil had engine trouble; she was tossed around the sea and wondered why she had ignored my suggestions about first class.

While you can come and go from Kowloon via China Hong Kong City (and I have done this very conveniently), there are departures every 15 minutes from Shun Tak Centre in Western, and you have more choices of types of craft at Shun Tak.

Departing Shun Tak is no easy task; pay attention when you line up to get your ticket. This is the second time I've mentioned this, so you can tell I think it's more than a bit confusing. Note that it can be outright difficult if you try to change tickets. We missed our return catamaran and had to buy new tickets on the jetfoil—no refunds, no exchanges, no credits.

The price of your ticket includes exit taxes for both Hong Kong and Macau. You will have to fill in immigration papers on both sides of Hong Kong, and yes indeedy, you need that passport. Allow 20 minutes for the paperwork on the Hong Kong side; it's quicker leaving Macau, but you must still exit the country and go through security.

Once you have your tickets, report to the departure area (after clearing immigration, of course). There you'll see people milling around and standing in line, and you won't know what to do. Get in the line, dummy, you need a seat. Then you can mill around. There are kiosks selling food, drinks, magazines, etc.

If you arrive early—as you may well do because you are so nervous about everything that has to get done—you may board an earlier boat. No matter what your ticket says, as long as they have seats, you can get on.

ARRIVING MACAU

You'll walk along a little gangway, enter a building, follow a walkway, and go through security. You are

Macau

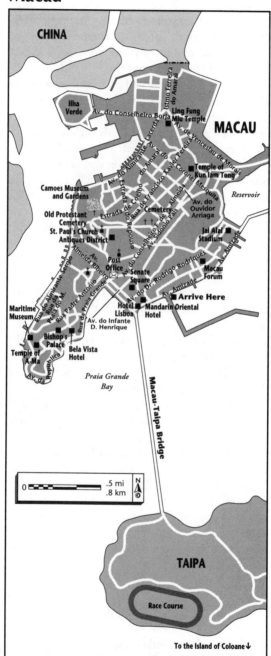

CHINA

Ilha Verde

Av. do Conselheiro Borja

Ling Fung Miu Temple

MACAU

Ístimo Ferreira do Amaral

Av. de Venceslau de Morais

Temple of Kun Iam Tong

Av. do Almirante Lacerda

Av. do Coelho do Amaral

Rua de Francisco Xavier Pereira

Av. do Coronel Mesquita

Reservoir

Camoes Museum and Gardens

Estrada do Repouso

Av. do Ouvidor Arriaga

Old Protestant Cemetery

Cemetery

St. Paul's Church

Av. de Sidónio Pais

Antiques District

Av. do Conselheiro de Almeida

Almeida Ribeiro

Jai Alai Stadium

Av. da Amizade

Post Office

Senate Square

Macau Forum

Rua do Almirante Sérgio

Av. do Dr. Rodrigo Rodrigues

Arrive Here

Maritime Museum

Rua da Praia do M.

Rua da Praia Grande

Av. Amizade

Hotel Lisboa

Mandarin Oriental Hotel

Bishop's Palace

Rua Padre Antonio

Av. do Infante D. Henrique

Temple of A-Ma

Bela Vista Hotel

Av. da República

Praia Grande Bay

Macau-Taipa Bridge

0   .5 mi
      .8 km

N

TAIPA

Race Course

To the Island of Coloane ↓

1462

now in Portuguese Macau. I spoke Portuguese to our taxi driver, who thought I was nuts. Better luck to you and yours.

Once you are outside the terminal, you'll note that there are bus stops and a hut for waiting for taxis. It's a little confusing, partly because so much construction is going on, and if you are used to the way it used to be, well, you'll find that everything is different.

LUGGAGE
. . . .

We were originally planning to spend the night at the Bela Vista and had overnight tote bags with us, plus camera equipment. We were rather weighted down (we always are), but were at least able to walk and carry our own luggage. Good thing. On our voyage from hell the stowed luggage was flying all over the place.

There is no luggage service per se; don't bring what you can't carry. Thankfully Macau is a casual kind of place; if you lose your shirt at the gaming tables, it will be one less thing to schlep back to Hong Kong with you.

There are some official regulations about luggage—locals ignore them, of course. Checked luggage is only allowed on the jetfoil and must be checked 30 minutes prior to departure. You will pay $HK 30 for each piece weighing from 10–20 kilos and $HK 40 for pieces weighing 20–40 kilos.

As the airport comes into use and there is more serious interaction between Hong Kong and Macau by tourists who are using both airports, it will have to devise a better luggage system.

If you do have serious luggage, consider calling your hotel in Macau and asking them if they can arrange pick up and delivery so you can travel scot-free.

If you are staying at the Mandarin Oriental in Hong Kong and go on to stay at the Mandarin

Oriental in Macau, you may arrange to have your luggage sent ahead. This is a brilliant notion.

GETTING AROUND MACAU

There are a million taxi drivers at the ferry pier who want to be your driver-cum-guide for a day and who will make a deal with you. It's harder to find a taxi to just take you some place. **The Mandarin Oriental** is essentially across the street—it's a busy street and not easy to cross, but you can walk there if you don't have too much stuff. This is only one of many reasons to book the Mandarin Oriental for your stay. Another perk: If you arrange beforehand, they will send a car to take you to either The Mandarin or the Bela Vista—they own the **Bela Vista,** too.

When we finally did get a taxi, I told the driver exactly where to go. In Portuguese. *No fala.* This driver acted as if he didn't speak any language we spoke—and between us we do know a few— and then handed me a map of Macau so I could point to our destination. Now let me tell you something, if I did not know where we were going, its location on the map, and the correct route, I would have had a nervous breakdown right then and there. Do study your *mapa turistico* while you're sitting on the jetfoil.

If this is a day trip, you want to go to see *Igresia São Paolo.* I'll guide you beyond that in a few minutes (see page 281). If you are staying awhile, you obviously want to go to your hotel. Make sure you know where it is on a map. Just in case.

If you are staying a few days, you might want to rent a mini-moke, a Jeep-like affair. We had ours booked through the hotel, but gave it up when we didn't get to stay over. Prices are about $35 per day from Avis, and they bring them right to your hotel. Many hotels offer a moke option as part of a package deal.

MONEY

. . . .

Macau has its own unit of currency, called a *pataca*. It is traded on parity with the Hong Kong dollar, which is also accepted interchangeably, although change may be given in local coins.

If you have an ETC card from the Hongkong and Shanghai Bank, you can use the cash machine at the bank—you will get Macau cash. You cannot get money if you just have a passbook; you must have the ETC card.

PHONE MATTERS

. . . .

If you are on a day trip but need to call home, go to the Leal Senado in the central square for a telephone marked IDD, International Direct Dial. You can direct dial Hong Kong from any phone; just use the proper area code (852) and have the right coins on hand. To call AT&T Direct from Macau, dial ☎ 0800-111.

SLEEPING IN MACAU

. . . .

📂 THE MANDARIN ORIENTAL MACAU
Ave. da Amizade, Macau.

If you want to be part of it all, the Mandarin Oriental is the logical choice, if not the romantic one. This high-rise poured-concrete hotel sits right at the harbor, a sneeze from the ferry terminal. It's got about 400 rooms, including several Mandarin suites; most rooms have views of the South China Sea. It's the only large five-star property in the heart of things, and it's where you want to be, if you need big and fancy.

Along with the usual Mandarin luxuries, the hotel has several famous restaurants, a beauty shop, business services, swimming pool, health club and spa, and all the features you come to expect from a Mandarin property. It is the best in town in terms of luxury, location, and complete facilities.

You can also get a promotional deal that will knock your socks off. Various weekday packages include Midweek Interlude and Macau Affair packages. (You know what I told you about Macau.) Packages include double accommodations, welcome fruit basket, jetfoil transfers, discounts on moke rental or tours, and either a dining credit or perhaps a meal on the property, depending on which promotion you luck into. Weekday promotional rates can be as low as $115!

Call ☎ 800-526-6566 for reservations in the U.S., or Leading Hotels of the World, ☎ 800-223-6800. Local ☎ 853-567-888; fax 853-594-589.

🛍 HOTEL BELA VISTA
Rua do Comendador Kou Ho Neng 8, Macau.

If I sound lukewarm about the Mandarin Oriental, it's only because I am wild about the Bela Vista. Book your room now, read the rest of this book later.

Once the grande dame hotel of Macau, the Bela Vista basically fell apart and became a dump. It was closed for 2 years' worth of renovations; it is now owned by the government and run by Mandarin. It is to die for.

Here's the problem: The hotel has only 4 rooms and 4 suites! Each is different; each is decorated to the gills with tiles and colonial furniture and touches of grandeur. Second problem: no pool or spa or health club.

If you are in Macau for a day trip, you won't mind the lack of rooms since you'll just be coming here to sniff the air and have lunch, which is not very expensive, by the way, and is an absolute must-do part of your day trip.

For those who are coming for the weekend or more: The hotel is drop-dead-chic gorgeous; it has

colonial proportions and makes a statement of refined elegance and old money. The rooms are not
cheap. In fact, you might need to sit down. The top
suite in the house goes for about $500 a night. And
that's U.S. dollars. It also happens to be worth it.
The Macau Suite, with fireplace, is about $300 a
night—and a bargain.

You can get all the charm and none of the expense by coming for lunch or tea (see page 278).
The hotel is not far from downtown, although to
get there your taxi may need to circle a part of the
island because of one-way streets. This hotel is not
really within walking distance to much of anything.
But who wants to go much of anywhere once you're
here?

For reservations in the U.S., ☎ 800-526-6566. If
you are booking for a holiday period, book as far
ahead as possible. They may be sold out for New
Year's Eve 1999. Local ☎ 853-965-333; fax 853-
965-588.

WESTIN RESORT MACAU
Estrada de Hac Sá, Coloane, Macau.

Way out on the island of Coloane, which is devel-
oping as the beach bunny resort area of Macau, this
hotel is a destination unto itself and is marketed as
such. There are plenty of places to eat and numerous recreational activities (including golf). There's a
complimentary shuttle to and from the ferry pier,
some 20 minutes away.

For reservations in the U.S., ☎ 800-228-3000.
Local ☎ 853-871-111; fax 853-871-122.

SNACK & SHOP

It is not easy to bump into a cute place to eat lunch
in Macau, so plan your day accordingly. If you come
on a day trip, I can't imagine doing anything other
than eating at the **Bela Vista.** But there are other

choices. There is also a gourmet grocery store on the main drag, and you can picnic. There may be tons of American fast-food joints as in Hong Kong, but I've never found them in my traditional shopping path. (There's a **McDonald's** on the main drag near the Senate Square.)

Also note that eating is one of the adventures that Macau is famous for. People in Hong Kong all have their favorite places, which they may not even tell you about for fear you will ruin them; they don't want tourists crowding in.

Decide on your lunch venue before you leave for Macau, especially if you are visiting on a day trip; then plan your schedule accordingly. You will more than likely have to taxi to lunch, so budget time and funds. If you are staying for a while, these choices also serve dinner. Do note that several hotels (**Mandarin Oriental, Hyatt Regency, Westin, Pousada De São Tiago**) are known for their dinner service as well.

Please note that the only one of these listed restaurants I have been to is the Bela Vista; the others are culled from the Macau Tourist Information Bureau, friends in Hong Kong, Mary Bakht at the HKTA in New York, *Gourmet Magazine,* and several guidebooks, which all agree with the others.

Here goes:

HOTEL BELA VISTA
Rua do Comendador Kou Ho Neng 8, Macau.

If you aren't sick of my ranting and raving about the Bela Vista, you'll simply trust me and book ahead. Weather permitting, you want to sit outside on the terrace.

The shocking thing about lunch at the BV (as some call it) is that it is very fancy without high prices. The most expensive entree on the luncheon menu is $10! The menu is huge; it's written in English and Portuguese and contains many local specialties as well as more exotic choices. The appetizers are huge; Ian's pasta could have fed two. He barely had room for his grouper and shrimp in banana leaf. The homemade cinnamon ice cream was the perfect finishing touch to a glorious day. There's a good wine list.

I am pushing BV so strongly because I firmly believe that my newfound fondness for Macau is rooted in the beauty, romance, good eats, and local charm of this single hotel. The combination of Macau's funky streets, markets, antique shops, and then this gorgeous colonial restoration offers exactly what I want out of China—the best of both worlds.

By the way, if you taxi here from St. Paul's or the main area, your taxi will circle around the waterfront drive on a one-way course. Don't be alarmed.

For reservations, direct dial from Hong Kong (or call from the U.S.) ☎ 853-965-333, or fax 853-965-5888.

HENRI'S GALLEY
4 Ave. da Republica, Macau.

You pronounce this *"Henry"* in the American fashion, not *"On-rhee"* like the French. You can also get yourself into gourmand controversy when you discuss this restaurant with foodies from Hong Kong. Glenn Vessa, who knows everything (but won't tell unless you ask), says that Henri's is very overrated and is worth skipping. I've never been. Food writers from around the world have been basking in the glory of Henri's for years. So if you are in town for a few days, you'll just have to try for yourself. (If you're here for only one lunch, you know I want you to go to the **Bela Vista**.)

Known for chicken, prawns, spicy dishes, and a choice of Chinese food, Henri's is on the waterfront, not far from the Hotel Bela Vista, in fact. It is not walking distance from town. For reservations, ☎ 853-556-251.

A LORCHA
289 Rua do Almirante Sérgio, Macau.

Glenn gives thumbs-up to this choice for Portuguese cooking; it's near the A-Man Temple on the southwestern part of the main peninsula. Known for their combination of Portuguese, Chinese, Indian, and African dishes. Reasonable prices. Lunch is served from 1pm to 3pm; dinner from 7pm to 11pm ☎ 853-313-193.

PINOCCHIO'S
4 Rua do Sol, Taipa.

On Taipa Island, and a good excuse to cross the bridge and see a little more of Macau than you planned on, Pinocchio's is huge, famous, and the kind of landmark place where "everyone" goes . . . at least once. Fred Ferretti gives it a rave, in person and in *Gourmet Magazine*. They open at noon. You can dine alfresco. ☎ 853-327-128.

SHOPPING MACAU

. . . .

The main reason people come to Macau to shop is simple: The prices are lower than in Hong Kong, and the specialty is antiques and "antiques." Yes, friends, it is possible to see antiques being made in front of your very eyes. These copies are so good that you will never buy another antique again, for fear that it just came out of the back room of a shop in Macau.

Quite frankly, if you could see what I have seen in Macau, you might be rattled to the very fiber of your being. The fakes were so good that I would never trust myself again. But I digress.

Macau is now more than just a hot spot for a day trip so visitors will be taking the shopping quite seriously. Just about everything is less expensive in Macau than Hong Kong, from hotel rooms to goods in the market to souvenirs to antiques.

Every local from Hong Kong has his or her own private sources in Macau. Indeed, Macau is the kind of place where you need an inside track. There's no doubt that the really good stuff is hidden. And maybe illegal.

The shopping must be considered fun shopping, unless you have brought with you a curator from a museum or Sotheby's or Glenn Vessa and really know your faux from your foo. If you give it the light touch, you're going to have a ball.

THE BEST OF MACAU

· ·

Since addresses are hard to find in Macau, and many places don't even have their names clearly marked, the best way for me to show you the best of central Macau's shopping area is to take you on my walking tour.

If you are visiting Macau on a day trip, take an early jetfoil from Hong Kong so that you hit St. Paul's by 10am. You can wander happily for a few hours and then taxi to the Bela Vista for a 1pm lunch. Book the 4pm jetfoil back to Hong Kong.

• Tell your taxi *Igresia São Paulo* (St. Paul's Church), or be able to point to it on a map. A *Macau Mapa Turistica* is handed out free in Shun Tak Centre. This particular map has a picture of the church, but no number or letter beside it, so it may take you some time to study the map and learn the basics of the town. If you have other tourist materials with a picture of the facade of the church, you may show that to your driver as well.

This church was built in the early 1600s; it burned to the ground in 1835, leaving only the facade, which is in more or less perfect condition. (It was recently restored.) Not only is this quite a sight to see, but it's the leading tourist haunt in town and signals the beginning of the shopping district. Exit the taxi at the church.

- The church is up a small hill, with two levels of stairs leading to a small square. If you go down both levels of the stairs, you will be at the major tourist trap area and flea market heaven where dealers sell mostly new antiques . . . although you always hear stories of so-and-so, who just bought a valuable teapot at one of these stalls.

- Before you go lickety-split down all the stairs to the stalls, note that if you go down only one staircase, there is a small alley on the right side of the stairs—an alley that runs alongside the church. It's only a block long and ends just past the rear of the church, where you will find a tiny shrine. Not that it's well marked, but the name of this alley is **Rua da Ressurreciao.** It is lined with tourist traps, porcelain shops, antique stores, and even a ginseng parlor. You've got **Keng Ngai Antiquano** (no. 5) and **Tung Ngai Antiquarios E Artisanato** (no. 3), etc. Don't expect any bargains in these shops and by all means know your stuff, but begin your shopping spree here. I must say that most of these stores are rather fetching: plates in the windows, red lanterns flapping in the breeze, maybe even a few carved dragons over the doorway. They all take credit cards, and you may have a ball here. I'm suspicious of any place that's too clean and too close to a major tourist haunt such as the church, but you could spend half a day happily enjoying these stores.

- After you've done this alley, work your way around the vendors at the main "square" in front of the church steps. Film, soft drinks, and souvenirs are sold here; there are no particular bargains. I once bought a very good Chairman Mao button here (ceramic), which has become valuable in the intervening years, but there isn't much that's particularly inexpensive. Be prepared to bargain; be prepared to walk . . . and possibly return later.

- Now then, normal people head into town by walking down the hill to the market and shopping as they go. The way to do this is to head down the Rua de São Paulo to the Rua da Palha, passing shops as you go. This walkway leads directly to the marketplace and the Senate Square, which is the heart of downtown. There are a few cute shops this way, and I have even bought from some of them. BUT, I am sending you down the hill the sneaky, nontouristy way.

  If you have the time, you may want to go down my way and then walk back up the main way, so you can see the whole hill (and shop it, of course). Also note that if you are with people and decide to split up, you can always meet back at the church stairway flea market area at an appointed time; this is a good place to get a taxi later on.

  The big red stall is not a loo; it's a postal box. You can mail postcards here.

  If you do head down Rua de São Paulo, be sure to look in at **Cheong Weng Trading Co.** (no. 26A), which sells handcrafted wooden items—toys for kids, nutcrackers, picture frames, and nontouristy items. Next door (no. 28) is **Chan Pou Maniek Hong,** where you can buy newly made porcelains for tourists. I bought a tea mug (with lid) for $HK 10. I bought the exact same mug in a street market in Hong Kong for $HK 18, so you can see where Macau got its reputation for lower prices.

- If you are standing with the church to your back, a major tourist trap called **Nam Kwong Arts & Crafts** should be to your right, with the red postal box in front of it. Shop here if you are so inclined, then make a hard right (under the laundry from the balcony above) onto a small unmarked street. (There are other branches of Nam Kwong in town.) Once you have turned right, look to the left for an alley called **Calcada do Amparo.** Enter here and begin to walk downhill.

It's not going to be charming for a block or so, and you will wonder where the hell you are and why all the tourists went the other direction. Trust me, you are headed into the back alleys of the furniture and antique area, which you will soon discover. You are wearing good walking shoes, I hope. This is called the Tercena neighborhood, by the way.

• The reason I haven't given you shop names and addresses should be now abundantly clear—there's no way of really even knowing where you are when you walk down this hill. In about 2 blocks your alley will dead-end into a small street called **Rua Nossa Senhora do Amparo,** which may or may not be marked. These little alleys are called walkways or *travessas* and may have names (look for **Travessa do Fagao**).

In terms of getting your bearings, you are now halfway to the main downtown square of Macau and on a small street that branches off from Rua do Mercadores, the main small shopping street that connects the main big shopping street to the area above at the top of the hill.

This will make sense when you are standing there in the street or if you look at a map. But don't do a map too carefully because part of the fun of the whole experience is wandering around here, getting lost and found, and feeling like what you have discovered is yours alone.

When you are back on the Rua Nossa Senhora do Amparo, you'll find a ton of little dusty antique shops (they start opening around 11am; don't come too early)—some have names and some don't. As a starting-off point, I send you to **Cheong Kei Curios Shop** (no. 10)—it's written **Ferros Velhos Cheong Kei** in black letters over the door on a big sign—this is the musty dusty antique shop of your dreams and is in the core of what I call "Antiques Heaven." Segue onto **Rua das Estalagens,** which has more antique shops as well as some fabric shops and jobbers.

I would not begin to vouch for the integrity of any of these shops here. I can only assure you that you'll have the time of your life.

• When you have finished shopping the antique trade, work your way laterally across Rua das Estalagens to Rua do Mercadores. If you turn right, you will connect in 2 short blocks to Avenida de Almeida Ribeiro, the main drag. I suggest instead that you keep moving laterally, so that you run smack into the market.

The market is called **Mercado De São Domingos**; it has an outdoor fruit and veggie portion tucked into various alleys, an indoor live-stock portion, and a dry goods portion. Wander through as much as you can take, and find yourself at the main fountain and a square (Senate Square), which instinct will tell you is the main square.

If instinct isn't enough, look for the restored colonial buildings, the tourist office, a large neon sign featuring a picture of a cow (I call this the Ma-Cow sign; Ian does not think this is funny), the main big post office, the deliciously dilapidated Apollo Theatre, and the Leal Senado, which is the Senate building. You have arrived in the heart of town. After you've spotted the spotted cow (I love that cow, sorry), you'll note that there are several pedicabs—rickshas drawn by bicycle—clustered here, you may book a ride. Or take a snapshot. It costs about $5 to get a ride to the waterfront.

There are a few shops clustered here; some are liquor stores, which specialize in old ports from Portugal, etc. After you poke around here and drop into the excellent tourist office (for postcards, no stamps), cross the street and head into the white stucco Leal Senado building just to stare—it is beautifully restored with tons of old Portuguese blue-and-white tiles, a garden, a library, and some magnificent colonial touches.

The address of the tourist office (in case you need help, a place to meet up with the people you came with, or someone who speaks English and can teach you how to use the phone or write something for you in Chinese) is 9 Largo do Senado.

The huge post office across the square is where you buy stamps, but beware, there can be long lines.

• Once finished at the Leal Senado, walk to the right—this is toward the water if the Senate building is to your back. You are now on Avenida de Almeida Ribeiro, the main drag. Here you can stare at the contrasts in architecture and note the old and the new, the shabby and the luxe. The stores here include the gourmet market I was telling you about, a branch of the local Chinese arts and crafts store **Nam Kwong** (no. 1), and an antique shop or two.

I fell in love with Chinese mirror boxes while at **Honeychurch,** on Hollywood Road in Hong Kong. I found an excellent example for 25% less than the Hong Kong price at **Wing Tai Curios Centre** on Avenida de Almeida Ribeiro—I cannot tell you if it was genuine or made yesterday; I can only tell you it was nice and less money than in Hong Kong. I can also tell you that schlepping a mirror box all the way home is my idea of hell. And I'm the type who judges the success of a trip by the size of the item I carry on the plane.

You can walk just about to the waterfront here, certainly to the **Hotel Lisboa,** where you may want to gamble at the Atlantic City–looking casino or look at the new Bank of China across the street.

• Get a taxi at the Lisboa; head for lunch at the **Bela Vista.** Congratulations, you've seen what I consider to be the best parts of Macau. Well, the best shopping parts, anyway. Do note that if you aren't going in for the fancy lunch break, you can grab a taxi instead for the **Kun Iam temple;** there are more tourist and antique shops there.

Chapter Thirteen

. . . .

TOURS

I created this tour for Richard Branson; it's been slightly updated so I can suggest it for anyone with only 1 day to shop Hong Kong.

1. Tour begins in Stanley at 9:30am; you can taxi there or take a bus—up to you. I'm giving you 1½ hours to shop Stanley; you can stay a little longer if you need the time or don't want to buy china in Aberdeen. Don't want to buy china? What are you, Communist? Also note that if you hate Stanley (it has changed a lot!), you may want to adjust the tour slightly and change the pace.

2. Grab a taxi at **Watson's** on Main Street in Stanley and head for Aberdeen. Wa Who for **Wah Tung.** See page 149 for the exact street address; this is in an industrial area that is not a common tourist area. Better yet, you've called Wah Tung, and they pick you up in Stanley. Why didn't I think of that before?

3. Spend 1 hour at Wah Tung, surveying four floors of china. Remind them to give you a discount for showing your copy of this book.

4. Now taxi back to Central by way of Pacific Place. If you are footloose and fancy free, it's lunch at **Golden Leaf in the Conrad Hotel,**

287

88 Queensway, above Pacific Place Mall. This is traditional Chinese gourmet food made with herbal cures—be sure to have the detoxifying dessert!

5. Now spend an hour in Pacific Place, making sure that you visit **Seibu,** the Japanese department store.

6. When finished at the mall, taxi directly to the **Pedder Building,** 12 Pedder St., and first shop **Shanghai Tang** and then the outlets inside the Pedder Building.

    The tour officially ends here; you can drop out whenever you want and head back to your hotel or have a refueling tea break at the **Mandarin Oriental Hotel,** the fanciest teatime hotel in Central.

7. If you're strong enough, you may either continue onto **The Lanes,** page 112, which are 1 block away or walk up to Hollywood Road and do some of the antique shops before you stop off at **Man Mo temple** for a final prayer. Pray for the strength to make it to the **Temple Street Market** after dinner.

TOUR 2: THE SHIP-SHAPE SHOPPER

This is a slightly easier day than the one above and was created for friends who were arriving in Hong Kong on the various cruise ships and wanted a nice overview but didn't want to exhaust themselves. Consult the maps "Kowloon" and "Central & Western Districts" (pages 114 and 124) for guidance.

1. Negotiate your way through the pier-and-mall combo, where your ship docks, out to Canton Road, and quickly walk through **Chinese Arts & Crafts** at the corner of Canton Road and Salisbury Road. Walk over 2 blocks to Nathan Road for the flavor of it—don't you dare buy anything in those junky camera and electronics shops—until you get to Haiphong Road; your back is to the harbor.

2. Turn left on Haiphong Road, walk 1 block to Lock Road, and enter **Haiphong Alley** to buy souvenirs (see page 125 for more precise directions and a description of the kinds of souvenirs available). Then stop at **Pan Am Pearls,** 9 Lock Rd., for fake pearls. There is also a jobber on Lock Road with clothing in bins. Yummy, the true flavor of Hong Kong is here.

3. Return to Nathan Road, cross over to **Granville Road,** and shop the bins for name-brand goods at bargain prices.

4. Head for the **Peninsula Hotel** or **The Regent Hotel** for a moderately priced lunch with a never-to-be-forgotten view.

5. Take the Star Ferry across the harbor; ride first class.

6. Walk up and down **The Lanes** (see page 112 for a more detailed description of the goods available here) just to get a look-see.

7. Shop the **Mandarin Oriental Hotel Mall,** and then have tea in the hotel.

8. Take the Star Ferry (second class, so you can see the difference) back to Kowloon and collapse—once you're back on board your ship.

TOUR 3: HONG KONG—CENTRAL & SANE

If you're a delicate flower, feel jet lagged or disoriented in any way, your first day in Hong Kong should be easy and breezy. The Hong Kong side, especially the Central District, is the place to start. This is the area where all of the large shopping centers, as well as the majority of office buildings, are located. It is more western in style and thinking than other parts of Hong Kong, so that if you aren't ready for the real world, this can ease you into the right state of mind.

1. If you are staying in Kowloon, come across the harbor on the Star Ferry. This is the best way to view Central for the first time, as the skyline is

Tour 3: Hong Kong—Central & Sane

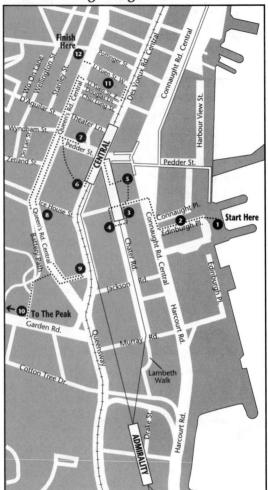

Finish Here

Start Here

To The Peak

1 Star Ferry Pier
2 Pedestrian Walkway
3 Mandarin Oriental Hotel
4 Prince's Building
5 Swire House
6 The Landmark
7 Pedder Building
8 The Galleria
9 The Hong Kong and Shanghai Bank
10 To Peak Tram
11 The Lanes
12 Lane Crawford's & Watson's

spectacular. Splurge for a first-class ticket; ride upstairs where you can hang out of the ferry window and gawk. The most obvious landmark—with the crisscross Xs built across the high-rise body—is the I. M. Pei–designed **Bank of China.**

2. When you get off at the ferry terminal, note the vendor who sells various teas from a huge brass samovar, an excellent bookstore, and a handful of ricksha drivers who will ask if you want a ride. There are also a few street vendors selling anything from fresh flowers to film to old coins and more, depending on the night action.

    From here there's a pedestrian tunnel that will bring you up between **Statue Square** and the **Mandarin Oriental Hotel.** If you don't use this walkway, you'll have a terrible time getting across traffic and metal bars on the curbs.

3. The Mandarin Oriental Hotel, home to two of the most popular tailor shops in town, is a good place to begin your tour of hotel lobbies, which is a national pastime. On the mezzanine level you will find **David's** (custom shirts) and **A-Man** (suits). Also on the mezzanine don't miss the jewelry shop, **Gemsland.** There's also a tiny but excellent book-postcard kiosk in the hotel. Bathrooms are on the mezzanine level, on the opposite side from the shops; you will have to tip the attendant.

4. Leave the hotel via the pedestrian bridge that connects the Mandarin Oriental to the **Prince's Building** across the street. Explore many levels of designer shops.

5. After leaving the Prince's Building, cross the street and walk to **Swire House** (in the middle of the block and before you get to Pedder Street). Swire House is a perfect example of an office building/shopping center. Within the Swire House arcade, you will find even more designer boutiques.

6. Leave Swire House via the Chater Road exit, take a right, and then an immediate left onto Des Voeux Road Central, where you will be in front of **The Landmark,** the most famous American–style upscale mall in town. One entrance into the building is between **Gucci** and the **Peninsula Chocolate shop.** Walk past Gucci, down a somewhat claustrophobic hallway, toward the throngs of people and center atrium. The biggest names in design are here. If you are looking for discount shopping only, don't waste your time . . . move on, or grab a bite to eat at the **Fountainside Cafe.**

   The Landmark could be an all-day adventure in itself, but I'd just as soon you spent 20 minutes here to get the idea and then beat it to the street. We're going to some outlets now!

7. Exit The Landmark via the Pedder Street door, cross at the corner of Queen's Road Central, turn right down Pedder Street, and look for the **Pedder Building** (no. 12: a small entryway right next to the **China Building**). If you get to the Mandarin House, you have gone too far. Look no further than **Shanghai Tang** then head upstairs. Not every store here is an outlet, and some of the outlets are not cheap. But this is as good a place as any to get a feel for Hong Kong's outlet scene and to know you've at least bettered the prices in The Landmark.

   I want everyone who visits Central to spend at least a half hour in the Pedder Building, where I know you'll wake up to the shopping realities of Hong Kong. The Landmark is not the real world.

8. If you still have the energy at this point to go on, exit the Pedder Building, take a right, and then another right onto Queen's Road Central. Walk toward the **Hongkong and Shanghai Bank,** another architectural landmark. In a block you'll hit **The Galleria,** a small mall devoted to many tony names who have defected from The

Landmark and a number of **Joyce's** boutiques, 9 Queen's Rd.

9. Exit Galleria and walk underneath theHong-kong and Shanghai Bank, where you'll see the Beam-Me-Up-Scotty escalators that actually lead to the bank lobby.

10. Exit the bank to your left, and walk 2 blocks to the **Peak Tram** station. Climb The Peak aboard the Peak Tram. Eat lunch at the **Peak Cafe,** enjoy the view, check out the souvenir stands and head for the small **Peak Galleria** that houses the discounter **Labels Plus.** Finished at the Peak, you can take the tram down or a taxi or bus into Central, then walk to the Star Ferry and bail out now. But really, you can't be tired yet. There's lots more to see and do, and now that you've gotten acclimated, you're ready to move into less western parts of Central.

11. Walk along Queen's Road in the westerly direction, stop for a spree in **The Lanes,** which are located before Pottinger Street, with Li Yuen Street East coming before Li Yuen West (unless you are very lost). Walk to your right, going down Li Yuen Street East and shopping your heart out until you get to Des Voeux Road; then walk the few yards it takes to get to Li Yuen West on Des Voeux, turn to your left into the lane, and walk back to Queen's Road along a shopping lane similar to the one you were just on. While you may not need a brassiere, do note that souvenir T-shirts cost only a little more than $1 and Hermès–style Kelly handbags cost less than $50.

12. Your last stop (well, one of your last official stops, anyway) should be the **Lane Crawford** department store, across the street from Mandarin Optical and farther toward Pottinger Street. This is the fanciest British-style department store in town. Prices are the highest in town also, but you can find a sampling of anything you want, from truly fine art to portrait

photography, from china and crystal to Mikimoto pearls. It's a great place to work on pricing the things you plan to buy later in the trip. Figure that whatever it costs at Lane Crawford is the most the market will bear. Lane Crawford also offers top-of-the-line quality, so you'll be able to get an idea of how price and value coordinate.

13. If you aren't exhausted, while you're at Lane Crawford you are also next door to the local chemist chain **Watson's,** which sells a little of everything, including makeup, toys, perfumes, panty hose, film, and more. Now you are surely exhausted and are ready to collapse for tea: You're only a block from the **Mandarin Oriental,** where high tea is almost a meal unto itself.

14. Use this break to get off your feet and rest up because after dinner, you're going to the **Temple Street Market** around 8 or 9pm. This is a very hot night market in Kowloon, where Chinese opera is performed in the streets and all sorts of silly items—from copy watches to vibrating pillows—are sold at bargain-basement prices.

TOUR 4: ANTIQUES, TEMPLES & MORE

Now that you've gotten used to Hong Kong, you're ready to see (and buy) a little bit more. Step this way. In your good walking shoes, please. This can be done as a half-day tour after working Central.

1. Begin your day in Central (via MTR or Star Ferry) at the foot of Pottinger Street, a very steep street with scads of stalls and an equal number of steps. Yes, you could hop on the escalator, but that would take all the fun out of it.

2. When you make it to the top of Pottinger Street, you will be at the crossroads of Chinese antiques and curios heaven, better known as Hollywood Road. Hollywood Road became popular for

antiques in the early 1950s, after the Revolution in China. At that time many Chinese had fled the People's Republic with possessions in hand. In order to raise cash, they pawned them on Hollywood Road. The tradition remained, and Hollywood Road is still the center of merchandise coming out of China. Most of what you see in the shops today is not antique, but antique repro. The true finds are in the back rooms and are saved for dealers. However, if you are an antique collector, let the shop owner know immediately. Often it is better to have an introduction to a dealer in town who can shop and negotiate with you.

For the majority of shoppers who want a curio to take home, rummaging through dusty shelves for the "perfect" piece is a lot of fun! Just remember that there are no Ming vases on the shelves. Ask lots of questions, and bargain. Make sure you get a receipt stating the age of your purchase. If you are buying a true antique, you are entitled to a certificate of authenticity. Customs will want to see these papers. If you are planning to buy in quantity for any reason, ask for the dealer price. Bring along your business card and negotiate on a quantity basis. Many of the shops are used to dealing with interior designers who buy for their clients.

Hollywood Road is actually an extension of Wyndham Street, with stores running for several blocks, right to the block after the Man Mo Temple. The closer you get to Ladder Street and the **Man Mo Temple,** the tackier the shops become, although the immediate block after the temple offers fancy dealers and tourist traps that pride themselves on being part of the action.

3. When you get to Man Mo Temple, take time out from shopping for culture, religion, or appreciation. You can buy any of the necessary prayer supplies right there in the foyer after you enter. There are candles, papers for burning,

Tour 4: Antiques, Temples & More

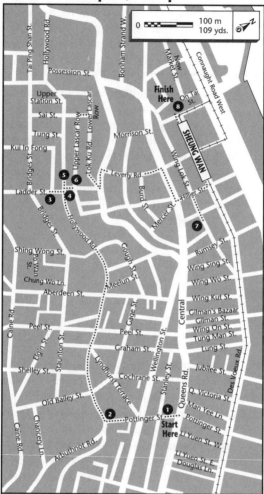

1. Foot of Pottinger Street
2. Hollywood Road
3. Man Mo Temple
4. Chinese herbalists & curio makers
5. Ladder Street Flea Market
6. Cat Street Flea Market
7. Man Wa Lane
8. Western Market

joss sticks, etc. You may also say a prayer and bang the drum slowly.

4. After the temple, the shops become a mix of Chinese herbalists, furniture makers, and curio stores. Be sure to go into a Chinese medicine shop and look at all the wonderful, exotic substances in glass jars. The wizened old men concocting remedies for any ailment you might have are probably the only true antiques left on Hollywood Road.

5. After you have exited Man Mo Temple, go to the corner of Hollywood Road and Ladder Street. You'll note that there is a street directional sign that says "Flea Market." Ladder Street is another of those wonderful stepped streets that looks like it has been there for centuries. Most of the street actually runs uphill, but you will be thrilled to know that you will be going downhill.

6. Step down just one level, and you are at Cat Street, the heart of the flea market. Turn left onto Cat Street and begin to browse the stalls and blankets and huts. The shopping opportunities stretch for almost 3 blocks; some alleys also have vendors; there are also real, bona-fide antique shops behind some of the street dealers.

   Farther along the street you will see workshops making furniture and forging metals. Dealers who sell mostly to the design trade have their showrooms in the **Cat Street Galleries,** which is in the middle of the block, in the **Casey Building** on the harbor side of the street. The actual address for the gallery is on the next street down the hill; so if you miss the building on Cat Street, walk to the end of Cat Street, turn right, duck under the hanging laundry, and turn right again on Lok Ku Road.

7. If you have the energy to walk, go down the steps of Ladder Street to Man Wa Lane, taking Hillier Street. If you can't walk, you can almost roll. Man Wa Lane is confusing to shop (unless

you read Chinese), but offers a wonderful photo opportunity and a unique shopping look-see. Here the chop dealers have their stalls.

8. If you have strength for one more adventure, walk the few extra blocks to Des Voeux and hang a left; you are now headed for the **Western Market.** Note that there are several card and stationery dealers on the street level, which have merchandise you don't find everyone else; there are fabric dealers on the mezzanine. There are clean bathrooms and even a good restaurant, if you need to eat. If you want a more adventurous eating experience, you are only a block from **Yat Chau** (262 Des Voeux Rd.), where you will be examined by a Chinese doctor and told what to eat in order to be cured. Refreshed, and possibly cured, pop into the Sheung Wan MTR station and head home.

TOUR 5: KOWLOON IN A DAY

Kowloon has many different shopping areas, each of which should be a day's adventure. In our 1-day tour we will cover only our favorites; there are many more in our listings. Begin your day early so that you arrive at the Jade Market at 10am, when it opens.

1. Begin the day with breakfast in the coffee shop at **The Regent Hotel,** so you get a good view of the harbor, of Central, and of Kowloon's glory.
2. Head for the Tsim Sha Tsui MTR Station on Nathan Road.
3. Your stop is Jordan Road for the **Jade Market,** which opens at 10am. If you choose to take a taxi, ask the driver for the corner of Reclamation and Kansu streets at the overfly. If taking the MTR, exit at the Nathan and Jordan roads terminal, walk past the **Yue Hwa department store,** past the **Wing On Bank and department store,** past the **Hotel Fortuna,** and take a left on Kansu Street. You will then see ahead of you

blocks of stalls with umbrellas. These are produce vendors. The Jade Market is an enclosed area just after you pass Shanghai Street. Note that there are two tentlike buildings that make up this market. There are almost 500 dealers.

Figure an hour or two for the market—after that you'll be cross-eyed or have a different notion of who the green-eyed monster is. And you may be getting hungry. Walk back to the MTR and head to the Tsim Sha Tsui station; exit at Haiphong Road because now you're going to **Granville Road,** the bargain-bin capital of the world. And yes, there's a **McDonald's** on Granville Road. You can also eat in any of the real-people places that line the street. Ian found one he loves, but I refused to write down the name of it because it was very Chinese.

4. Don't eat too much lunch—bargains can't be tried on in the stores on Granville Road, and they won't be bargains if they don't fit.

   Granville Road is the street on your right-hand side, if the harbor is to your back and you have just passed the entrance to the **Burlington Arcade.**

5. If you are having a fitting at **W. W. Chan,** now is a good time to pop in. Otherwise, it's Granville Road. The first block is mostly boring; there's that McDonald's.

   In the next block, you'll find shop after shop of bargain basements with bins, racks, and an amazing selection of labels for less. It can be feast or famine. Dive in.

6. When you get to the end of Granville Road, turn around and walk back to Nathan Road. Cross to the mosque side of Nathan Road; note that there's an **American Express** in the **Park Lane Shopper's Boulevard,** in case you now need more money. You are now headed toward the harbor and **The Pen.** At the end of the mosque block, turn right on Haiphong Road. Walk over to Lock Road and turn left until you get to **Pan Am Pearls**

Tour 5: Kowloon In A Day

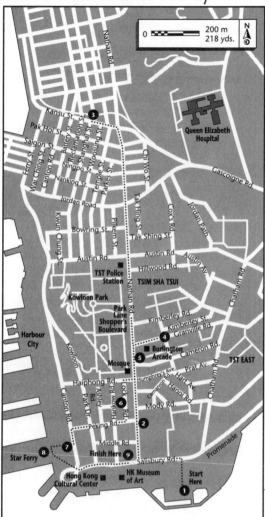

1 The Regent Hotel
2 Tsim Sha Tsui MTR Station (Closest to the Regent)
3 Jade Market
4 Bargain Shopping on Granville Road
5 W. W. Chan
6 Pan Am Pearls
7 Omni Hong Kong Hotel
8 Ocean Terminal
9 The Peninsula Hotel

(no. 9), which is upstairs and where you'll find some of the best fake pearls in town.

7. Now that you've had enough tacky cheap stuff, walk over to Canton Road (1 block) and enter **Ocean Terminal** through the **Omni Hong Kong Hotel.** You'll see signs for **The Silk Road,** which is a gallery of antique dealers, some real, some fake. You can do this if you have the courage. Me? I'm just sending you to **Fook Ming Tong,** which is awfully touristy and upscale, but I feel like you deserve it after seeing some of the less tony parts of Kowloon. This tea shop has expensive but fun tea souvenirs with wonderful packaging and beautiful shopping bags. Whether you do The Silk Road shops or not, be sure to poke in at **Charlotte Horstmann,** one of Hong Kong's best-known antique dealers.

8. If you're a glutton for punishment, you'll roam around Ocean Terminal and the miles of designer boutiques. I say, high-tail it out of there while you still have the strength.

9. Head for the **Peninsula** and their basement filled with fancy stores and a strong cup of *cha* in the lobby where the *tai-tai* gather. Gather your strength as well.

10. Fortified with tea at The Pen, you're ready for a final Kowloon-style down-and-dirty adventure: a trip to Fa Yuen Street topped off by the **La-dies' Market,** which opens in the late afternoon. Take the MTR to Prince Edward and walk south along Fa Yuen Street (see page 128 for precise instructions). When you finish at these Granville Road–style bargain outlets, if you can still walk with all those shopping bags, head over 1 block to Tung Choi Street and the Ladies Market. At the market you can find Fila shirts, Japanese toys, underwear, watches, electronic goods, and knits. Hopefully there's even a vibrating pillow for your back, which you will need after a day like this one.

Size Conversion Chart

. . . .

Women's Clothing

American	8	10	12	14	16	18
Continental	38	40	42	44	46	48
British	10	12	14	16	18	20

Women's Shoes

American	5	6	7	8	9	10
Continental	36	37	38	39	40	41
British	4	5	6	7	8	9

Children's Clothing

American	3	4	5	6	6X
Continental	98	104	110	116	122
British	18	20	22	24	26

Children's Shoes

American	8	9	10	11	12	13	1	2	3
Continental	24	25	27	28	29	30	32	33	34
British	7	8	9	10	11	12	13	1	2

Men's Suits

American	34	36	38	40	42	44	48	48
Continental	44	46	48	50	52	54	56	58
British	34	36	38	40	42	44	46	48

Men's Shirts

American	$14^{1}/_2$	15	$15^{1}/_2$	16	$16^{1}/_2$	17	$17^{1}/_2$	18
Continental	37	38	39	41	42	43	44	45
British	$14^{1}/_2$	15	$15^{1}/_2$	16	$16^{1}/_2$	17	$17^{1}/_2$	18

Men's Shoes

American	7	8	9	10	11	12	13
Continental	$39^{1}/_2$	41	42	43	$44^{1}/_2$	46	47
British	6	7	8	9	10	11	12

INDEX

ABOUT THE AUTHOR

Suzy Gershman is an author and a journalist who has worked in the fiber and fashion industry since 1969 in both New York and Los Angeles and has held editorial positions at *California Apparel News, Mademoiselle, Gentleman's Quarterly,* and *People Magazine,* where she was West Coast Style editor. She writes regularly for various magazines, and her new essays on retailing are text for Harvard Business School. She frequently appears on network and local television; she is a contributing editor to *Travel Holiday.*

Mrs. Gershman lives in Connecticut with her husband, author Michael Gershman, and their son, Aaron. Michael Gershman also contributes to the *Born to Shop* pages.